Reading the Bible Through New Covenant Eyes

Alan Bondar

PublishAmerica
Baltimore

First printing

PublishAmerica has allowed this work to remain exactly as the author intended, verbatim, without editorial input.

Hardcover 978-1-4489-6489-5
Softcover 978-1-4489-8428-2
PUBLISHED BY PUBLISHAMERICA, LLLP
www.publishamerica.com
Baltimore

Printed in the United States of America

Dedicated to Gail Ann Bondar,
for loving a man like me,
and for standing by me through tough times for the sake of truth.

I love you with all of my heart.

People will tell you that this book is dangerous.

I say think for yourself.

Table of Contents

Acknowledgements

This book took two years to write. The reason it took two years to write is because I never realized where the implications of the original manuscript would take me. The first three chapters of this book were the contents of that original, incomplete manuscript. My intention was to help people learn to read the Bible in context. I had a totally different direction in mind for the rest of the book. But as I began to put my own words into practice, I realized that my intended conclusions for the rest of the book were not being drawn from my prescribed method of reading the Bible.

It wasn't until a year and a half after the beginning of writing that I was finally able to read the Bible through New Covenant Eyes. It wasn't as if I didn't believe what I was writing; it's just that, like many people, the things that I prescribe in the first three chapters of this book for reading the Bible were tainted with presuppositions that are very hard to break with. Those presuppositions are numerous and would convolute the point here were I to record them for you. Some of them will be seen as you read this book. The point is that learning to read the Bible through New Covenant Eyes takes time to develop because we all have presuppositions with which we read the Scriptures. Old habits die hard, but when they die, the things that you'll discover as you learn to read the Bible through New Covenant Eyes will surprise you.

The implications in the last three chapters of this final product you now hold in your hands surprised me. I never saw it coming. I discovered a doctrine called *full preterism*. My journey towards full preterism has been a long one, and I want the reader to know up front, once again, that it wasn't easy for me to part with my presuppositions in order to embrace this doctrine. I expect that it will be difficult for you as well. But it is worth the long journey. I hope to make your journey easier by providing you with this book.

My journey towards full preterism has gone through many stages of development, which would take another book to show. But that book would require joint authorship with my friend, Jeremiah Thompson. I would not be where I am today theologically if it were not for him. He doesn't let me get away with anything. He makes me prove everything from the Scriptures. I came to realize long ago that if I can't persuade him, then it isn't right. He is one of the greatest minds of our time. He keeps me centered on sound theology and corrects my thinking along the way. I am grateful to him for his many years of friendship.

In addition, I want to thank Jeremiah for being one of the editors of this book, along with Denise Defrehn, Mariel Courtwright, and Wanda Short, whom I have to thank for correcting my grammar mistakes, and providing guidance in producing a book with content that is readable and understandable. I would also like to thank Jeremy Defrehn and Brennan Courtwright for checking that my content was indeed Scriptural. I am grateful to all of the members of Messiah Reformed Church in Fort Myers, Florida, for their support with this book. In addition, I want to thank Ed Lamb for providing a non-preterist critique of this book. His insights were very helpful in some of the weaker areas.

I would also like to thank Sam Frost, Ed Stevens, and Kelly Nelson Birks for befriending me in a time of need. Thanks to these men, the materials that they gave me challenged and sharpened my thinking on full preterism. They were there for me when I first recognized full preterism in the Scriptures and had nowhere else to turn. Further, Dr. Birks was instrumental in helping us during the beginning stages of Messiah Reformed Church. God used him to save us from making a lot of mistakes that we otherwise might have made.

Finally, saving the best for last, I want to thank my wife, Gail Ann, for editing the first three chapters of the original manuscript and, more importantly, for being my joy and my crown, making me feel like a king, and for remaining by my side throughout my journey. It hasn't been an easy journey for us, but she has stood by me through thick and thin. If it were not for Gail Ann, this book would not have been possible. She is the most patient, loving, and submissive wife that a man could have. Why God would bless me with her is incomprehensible. Short of my salvation in Christ, Gail Ann is the best example of God's grace in my life. I love her dearly and I dread the thought of living my life without her. I present this book to you, the reader, because Gail Ann loves truth, and is willing to sacrifice whatever it takes for truth to be known. That is why this book is dedicated to her.

Forward

Don K. Preston

Modern Bible students are inundated with "personal Bibles," lessons on the "relevance of the Bible," and an almost overwhelming amount of emphasis on the individual application of the Bible. We are told that the Bible was written for our times! It was written to me, today! Believe it or not, this view of the Bible is narcissistic and misguided. The Bible is a book of Covenant, God's Covenant with a Covenant people, and was written to those people 2000 years ago! The Bible must be read through Covenant Eyes!

In this important book, Alan Bondar challenges the reader to read the Bible through the prism of Covenant and covenant people, not as a book of personal letters to the modern individual! Now, make no mistake, this is a challenge to most Bible readers, but it is an important lesson to be learned and applied. Bondar does a great service by pointing out that modern readers have no right to make "personal" and "modern" applications without first determining what the Bible meant in its original context. This does not, by any means, indicate that Bondar believes the Bible has no modern relevance. On the contrary, the author shows that the greatest relevance for today is to discover the original meaning of Scriptures. Then and only then can we make the proper application.

Bondar meets the challenges of most of the futurist eschatologies, demonstrating their failure to honor the actual text of Scripture. With candor, yet tact, the author emphasizes that we must see the Bible as a book written about the fulfillment of God's promises to Israel, with the attendant blessings for men of all ages flowing from that fulfillment.

This book will guide the modern reader into a fascinating and meaningful world of covenant thought, and covenant fulfillment. Bondar shows that we must honor the overwhelming sense of the nearness of the end that is found on virtually every page of the New Testament. This simple, but very effective study will help many Bible students to see the problem confronting the modern church. Yet, Bondar not only demonstrates the problem, he offers solid, logical, textual solutions to the problem. In addition, the author offers in-depth analysis of some of the more difficult end-times passages and offers solid analysis that will open your understanding in a wonderful way. There is something here for everyone.

It is very clear from this book that Alan Bondar has done his homework. He has engaged in countless hours of research and soul searching. He has paid the price of rejecting the religion of his "fathers," and for challenging the status quo. This book is the result of that research, that struggle, that love of truth that has exemplified reformers through the centuries.

And speaking of Reformers, Bondar does an excellent job of demonstrating that many of the more prominent reformed thinkers of the day are in fact turning their back on their own tradition of Sola Scriptura, and "Reformed, but ever reforming." Very revealing information!

We live in exciting times. A "New Reformation" truly is afoot, as more and more Bible students like Alan Bondar grapple with age old questions and challenges, and find the answers that they need by reading the Bible as it was supposed to be read: Through New Covenant Eyes.

Will you agree with everything Bondar has to say? No. Will your views be challenged by reading this book? Yes. Will you benefit from reading this book? Definitely!

Don K. Preston
Ardmore, Oklahoma
September, 2009

Preface

The Church by and large has lived her life embracing the creeds. Some churches have done this more expressly than others, but the fact remains that there are basic beliefs that have been passed down through the years that have come to be known as orthodox Christianity. Many denominations are not even aware of the presuppositions to which they hold, which are based on these orthodox views, yet they embrace them none-the-less. In other words, those who would not expressly state that they are creedal or confessional still embrace, at the very least, the doctrines stated in the creeds. This simply means that these denominations are implicitly creedal whether they expressly admit it or not.

On the other hand, there are denominations that are intentionally creedal and believe that everything stated in the creeds is accurate simply because of their historical longevity. These denominations are also typically confessional, and believe that at least the major views stated in the various confessions are considered to be orthodox.

Being creedal and confessional is not a bad thing. In fact, it's a necessary thing. A statement of what you believe is a creed; a detailed dictation of those beliefs is a confession. To say, "I have no creed but Jesus," is a creed. And to express the details of what you believe about Jesus is a confession. Therefore, being creedal and confessional is not the problem this preface intends to deal with.

The problem is that the confessions and creeds of the historical Church, and especially the creeds, have become a sort of magic decoder ring,[1] which a person must use to interpret the Scriptures in order to be considered orthodox. But at the time the confessions and creeds were composed, the various councils that met and discussed the issues were only able to determine what they thought to be accurate according to their interpretation of the Scriptures. These councils didn't use a creed to determine a creed, or a confession to determine a confession. Rather, they used the Scriptures to determine both the creeds and the confessions.

The point is, the statements in the creeds and confessions were determined by the use of the Scriptures and were never intended to be magic decoder rings by which to determine what the Scriptures teach. In other words, the creeds and confessions were always believed to have the possibility of error, but the Scriptures were believed to be inerrant. Thus, the creeds and confessions were to be an expression of what the various councils believed the Scriptures taught according to the interpretation that was had at the time.

A confession or creed, therefore, is a statement or expression of beliefs determined *by* Scripture and so neither of them should be used as a guide for interpreting Scripture. When used as a guide for interpreting Scripture, these confessions and creeds become magic decoder rings that are placed over the Scriptures to make sure that they are interpreted "correctly." The assumption is that our Church Fathers must have gotten the major issues right. There is general agreement amongst everyone, however, that they may have erred on some of the minor issues. The question is, who gets the right to determine the difference between major issues and the minor issues? Apparently, the creeds contain all the major issues and are not to be questioned or challenged.

Yet time and time again, there arises disagreement amongst Christians about some of the teachings in the confessions and/or creeds to which the solution to the disagreement is typically determined *not* by use of the Scriptures, but by the confessions and creeds themselves. Anyone who does not hold to the "major doctrines" defined within are considered heretics, or at the very least, unorthodox, and are, therefore, not interpreting the Scriptures accurately. So the particular contention with the confession or creed that may arise for discussion is determined to be true or false by whether or not the confession or creed teaches that particular view. In other words, the creeds and confessions have become the ultimate authority in the Church even though the confessions themselves teach that the Scriptures must remain the ultimate authority.

Consider the following possibility: Someone arises and says, "The confessions are the ultimate authority." The confessionalists then say in response, "No, the confessions say that Scripture is the ultimate authority." We now have a stalemate.

The confessions and creeds have become, in many churches, the magic decoder rings through which we are required to understand the Scriptures. This is especially true of the creeds. If you think this is an unfair exaggeration, consider the following words from Keith Mathison, director of curriculum development for Ligonier Ministries, where he speaks of the creeds as the ancient rule of faith:

> ...[A]lthough Scripture is the sole infallible authority, it must be interpreted by the Church within the boundaries of the ancient rule of faith or regula fidei. According to the teaching of the early Church and of the magisterial Reformation, a rejection of this rule of faith as a hermeneutical boundary is a rejection of the perspicuity of Scripture; a rejection of the promise of Christ that the Holy Spirit would teach the Church; and a rejection of the Christian faith.[2]

According to Mathison, then, the Scriptures are no longer the ancient rule of faith, but are bound by the creeds, which have somehow become the ancient rule of faith through which to interpret the Scriptures. Here is what this amounts to: We have the ancient rule of faith that puts a box around what the Scriptures are allowed to teach us. "Here is your box, Mr. Bible. You may not enlighten future generations about anything that is not in this box."

Further, Mathison's following comment, informing us that the early Church and the magisterial Reformation determined that this rule of faith must be followed, is nothing more than another ancient rule of faith to put us in the box of the first ancient rule of faith. So Mr. Bible's box just got a little smaller, and more confining. If we follow the logic here, the ultimate ancient rule of faith isn't the creeds after all. The ancient rule of faith is the early Church and the magisterial Reformation dictating to us that we must follow the creeds. What is even more astounding than all of this is that this very "rule of faith" defended by Mathison actually contradicts the only rule of faith allowed for by the Westminster Confession of Faith (WCF) itself.

In the WCF 1.1, after listing the sixty-six books of the Bible, we read these words: "All which are given by inspiration of God to be the rule of faith and life." If these sixty-six books were given by inspiration of God to be *the* rule of faith, then how can anything else be considered *the* rule of faith? If we are going to uphold the Westminster Confession, which I surmise that Mathison does, then the only rule of faith that the WCF itself allows for is the Word of God. If anyone wishes to argue that the creeds are the ancient rule of faith, they must acknowledge that the WCF, at the very least, has erred in it's teaching regarding the Word of God. This would be considered a "major doctrine," would it not?

Thus, if a doctrine within the creeds themselves contradict the Scriptures, then we must either change that doctrine, or change chapter 1 of the WCF. In fact, if we are going to be required to determine truth by using "the boundaries of the ancient rule of faith" proposed by "the early Church and the magisterial Reformation," then we most definitely have to change the statement in the WCF 1.10, which reads, "The supreme judge by which *all* controversies of religion are to be determined, and *all* decrees of councils, opinions of ancient writers, doctrines of men, and private spirits, are to be examined, and in whose sentence we are to rest, can be no other but the Holy Spirit speaking in the *Scripture*" (italics mine). Did you catch what that said? All decrees of councils and opinions of ancient writers are to ultimately be examined and determined to be true or false by the Holy Spirit speaking in the...creeds. That is what the statement would have to say in order for us to interpret Scripture within the boundaries of the "ancient rule of faith" proposed by Mathison above. But that isn't what the confession says. Elsewhere in the same article, Mathison states the following:

The ecumenical creeds represent the hermeneutical consensus already reached by the Church. They declare the basic essential truths which have been confessed by all Christians from the first days of the Church until today. They represent that which the entire Church has seen in Scripture....[I]f the Holy Spirit has been promised to guide the Church into the knowledge of the truth of Scripture; if the entire Church for thousands of years confesses to being taught by the Spirit the same essential truths in Scripture, then it follows that those truths are what Scripture says.[3]

There is a pressing question that is staring us in face here: Aren't we today part of that same Church? Why then is Mathison limiting the work of the Holy Spirit to only a portion of the Church in one small period of time? Mathison, being a postmillennialist,[4] should know better than this considering the postmillennial belief that the church could potentially remain on this earth (prior to Christ's future coming) for a far longer period of time than the amount of time the historical church has existed up to the present. Does he mean to suggest that all the boundaries possible for understanding the Scriptures were discovered and written down for us by a portion of the Church in such a short period of time (relative to his eschatological position)?

Following his logic, Mathison's reasoning should cause us to wonder why he is a Presbyterian instead of an Episcopalian. The Episcopalian form of church government is entirely based on the exact same lines of argumentation. And if, once again, you think this statement is unfairly exaggerated, I refer you to the Reverend Dr. Peter Toon's chapter in, *Who Runs the Church? 4 Views on Church Government,* where he provides such a historical defense of the Episcopalian polity[5] that can be summarized by the following quote:

> ...it is difficult to believe that Almighty God, the Father of our Lord Jesus Christ, would have allowed the church in its formative years of growth and expansion in Europe, Africa, and Asia to go so seriously wrong as to make a major mistake in terms of its general polity and church government.[6]

Like Mathison, Toon argues for his church polity using an ancient rule of faith instead of Scripture. In defense of Toon, however, he at least believes that the Bible doesn't speak to us clearly on the issue of church polity. So he uses history for his argument. Mathison, on the other hand, does believe that the Scriptures speak clearly on eschatology (the study of last things), but his eschatology is driven by the confessions and creeds, not Scripture alone. The point being made here is that both Toon and Mathison use the same argument to arrive at their conclusions. The difference is that Toon is consistent (at least here) and Mathison is not. For Mathison, the church polity that was established during the Reformation trumps the church polity that was established during the first five centuries of Christendom. Does anyone else see a problem here? For Mathison, it's okay for the Church in the 16th century to alter the beliefs of earlier generations, but it is not okay for the Church today to alter the beliefs of earlier generations.

Unfortunately, as Mathison has shown us, what was originally intended to be a dictation of beliefs has become a dictator of beliefs. It is fine and good for any denomination to hold to a set of beliefs. But when those beliefs become the grounds to determine that anything contrary is false, then those beliefs have become the authority over Scripture.

Mathison edited a book entitled, *When Shall These Things Be? A Reformed Response to Hyper-Preterism*. This book enlists the authorship of eight well-known men in the Reformed tradition. These eight men are: Keith Mathison, Charles Hill, Richard Pratt Jr., Kenneth Gentry Jr., Simon Kistemaker, Douglas Wilson, Robert Strimple, and RC Sproul Jr. A quick look at the biographies of these men in the back of the book shows that they have multiple degrees, including doctorates, are pastors at various churches, teachers at seminaries, and authors of multiple books. These men are leaders in the Church today and are guiding the thinking of lay people, as well as present and future pastors of the Church. It is easy to look at all that these men have accomplished and thereby be drawn to what they teach and write. The reason that these men are all mentioned here is because it is important to recognize that, as coauthors of *When Shall These Things Be?*, these highly educated and respected men put their stamp of approval on the following quote from Kenneth Gentry that you are about to read. If the following quote does not bother you, then stop reading this book now, because you'll never get it.

> ...[O]rthodox Christians believe that *doctrines* contained in the creeds are the doctrines of *Scripture*, and therefore the doctrines are deemed infallibly certain because they derive from God.[7]

> A critique of any new theological construct or religious movement must consider it on the basis of the historic creeds of orthodox Christianity as an important *first step*...Only *after* obtaining such a theological orientation may we move on to consider exegetical and theological issues.[8]

All of the contributors for, *When Shall These Things Be?*, stand side-by-side with Gentry here. According to the authors of When Shall These Things Be?, who represent many in the Church today, the doctrines stated in the creeds are determined to be true or false not by the Scriptures, but by the sheer fact that those doctrines are stated in the creeds. Their logic teaches us that we cannot possibly know what the Scriptures teach without the creeds. But if that is true, then how could the creeds have possibly been developed in the first place?

It is time that we stop throwing our confessions and creeds at views that disagree with statements therein. If we cannot search the Scriptures together on these issues without needing a confession or creed to do so, then the confessions and creeds have become our final authority. Truth is not proven simply because a person can argue against an opposing view by stating that a particular confession or creed teaches otherwise. If we wish to defend a particular view that is stated in the creeds that we embrace, then we should be able to defend it from Scripture. If our creeds stand at the end, so be it. If they fail to stand under the scrutiny of Scripture, then we need to change our creeds. Let our confessions and creeds be statements of what we believe and no longer statements of what we *must* believe. This goes for using quotes from church fathers as determining factors as well. Using these things as additional support for a Biblical position is one thing. Using them to determine a Biblical position is quite another.

Please understand that the creeds and confessions contain truth and should not be abandoned until proven otherwise. They are innocent until proven guilty by the Scriptures. The entirety of the creeds and confessions do not crumble simply because one part needs to be fixed. This is like going to the hospital to fix a broken arm. It is an illogical fallacy to hold to the "all or nothing" principle. Just because the Spirit was working in the church throughout history doesn't mean that He has worked in every "major" theological area already. Most of the statements in the creeds and confessions can be verified by Scriptures and we are indebted to the historical Church for her work. But this does not mean that if they erred in one point that, therefore, all of it must be wrong. Or, if the Church today discovers that the Scriptures teach a view contrary to a portion of the creeds, this does not mean that we are abandoning orthodoxy or disconnecting from the historical Church.

Interestingly enough, several of the framers of the WCF refused to put their signatures to it after it was formulated because of the undesirable process they had to undertake to develop it. Calvin refused to be bound by the Apostle's Creed because he recognized the potential problem being dealt with in this preface. In addition, when the original WCF was brought to America from England, it was revised because America didn't have kings. What gave us the right to alter the confession? It appears we are willing to amend the confessions for practical reasons, but not for Biblical reasons.

Being willing to alter the creeds and confessions leads to another issue. If we suggest that the creeds and confessions (passed down by the historical Church and believed for generations and generations) must be evaluated in light of Scripture and altered as necessary, then we must also evaluate the grounds on which we hold firmly to the sixty-six books of the Bible. Is it not because of the historical Church that we embrace these sixty-six books? Certainly it is. Why then do we trust that the formulation of the Canon of Scripture that was handed down by the historical Church is indeed the Holy Scriptures? The answer is that we have no reason to doubt that the Holy Spirit worked in the Church to give us His Word. If another one of Paul's letters were to surface all of a sudden, then we would have reason to doubt that we did not have all of the books of the Bible. Is this a possibility? Most certainly not.

Greek scholars, Kurt and Barbara Aland, explain why: "Any reading ever occurring in the New Testament textual tradition, from the original reading onward, has been preserved in the tradition and needs only to be identified."[9] Dr. Charles Hill, professor of New Testament at Reformed Theological Seminary, explains the implications of this in a personal e-mail exchange with me on March 19, 2009: "That means, they have confidence that we haven't lost anything of the originals, that even when we are unsure which variant was original, the original reading is somewhere among the variants we have... You might simply say that we are finding more and more fragments of early copies of the NT writings which confirm that the text we have always had is essentially accurate and that the original text has not been lost."

Since this is the case regarding the sixty-six books of the Holy Scriptures, on what grounds can we, and should we, alter the creeds and confessions? Clearly, the answer is, when the Scriptures contradict them. If we embrace the Canon of Scripture handed down to us by the historical Church, then we cannot also embrace a doctrine that the historical Church has handed down to us that contradicts those very same Scriptures.

Here we must make a choice: We may either embrace the Scriptures, for we have no reason to doubt that the sixty-six books of the Bible are indeed the very Word of God, or we may embrace a doctrine that contradicts those Scriptures and thereby deny that the Scriptures are accurate. But we cannot embrace both. That is an inherent contradiction. If we embrace the Scriptures as the very Word of God as a closed Canon, then it is the final inspired Word from God. If we believe that to be true, then no other document, no matter how old it is, can be equal to it in authority because no other document is inspired by God. Thus, if no other document can claim to be inspired as the authoritative Word of God, then to question a creed or confession is actually common sense. Further, to claim that a portion of a creed or confession is wrong because the actual inspired Word of God contradicts it is actually more orthodox than it is to hold to the creeds and confessions in such cases. It is here that we discover that those who refuse to submit to what the Scriptures teach over against portions of the creeds and confessions that contradict those Scriptures are the ones that actually fail to uphold their own standard.

Brothers and sisters, we must be willing to engage the Scriptures with one another without the use of the confessions and creeds as authoritative even if we hold to them as expressions of what we believe at the time. We must be willing to discuss our disagreements using the Scriptures as our sole authority, and bring in external sources such as church fathers and confessions only as they help shed light upon what the Scriptures actually teach. It is frequently helpful to search history to see if the events that the Scriptures speak of are recorded anywhere. But where these external sources contradict the Scriptures, they cease to remain reliable sources. And just because we cannot find external support does in no way defeat an interpretation. Scripture must remain the *sole* authority.

Does that mean that truth is determined by anyone who brings about any doctrine they wish by saying it is Biblical? Of course not. It has to be Biblical. Why are we so afraid of this? It is because it is construed as arrogance to determine that someone else's view is wrong unless we have a creed to back up our statements. And we are called arrogant if we think that our understanding of Scripture is right and two thousands years of a church doctrine is wrong. To the contrary, it is arrogant to maintain a belief that we know conflicts with Scripture simply to uphold a particular view that has been predominant throughout history. To put it bluntly, this is the "longevity and majority rules" mentality.

This book will challenge that very mentality. Full preterism is a Biblical doctrine that conflicts with the confessions and creeds, particularly in the area of eschatology. Since full preterism disagrees with the confessions and creeds, many will say that it must be wrong. It must be noted, however, that there has never been a council throughout history that has used the Scriptures in a debate or discussion to verify the expression of the Church's view of eschatology in the creeds or the confessions. Mathison himself confirms this in the following two quotes from *Postmillennialism: An Eschatology of Hope:*

> Only recently in the history of the church has the doctrine of eschatology become a topic of intensive study...these doctrinal statements [concerning the coming of Christ and the end of the present age] were often left undeveloped and their implications were left unexplored due to more pressing controversies.[10]

> The basic eschatological beliefs of the apostolic fathers were accepted by the next generation without question. They continued to believe that Christ would visibly return in glory and that the dead would be resurrected for judgment. However, as J. N. D. Kelly notes, these doctrines "were held together in a naïve, unreflective fashion, with little or no attempt to work out their implications or solve the problems that they raise."[11]

You will notice in the confessions that the only doctrine expressed which allows for more than one view is eschatology. A person can be Premillennial, Amillennial, or Postmillennial. Does it not strike us as odd that such a variety of allowance is set forth here and nowhere else? Yet the Church, particularly the intentional confessionalists, continue to use the confessions, the creeds, and tradition as their guide for eschatology. But how can the confessions, the creeds, and tradition be a guide when three views are acceptable? Isn't it just as possible, if not probable, that since there was no definitive stance on how we get *to* the second coming that it was never really studied in depth?

The hope for this book is that the readers will abandon the confessions, the creeds, and tradition as magic decoder rings and visit the Scriptures without them. Those who do not consider themselves to be confessional or creedal will still have to set aside their unintentional creedal and traditional presuppositions in order to deal with the arguments as set forth from the Bible. If it can be demonstrated from the Scriptures that the creeds and confessions are correct, so be it. If not, then let's revise the creeds and confessions so that full preterists are no longer considered unorthodox.

I trust that you will weigh out the arguments from both sides equally and fairly. My prayer is that, after you read this book and the responses to it, all of us will understand God's Word better than we know our confessions and creeds.

Because of His grace,
Alan Bondar

Foreword

Samuel M. Frost

We live in changing times. It's not the first time, though. Throughout church history radical changes have sometimes taken place. Sometimes, these changes attempt to come at the Church from the outside. Those usually fail. However, sometimes the changes come from within the Church, and after some posturing and heated exchanges, the Church comes to grips with them as necessary to guard the once and for all delivered Truth of the Bible.

Jesus lived during the times when Traditions were in full swing within Judaism. From the time of Rabbi Ezra, through the dark period of the Seleucid terror, rabbinical thought and opinion came to dominate the exegesis and promulgation of Scripture (now translated into the Greek Septuagint). With the rise of the mighty Roman Empire and the selection of the Herodian dynasty, Judaism was poised in such a way as to hold sway over its people through Tradition interpreting Scripture.

As we can see in the biblical record of the gospel accounts, most characters we encounter were deeply influenced by this Tradition as they went about their daily lives as Jews. Merchants, tax collectors, carpenters, fishermen, bakers, and banquet caterers lived under the comfort that the Pharisees were looking out for their best interest, and they heeded their words without much dispute as they held Sabbath and other festivals of the Jewish calendar.

Then, Jesus came along. There were others like him before. Others had claimed a sort of messianic title and following. But they briefly existed. A lone self-proclaimed messenger proclaimed the kingdom of God in the desert, and he too gained a following. Then he saw this Jesus from Nazareth. Everything, well, almost everything, started to make sense. This was the One!

Jesus proclaimed the Kingdom of God was near. He gathered up twelve students willing to follow him from all walks of ordinary life. His preaching was different. He wasn't afraid, perhaps as they were, to question the injustice of the Temple priests, the Traditions of the Pharisees, which sometimes appeared to go against what Torah said (but no one dared question loudly). He even confronted the Roman authorities. Jesus' movement was not from the ground up only. His confrontations were with the nobility of the Jewish leadership. He would deliver scathing rebukes to their very faces. His following grew from upper echelon people to the bottom prostitutes. His message would change Judaism forever, as well as the whole world.

This spirit of Jesus was the spirit of a reformer. Someone who saw the Scriptures, compared them with the Traditions, and saw that the two did not quite line up. In order to further the words of God, the Traditions would have to be followed so that the words of God could continue to reap their success. That's what reformation is. That is the sincere intention behind it. It is not a lust for power, but a love for the power that God alone has to give when the shackles of error fall to the ground. It is not a revolution that wants to overthrow the existing institution. It is a *reformation* of that very same institution. The love for the institution is what compels reformers' ideas. As you read this book, this must be kept in mind on every page.

Alan Bondar has written such a work that will, no doubt, spark a heated debate. There will be posturing. It is always a dangerous enterprise to go against the grain in the name of the very source that supposedly upholds the institution one seeks to reform. Alan Bondar does just that. The Church claims to be built on the foundation of the apostles and prophets, upon the words of God as inspired in the Scriptures. Yet, when one looks at certain Traditions, one notices that they do not line up.

Martin Luther, the great Reformer of the 16th century, brought about a change that the Church still has not come to complete grasp of yet. I suppose that if many of Alan's ideas are accepted, or challenged, the Church will not be the same once they encounter them. It will have to posture itself and defend its Traditions, just like the Pharisees. Alan is in this for the long haul. This is not a matter of a slight change, any more than Luther's was. It was a massive change. Alan is challenging the very notion of a final, physical and bodily coming of the Lord Jesus at the end of history. Some have already began to make the proper changes in this area by teaching that such things as we popularly hear on the radio and television like the "end is near" and the "Great Tribulation" is here are false interpretations. Alan goes further, though. If a growing number within the Church has taught that the Great Tribulation was something that happened in the Jewish-Roman war of 66-70 C.E., then we must also at least be open to the idea that Jesus' "second coming" occurred, too.

But that's the problem. That's where many within the Church would stop. And, why do they stop there? One reason: Traditions. What Alan calls "full preterism" is a form of eschatology that does not entertain an "end of the world" scenario. God may end the world at some point, but such knowledge is entirely out of our range as believers. This single fact would cause an overhaul of the Church, mainly in its practices and doctrines as it relates to this issue. It does not seek, for it has no reason to seek, to understand God differently in terms of His Nature, and the Divine Nature and Human-ness of the Son of God. Preterists rest quite comfortably in those Traditions. It also champions the Tradition of the Bible as the word of God. In many ways, it is a Fundamentalist movement, stripping away some Traditions that have come to cloud the work of God in Christ and the Cross.

Jesus' twelve followers "got" what he meant. They, in turn, challenged the same authorities and Traditions their Master did. The final proof of their message was the fall of the Temple, some 30 years later, and the carrying away of the most holy things to Rome. What will this reformation look like? How, if adopted, will it effect change?

Already, since the last 30 years, the preterists have been making headway *within* the Church. Bondar's book is one among many that are starting to crop up. And, they are being heard. Some wanted us to go away. A few years ago, many thought we would go away, only to find out that we have not: We have grown in virtually every denomination, including many with the Roman Catholic Church. Churches are being planted around the world. If things keep going this way, the Church will have to ultimately deal with this issue. They don't have a lot of time, since the end is always "near." Preterists, on the other hand, have all the time in the world!

Anyone who has studied the history of Eschatology, the doctrine of "last things" on earth, comes away bewildered. It is the most diverse doctrine of the Church out there. There are so many forms of it, that many Christians do not bother even studying it. They just leave it to the leaders to dissect it and trust them. Some see the problems, but won't voice any opposition. Alan Bondar is tired of that. His voice in this book is loud and clear, and he shows all the characteristics of a cannon! Deal with this book, or you will deal with it later.

I can endorse this book because it is bold. It is a step, I believe, in the right direction. Although I don't agree with everything in it, perhaps because I don't yet see properly, I can still say it's a must read. I ask the reader to hear the heart in it. Read between the lines. Hear the ache. Hear the impatience. Hear the soul of a person who wants the Church to be the most relevant institution on earth again. Hear the voice of a disciple of Christ who loves his Church, and would gladly suffer shame for the Church. If you get at least that from the book, then, perhaps, you will agree with the author that, yes, something is amiss here. Something is wrong. If it motivates you to "search out the matter" for yourself, as did the wise Bereans, then I think the author would be pleased. If you just shut your eyes and pray that this goes away, you have not even begun to know the problem.

Samuel M. Frost
Tampa, Florida
July, 2009

Introduction

Books and lectures bombard the Christian community on how to make the Bible relevant to us and to our time. These books and lectures claim that the Bible is already relevant, but then, in an attempt to personalize the texts and apply them to us and to our time, the writers and speakers fail to realize their inherent contradiction by providing ways to make the Bible relevant. For example, a product called, *The Personal Promise Bible™* , says this:

> Have you ever inserted your name as you read the Bible to make it more personal? Now you can experience the reality of God's love and promises in a way you never thought possible. In the Personal Promise Bible, you will read your first name personalized in over 5,000 places throughout the New Testament with Psalms and Proverbs.[12]

I sampled this Personal Promise Bible by giving them my name. Here are some samples that my name produced:

> I Cor. 3:16 *Alan is God's temple.*
> Don't you know that Alan is a temple of God, and that God's Spirit lives in him?
> Eph. 1:5-6 *Alan has been adopted by God as His son.*
> Having predestined Alan for adoption as a son through Jesus Christ to Himself, according to the good pleasure of

His desire, to the praise of the glory of His grace, by which He freely bestowed favor on Alan in the Beloved.

Eph. 1:11 *Alan has an inheritance in Christ.*

In Him also Alan was assigned an inheritance, having been predestined according to the purpose of Him who works all things after the counsel of His will.

Col. 1:27 *Christ Himself is in Alan.*

To whom God was pleased to make known what are the riches of the glory of this mystery among the Gentiles, which is Christ in Alan, the hope of glory.

John 3:15-16 *Alan has eternal life in Christ.*

Alan, believing in Him, shall not perish, but have eternal life. For God so loved Alan, that He gave His one and only Son, that Alan, believing in Him, should not perish, but have eternal life.

I John 5:4-5 *Alan has overcome the world.*

For Alan is born of God and overcomes the world. This is the victory that has overcome the world: Alan's faith. Alan overcomes the world because he believes that Jesus is the Son of God.

Phil. 2:5-7 *Alan has Christ's mind.*

Have this in your mind, Alan, which also was in Christ Jesus, who, being in the form of God, didn't consider it robbery to be equal with God, but emptied Himself, taking the form of a servant, being made in the likeness of men.

Eph. 4:32 *Alan has been forgiven in Christ.*

And Alan is to be kind to others, tenderhearted, forgiving others, just as God also in Christ forgave Alan.

These are just a tiny sample of the 5,000 plus places in the Bible that my name could appear! Perhaps *now* people can read the Bible and understand it better. But this is not the case. This *Personal Promise Bible*™ is a clear-cut example of the modern tendency to find relevance in the Bible for our personal lives. However, it is important to realize that such personalization completely removes the Scriptures from the context(s) that God has placed them.

American Christianity has become individualistic and has created a failure to see that God speaks in His Word to a corporate people.[13] The irony is that Christians are no longer satisfied with God's promises; instead, a desire has arisen to peer into the Book of Life to make sure our names are written there without having to embrace God at His Word. Thus, the *Personal Promise Bible*™ actually accomplishes the opposite of its intent (see endnote 13).

So one way that this modern phenomenon has played itself out is seen in the numerous modern translations of the Bible (though few are as obviously bad as the *Personal Promise Bible*™). But beyond even the translations themselves is the way that Bibles are being packaged today. Apparently, the Bible is not relevant anymore unless people are "tricked" into reading it by packaging it within a magazine or a devotional. For example, if Bibles are promoted with boy/girl interviews about "what's hot and what's not," this way of packaging might just be able to sneak in a little Bible reading here and there. If an individual can't get anything out of the *Revolve BibleZine*™ for teen girls[14], perhaps it's because that individual is a Baby Boomer, and they need a special BibleZine just for them. Great news! They have one:

Redefine, NCV
The Complete New Testament
Full-Color, Trade Paper
Does the phrase "Forever Young" mean something to you? If so, you are one of 80 million Baby Boomers born between the years 1946 and 1964, and Redefine is just for you and your generation. This BibleZine brings forth truth from Scripture which helps Boomers look at life from a Christian perspective, particularly as you begin to deal with the many facets of change life brings. With practical insights on a variety of topics, Redefine is a great gift for any Baby Boomer!

✓ Financial management & the fear of insecure retirement
✓ Dealing with empty nest
✓ Children who aren't leaving home, parents who are coming home
✓ Grandchildren
✓ 2nd Careers
✓ Life fulfillment
✓ Health
✓ Travel
✓ Charities/Social Activism Opportunities
✓ Biblical essentials
✓ How to read the Bible for what it's worth
✓ Profiles on Bible personalities
✓ Faith notes

Since people aren't reading their Bible, this solution places it in a magazine that they might read. As Jeremiah Thompson has pointed out, the idea appears to be that such packaging is aimed at conforming the Bible to people instead of conforming people to the Bible.

This "relevantizing" is often formed in the question, "What does this mean to me?" Being products of our culture, it seems that people who initially do not have the question of how to understand the Bible suddenly find themselves saying, "I don't know how to understand the Bible—it just seems so archaic. What difference does this make for me?" Thus, the problem of relevance has been created by proclaiming that it's a problem. Perhaps the problem isn't with relevance, but with the heart. Yet, because of the inadequacy to handle the Scriptures and share the

Gospel with friends, families, and church members, a Bible is placed in their hands by any means possible along with the claim, "The Bible has power, so I just have to get it into their hands."

What has resulted from this, then, are the attempts to modernize the Bible. And these modernizing attempts even go beyond modern translations of the Bible, to such degrees as taking passages of Scripture and trying to allegorize them to meet some present day struggle in daily life: "What is your Goliath?" "Have you stepped out of your boat of worries and walked to Jesus on water?" This sort of preaching has caused people to open their Bibles and find themselves unable to understand what they are reading because they can't figure out what their two turtle doves and a pigeon are from Genesis 15:9 and Leviticus 12:6. Thus, the only conclusion that is surmised is, "My pastor must have some special insight because he knows how to apply this to me."

This isn't to say that these types of applications cannot be made; but more often than not, they are made at the cost of understanding the original context. Thus, many people have been trained by their pastors to bypass what the text means and skip directly to personal application. This has the effect of teaching people to think that personal application is the interpretation of the text. In the mind of many, then, interpretation and application have become synonymous terms.

Such poor handling of the Scriptures ought not to be so. These man-made complications have burdened the joy of reading the Bible for what it is: The unfolding story of God's faithfulness to Israel. And since an understanding of how God deals with His people has been lost, so too, has the understanding of who God really is. Therefore, in order to assist the reader toward a better understanding of the Bible, three basic issues surface that would make Bible study far more reasonable: First, we must understand that the Bible was written to a particular audience; second, we must understand that the Bible was written in a particular time; third, we must understand that the Bible was written for our joy.

Thus, the first part of this book is entitled, "How to Read the Bible Through New Covenant Eyes." The second part of this book is entitled, "Implications of Reading the Bible Through New Covenant Eyes." In that section, we will flesh out one doctrine in particular as an example of reading the Bible in this way. May your study of the Scriptures be invigorated as a result of learning how to read the Bible through New Covenant Eyes.

PART I:

HOW TO READ THE BIBLE THROUGH NEW COVENANT EYES

Chapter 1:
THE BIBLE WAS WRITTEN...
TO A PARTICULAR AUDIENCE

COVENANTS: WHERE DID THEY GO?

Throughout the Scriptures, God makes it plain that He deals with mankind through covenants. Therefore, it should go without saying that at the very least, God's people need to understand covenantalism. That is, we have to understand that God primarily speaks to specific people *groups*, who are in covenant with Him, corporately, even if *through* individuals. Individuals can only be in a right relationship with God through His covenant community, not apart from it. Every individual is in *a* covenant relationship with God because every individual is part of the human race. But being in a covenant where the terms have already been broken only brings death. Yet, that is one type of relationship with God—being enemies.

To have a reconciled relationship with God, one must be in a covenant community where redemption and life can be found. Thus, individuals can only be in a right relationship with God through His covenant community. Here we arrive at something that is typically missing from the mind of the average reader, but that is extremely relevant to Bible reading. Just to be clear here, making the Bible relevant and understanding something that will be relevant to Bible reading are two entirely different things. One of the goals of Bible study is to bring forth *from* the text the relevance that is already inherent *in* the text. We do not create relevance; we discover relevance. So understanding covenantalism becomes necessary for the reader of God's Word who wishes to discover the actual relevance in a particular text so as not to subjectively create false relevance due to ignorance.

Somewhere along the history of the church, the foci of true covenantalism has given way to a Christianity today that predominately teaches its people that the most important thing is "a personal relationship with Jesus." This is precisely why *Personal Promise Bibles*™ and *BibleZines*™ have a corner on the market. The more individualistic our approach to Scripture strays, the more individualistic our lives with Jesus will become. To put it another way, the further away we move from a covenantal approach to Scripture, the less fellowship we will have in the church.

More than ever, a covenant needs to become far more than a theological term. The Gospel is intimately connected to the covenants, and so an improper understanding of the covenants, or at the very least, covenantalism, inescapably produces an improper understanding of the Gospel. Yet, time after time, the word "Gospel", is thrown around like some magic spell by well-meaning people who would readily admit they haven't a clue what it means. Sermons they've heard have taught them to share "the Gospel: Your personal testimony or story about how Jesus saved you." Is it any wonder that the prevailing view today is that truth is relative?

If the Bible, the direct revelation of God in words, means something different to you than it does to me, and we believe both meanings can be correct, then everything else in life becomes relative as well. Wherein, then, are the grounds for the proclamation of Jesus, the crucified and risen Lord for the salvation of sinful men? "What works for you might not work for me." Without a recognition of covenantalism (at the bare minimum), we are on a slippery slope to absurdity. Every person in the Church should recognize covenantalism in the Bible, for what is the Gospel if not objective truth for a corporate, covenant people? God has always dealt with His people in covenants, and He continues to do so today.

The loss of the understanding and passion for covenantalism is especially apparent in America. One can see, after reading the introduction of this book, why that is. Perhaps the beginnings of this can be traced back to the revivalist era of the Church where traveling preachers toured the country calling for personal decisions of faith by walking an aisle or saying a prayer. It seems that this decisionalistic Christianity, which probably arose out of a genuine concern for apathetic times, became the litmus test for whether or not a person was a Christian and, no doubt, became a source of encouragement to the preachers to see so many people signing their names on a card that read, "I was saved on this date." Whatever one may think of that type of Evangelism doesn't change the fact that the *predominance* of having a personal relationship with Jesus arose out of this time period, or at the very least, reared its ugly head from hiding to become the norm of the day.[15]

During this time, the converts, of course, had to be able to display a change in their life-style to show that they were now Christians. Again, what probably began as a noble desire to see lives changed, became a very legalistic Christianity. Now, being a Christian meant that you could no longer drink, smoke, dance, and so on. As time went on, and the excitement of seeing hundreds, if not thousands of people walk an aisle after a preacher has preached a powerful, convicting sermon, the list of do's and don'ts grew with the culture. Even today, the remains of the revivalistic era are hanging on. For example, there are many folks who refuse to go to movies or play cards because they believe that those things are worldly.

The good news is that much of this legalism appears to be losing its grip in the Church today. The bad news is that individualism has developed into a full market-driven monster. While there is no way to know the true motivation of a person, one must wonder if there are many people in the Christian market who are just out to make a quick buck. There are, no doubt, many who mean well—just like many of the revivalists meant well. The goal here is simply to demonstrate that Christianity in America has become a money-maker because if you package something well, and you play on people's beliefs and emotions, you can get them to buy just about anything.

To bring this point home, it is next to impossible anymore to find a product sold in the secular market that has not been "Christianized" and sold especially in Christian stores. Even candy bars now have Biblical packaging. Consider some of the following examples of such "Christianizing":

If you like Role Playing Games, don't play Magic™ because that's evil; play the Christian version called Redemption™ instead. Or in the music realm: If you like Evanescence, listen to Barlow Girl instead, because that's a Christian group. Even on the web: godtube.com (now tangle.com) is the Christian replacement for youtube.com. And by all means, don't wear a shirt that says, "This bud's for you," where a shirt that says, "This blood's for you."

Thus, Christianity, for many Christians in the Church in America means, "How 'different' from the world can I, as an individual, be?" What is so heartbreaking about this is that these Christians rarely concern themselves anymore with what God's Word teaches about righteous living and have replaced those teachings with market-driven Christianity. Few Christians today are convicted over how much they gossip about others, but if they accidentally say a "curse word" that they have been taught to think is bad and sinful to say, then they find themselves repenting. Never-mind that this is completely unsupported Scripturally. It doesn't matter to them because learning God's Word is of secondary importance to looking like a good Christian as defined by American Christianity.

Just ponder for a moment the following questions: How many Christians do you know, including yourself, who read their Bibles other than on Sundays? And if they do read their Bibles during the week, how many of them are more concerned about what the verses mean to them personally than they are about what the verses actually mean in their context?

Now here's the point of all of this: If American Christianity is as individualistic and market-driven as it shows itself to be, then staring us in the face is the hard truth that Christians in America have little recognition that the Bible was written for the benefit of a covenantal people, but specifically to a particular audience in a particular time, also known as audience relevancy. But the American mindset of, "It's my money and I want it now,"[16] demands that the Bible speak to the individual personally just as God spoke to Moses through a burning bush.

But even the prophets of Israel themselves were unique among the people in that they were the mouthpiece of God to the general populace.

God didn't speak to every individual in those days to tell them about the special plan he had for each of their personal lives; nor does God do so today. He does not reveal to individuals what job they should take or whether or not they should move to another location but, rather, speaks to the corporate people of Christ through the Word of God. As simply put as possible, this means that the passages of the Bible that Christians read were not written so that individuals could put their names in the verses. Rather, they are to be understood from a covenantal perspective. So if we are going to regain a Biblical understanding of Christianity as defined by Scripture, we're going to first have to return to the basic fact that God primarily deals with His people corporately through covenants.[17]

UNDERSTANDING COVENANTALISM

The aspect of covenants that specifically concerns us here is the corporate-ness of a covenant. Covenants are taken very seriously. When God enters into a covenant, He always fulfills the terms of the covenant. While God first establishes each covenant by means of an individual, the covenants are always corporate in nature. Sometimes God makes a covenant with the whole human race (cf. Adam and Noah). Other times, God makes a covenant with a single nation (cf. Abraham and David). Whichever the case may be, God always fulfills the terms of each covenant in the life of the people as a whole.

The important thing to realize is that each of these covenants effects the people of the covenant as a whole, not simply as individuals within the covenant. It is not about individualism, but about the corporate people. While God does indeed speak to people in covenant with Him through leaders of the community, the Word from God to the people is not an individual thing. He speaks to all regarding certain commands or prophecies and no one individual has a special word from God that the rest were not given (except for the leaders *through* whom the word was given). This same understanding is provided by president Todd Williams, and professor Brian Toews, of Philadelphia Biblical University:

In both testaments we see that there were special people who spoke for God, performed miracles, interpreted events prophetically and wrote the inspired text of Scripture. They stand in contrast to the vast majority of believers who looked on, listened to, or read the writings of these special servants of God. This is the position that we stand in today. Like the church at Pentecost, when reading the Bible we look on the great miracles and listen to the great words of the prophets and apostles (Acts 2:41-43). The most important issue in this is that we cannot expect God to reveal a specific path for our lives in the same way that He did to the prophets and apostles. We can be assured, however, that His will is deposited for us in their writings, the Holy Scriptures.[18]

When we consider the audience that received the Old Testament Scriptures, we recognize that they were written to Israel, for they were God's covenant people through whom He chose to bring about the plan of redemption. The things written within the pages of the Old Testament Scriptures are about God's dealings with mankind through covenants, particularly with Israel. The focal point of what happens to Israel through the Old Testament hinges upon the covenants God made with them. Whenever He acts on behalf of Israel, it is always because of the promises made to Abraham, Isaac, and Jacob:

"So God heard their groaning; and God remembered His covenant with Abraham, Isaac, and Jacob" (Ex. 2:24).

"I will bring you to the land which I swore to give to Abraham, Isaac, and Jacob, and I will give it to you for a possession; I am the LORD" (Ex. 6:8).

"It is not for your righteousness or for the uprightness of your heart that you are going to possess their land, but it is because of the wickedness of these nations that the LORD your God is driving them out before you, in order to confirm the oath which the LORD swore to your fathers, to Abraham, Isaac and Jacob" (Deut. 9:5).

"But the LORD was gracious to them and had compassion on them and turned to them because of His covenant with Abraham, Isaac, and Jacob, and would not destroy them or cast them from His presence until now" (2 Kings 13:23).

Whatever was revealed to Israel through the Old Testament Scriptures was to be applied corporately. Individuals did not discover special revelation from God for them personally by reading the Scriptures. What applied to one applied to all. The New Covenant works the same way.

God spoke in His Word concerning all the terms, commands, and prophecies of the New Covenant to His people as a whole, not as individuals. The Bible is not concerned with giving a special word to an individual today who wants to know which job they should take. Actually, the New Testament was written to people in the first century (see chapter 2 and appendix A). We should be careful to understand the context of the circumstances and the audience of the time before we consider how it applies to our lives. Unfortunately, many people only want to know what God is telling them through a particular verse without knowing what the text is actually teaching.

An example of this can be demonstrated from James 1:2-3: "²Consider it all joy, my brethren, when you encounter various trials, ³knowing that the testing of your faith produces endurance." It is easy for an individual to jump into a text like this and simply walk away with a personal application to count it all joy in a present day trial that they may be encountering. And perhaps, in a text like this, that becomes the proper application. But how can we know for certain unless we understand the circumstances and are aware of the particular audience to whom these words were written. It doesn't take much to see that these words were written to the twelve tribes who were scattered abroad during the first century (v. 1). What kind of trials is James talking about? During the first century, there was much persecution (both spiritually and physically) against the Christians. It was during a time when the Law of the Old Covenant was being upheld by the Jews while Christians were being ridiculed and persecuted for following the law-free Gospel.

Whatever else may be discovered in this context, the point is that the individual today who is facing a trial is in no way facing the trials that the first century Christians were facing. In the case with James 1:2-3, we are fortunate that poor interpretation does not necessarily lead to poor application because since we are living in the New Covenant, we certainly know that we can count it all joy when we encounter various trials. But there may be more or less application that can be made in any given text depending on the actual context.

Here in James, while the problem with personal application before proper interpretation is minimal, it can still be pointed out that James was in no way teaching *us* today to count it all joy when we encounter various trials. He was writing to Christians that were suffering for the Gospel during the first century. This is quite different than the trials that the majority of people who read these verses encounter. One can see the danger of failing to interpret each text in its context before seeking application. The verses of the Bible were not written to me as an individual. As an individual, there are certainly applications that can be made to my life from the Bible, but those applications are no different for me than for anybody else, because the Scriptures are written to and for a corporate people, not to individuals.

SUMMARY

The Bible was written to a particular audience. The Old Testament was written to Israel, God's covenant people; the New Testament was written to God's covenant people in the first century. Before we, today, can begin to apply the Scriptures to our lives, we must first understand how they affected the audience they were written to. Once we understand the true meaning behind the texts as they applied to the people they were written to, we can then seek application for our lives, some texts more or less than others. The application that we discover for our lives will be the same for all of God's people.

Chapter 2:
THE BIBLE WAS WRITTEN…
IN A PARTICULAR TIME

DATING OF THE SCRIPTURES

What does the dating of the Scriptures have to do with understanding the Bible? The bottom line: Context. We would do well to heed the caution of Tremper Longman III and Raymond Dillard regarding context:

> Even new Bible readers hear the warning to read the Bible "in its context" and not to treat passages in an isolated fashion. However, many understand the context to be literary only and then forget to read the Bible in its historical context, that is, the time period in which it was written and about which it narrates.

One cause is the misunderstanding that describes the Bible as a timeless book. The Bible is a timeless book in the sense that it has an impact on every generation. The books of the Bible are also culture-bound. They were written for people in antiquity in a language and culture and with literary conventions that they understood.

As modern readers, we are distanced from the events that motivated the writings of the book. So even though the authority of the Bible is focused on the text and not on the events it narrates, it is still of utmost importance to read the Bible in the light of the time period from which it comes.

As such, the books of the Bible are careful to signal their relative age. Not every book is able to be dated with precision, but with few exceptions, each book informs the reader of its time of composition and describes events of a historical character.[19]

Deciphering the particular audience who received the letters that were written as well as deciphering the particular time period in which they were written provides a certain context to be able to understand the circumstances that those particular people were dealing with in their particular time. Knowing the people and their circumstances can make a huge difference in the meaning of a text. While it is true that the Scriptures were written *for* the modern church, they were not written *to* the modern church.

Many people read the Bible looking for God to speak to them directly concerning such things as where they should live or whom they should marry. But while God spoke this way directly to a select number of people in the Old Testament, He does not speak to any of His people that way anymore. Hebrews 1, for example, tells us that while God used to speak to His people in various ways in the past, He now has spoken to us finally in His Son. Second Peter 1 says that God "has granted to us all things that pertain to life and godliness." We must understand that the Bible was written to a particular audience, in a particular time. This chapter will focus on the particular audience and the particular time of the writing of the New Testament in order to help the reader to understand that all of the New Testament was written before 70 AD.

One major problem with a post-70 AD dating on any of the books of the Bible is that it takes interpreters on a quest to figure out if God is speaking to individuals today directly as He did then. Indeed, God's dealings with Israel are recorded in the Scriptures for our benefit. God deals with Israel from Genesis to Revelation. The Bible is the story of God's faithfulness to Israel. It is a complete book. He is not still revealing things to the Gentiles (or the Jews, for that matter) because He has already communicated everything His people need to know by telling the story of His faithfulness to Israel. In addition, the Scriptures teach that all of His children, in every generation, constitute the True Israel, descendants of Abraham by faith (cf. Rom. 2:28, 29; Rom. 4; Gal. 3:6-9, 29; Eph. 2:11-16). That being the case, we can look to the Scriptures to see how God deals with His people and how He has been faithful to them.

While the story of national Israel ended at the destruction of Jerusalem in 70 AD, the story of God's faithfulness to the True Israel continues. His True Israel will never be destroyed. She has been saved. She will live on into eternity as she continues to heal the nations with the Gospel. New revelation today is not necessary in order to know what man is to believe concerning God and what God requires of man. God has already revealed that in the story of His faithfulness to Israel.

In a pamphlet entitled, *Knowing the Will of God*, Brian Toews and Todd Williams summarize how to know what the will of God is for our lives. It is an excellent pamphlet and well worth reading.[20] After showing how to know the will of God from the Scriptures, the writers go on to explain the following:

The Will of God Cannot be Known By: Irresponsibly Using the Content of Scripture to Lead Us

"God Gave Me This Verse Today…"
We do not use the Bible indiscriminately by randomly opening it and finding some specific message from God. We are to work hard to handle accurately the word of truth (2 Timothy 2:15).

They go on to discuss several more ways by which the will of God cannot be known. A common thread among all of them is individualism, a sort of God-speaking-personally-to-me type of thinking. Much of this type of thinking stems from a failure to recognize that the Word of God was written to a particular audience, in a particular time. It was not written "to me."

THE VERACITY OF JESUS AND THE APOSTLES

There is enough evidence, both external and internal, to validate an early (i.e. pre-70 AD) date for every book of the New Testament (see appendix A). Most of the difficulties of each book are simplified by understanding them in light of God's dealings with natural Israel and/or in direct relationship to the 70 AD destruction of Jerusalem.

In his book entitled, *Why I'm Not a Christian*, Bertrand Russell argues, "I am concerned with Christ as He appears in the Gospels, taking the Gospel narrative as it stands, and there one does find some things that do not seem very wise. For one thing, He certainly thought that His second coming would occur in clouds of glory before the death of all the people who were living at that time."[21]

Russell then sites the following examples: "'Ye shall not have gone over the cities of Israel till the Son of Man be come'...'There are some standing here which shall not taste death till the Son of Man comes into His kingdom.'"[22] While Russell is not interested in putting forth an intelligible exegesis of the texts, he does see a problem with the traditional interpretation of the teachings of Jesus. The intelligible exegesis that both he and many others miss should be to understand these teachings to be speaking about the prophesied events surrounding the destruction of Jerusalem in 70 AD.

RC Sproul comments, "One of Russell's chief criticisms of the Jesus portrayed in the Gospels is that Jesus was wrong with respect to the timing of his future return. At issue for Russell is the time-frame reference of these prophecies. Russell charges that Jesus failed to return during the time frame he had predicted."[23] Russell is only dealing with the Gospels here, but the problem becomes even greater when this same reasoning is applied to the rest of the New Testament texts. Many of them contain time-frame references that, unless fulfilled in 70 AD, create problems with the veracity of the New Testament writers.

This is one of Russell's reasons, albeit the strongest one, for not being a Christian. While an argument from an atheist is by no means a conclusive argument for the early dating of all the books of the New Testament, his condemning words do ring true. Some might say to this that Russell's problem is that he is unable to understand the Scriptures without the Spirit; but that is an entirely different matter. Russell is not here arguing for how the Scriptures cause one to be changed by them (as 1 Corinthians 2 is teaching), he is arguing for a failure to understand what the words on the page are saying as far as the plain reading of the text is concerned.[24]

Russell proposes a valid criticism, unless there is a sound explanation to these time-frame prophecies, namely, the events surrounding the 70 AD destruction of Jerusalem. This is precisely why a vast number of believers can't understand the Bible. If any of the New Testament books are dated after 70 AD, then any specific point of reference for the plain understanding of what was written has been removed. To some degree, the Scriptures have been turned from being a book with actual words that can be understood into a sort of mystical writing that can only be understood by the greatest of minds.

An example of this is found in what was known as the Quadriga, a hermeneutic[25] established during the medieval period. The Medieval Quadriga taught that words on the pages of Scripture had a deeper meaning than just the exegetical. The words contained three other layers that had to be interpreted. These layers consisted of the ethical or moral, allegorical, and anagogical[26] meanings. Doug Wilson explains, "...the quadriga [sic] was a distorted hermeneutic because it confounded exegesis and application."[27] In other words, the text no longer had any *actual* meaning because it could mean anything.

Consider for a moment that you have a difficult decision to make about buying a house. If you think a rock on the ground in the historical narrative of the book of Genesis contains some allegorical meaning for you, then you might conclude that the rock actually means that you should finally make your decision firm—firm like a rock.

Now the Quadriga did have an exegetical layer, but it became confused with the other three layers. Application was no longer what one did with what the text said, but rather what one did with what the text said to him. Unfortunately, this hermeneutic has infiltrated the minds of many Bible readers today. And this has led to the inherent belief that certain prophecies that were written to a particular audience in a particular time have direct relevance for us today.

If the actual context surrounding the words on the page is removed, then it becomes necessary to find meaning outside of the intended context. But if the New Testament canon was completed before 70 AD, then a beautiful story of God's faithfulness to his people unfolds, and the time-frame prophecies that Russell and others have a problem with are no longer a problem. Personal Promise Bibles™ would become extinct because people would believe that God's promises and prophecies always come true, just as they did for Israel, without the need to have our names written in the text. But if fulfillment of God's promises and prophecies are brought into question, then futile attempts will be erroneously made to make sure they come true, thus creating our own god rather than truly embracing the God of the Bible.

To be sure, this flows from a desire to have a God who we believe is real. But to produce a god that is real according to what we believe is a different god than the God who has produced what we believe. Faith doesn't create God; God creates faith. Faith doesn't assume anything about God; faith actually believes God because He always keeps His promises. What if the people of God actually took God at His Word instead of making sure their names are placed within His Word? Until it is understood that God meant "soon" when He said "soon," there will be skepticism as to whether or not God will do what He said He would do. Granted, Christians will verbally claim that He will, but are we really convinced of it because we have seen Him do *precisely* what He said He would do in His Word or because we have been told to think that way?

This may anger many Christians, but the truth of the matter is that more Christians today live by experience rather than by God's Word. They know that God is faithful to them because they've never missed a meal or because they have a roof over their head. But what if they lost their house and found themselves to be starving? What promises would they hold on to then in order to confirm God's faithfulness? Receiving things that are considered good in America are all too often contributed to God's faithfulness. Perhaps they should be. Yet attempting to determine that God is faithful to us by our experiences will eventually fail. It is no different than reading tealeaves. While our experiences may *prove* God's faithfulness if He has promised to do something and it comes to pass, our experiences do not *determine* God's faithfulness. Rather, God's promise to be faithful to us determines our experiences. To say it another way, God is not more or less faithful to us if we live in want or if we live in plenty. Yet, because God is faithful to us, this fact is true whether we live in want or in plenty. So His faithfulness determines our experiences. For some, His faithfulness determines that they should live in want. For others, His faithfulness determines that they should live in plenty. These different experiences are not the determining factors of God's promise to be faithful. God's promises are verified in His Word because He has never failed to do what He said He would do in the life of Israel.

THE COMPLETION OF THE SCRIPTURES

A final thought regarding the dating of the Scriptures comes from the establishment of apostolic authority and the work of the Holy Spirit among the Gentiles. What was the purpose of the prophets and the apostles? The prophets communicated God's Word to the people of Israel. They did not have the complete canon of Scripture, and so God would speak to them directly many times and in many ways (Heb. 1). With the coming of Jesus, He prophesied that the Jewish age would come to an end (Matthew 23-24). Through the apostles, He established the New Covenant church as an entity consisting of Jews and Gentiles spreading throughout the world. No longer was the Gospel found exclusively in Israel as a nation (Mark 16:15). God broke down the division between Jews and Gentles and created one body out of the two (Eph. 2:15).

Throughout the book of Acts, the work of the Holy Spirit among the Gentiles continued to prove to the natural Jew that the Gospel had indeed been given to the Gentiles as well. So the Gospel spread throughout the world, that is, the Roman Empire. Beginning with Jerusalem, it spread to Judea, Samaria, and to the utter ends of the earth. That is what the book of Acts is about—the fulfillment of that commandment given in Acts 1:8. Paul himself even claims that this happened while he was alive:

> Colossians 1
> [3]We always thank God, the Father of our Lord Jesus Christ, when we pray for you, [4]since we heard of your faith in Christ Jesus and of the love that you have for all the saints, [5]because of the hope laid up for you in heaven. Of this you have heard before in the word of the truth, the gospel, [6]which has come to you, *as indeed in the whole world it is bearing fruit and growing...*[28]

> [21]And you, who once were alienated and hostile in mind, doing evil deeds, [22]he has now reconciled in his body of flesh by his death, in order to present you holy and blameless and above reproach before him, [23]if indeed you continue in the faith, stable and steadfast, not shifting from the hope of the gospel that you heard, *which has been proclaimed in all creation under heaven*, and of which I, Paul, became a minister.[29]

> Romans 10
> [14]How then will they call on him in whom they have not believed? And how are they to believe in him of whom they have never heard? And how are they to hear without someone preaching? [15]And how are they to preach unless they are sent? As it is written, "How beautiful are the feet of those who preach the good news!" [16]But they have not

all obeyed the gospel. For Isaiah says, "Lord, who has believed what he has heard from us?" [17]So faith comes from hearing, and hearing through the word of Christ.[18]But I ask, have they not heard? Indeed they have, for *"Their voice has gone out to all the earth, and their words to the ends of the world."*[30]

With the destruction of Jerusalem in 70 AD, many of the remaining Jews who did not believe, but continued with their Old Covenant sacrifices, were destroyed along with the Temple. What, then, became of the need for the ministry of prophets and apostles? The Scriptures had been written: The prophecies regarding the nation of Israel were given and fulfilled through the signs culminating with the destruction of Jerusalem (Matt. 24; Mark 13; Luke 21). The destruction of Jerusalem verified the establishment of the New Covenant, the coming of Christ, and the end of the Jewish age. In chapter 8 of Hebrews, the writer communicates that the fulfillment of Jeremiah's prophecy about the New Covenant coincided with the disappearing of the Old Covenant:

[7]For if that first covenant had been faultless, there would have been no occasion sought for a second. [8]For finding fault with them, He says,?"Behold, days are coming, says the Lord,?when I will effect a new covenant with the house of Israel and with the house of Judah; [9]not like the covenant which I made with their fathers?on the day when I took them by the hand?to lead them out of the land of Egypt; for they did not continue in my covenant, and I did not care for them, says the Lord. [10]For this is the covenant that I will make with the house of Israel?after those days, says the Lord: I will put my laws into their minds, and I will write them on their hearts. And I will be their God, and they shall be my people. [11]And they shall not teach everyone his fellow citizen, and everyone his brother, saying, 'Know the Lord,'?for all will know me,?from the least to the greatest of them. [12]For I will be merciful to their iniquities, and I

will remember their sins no more." [13]When He said, "A new covenant," *He has made the first obsolete*. But whatever is becoming obsolete and growing old *is ready to disappear*.[31]

The elimination of the Old Covenant happened by means of the destruction of the Temple in Jerusalem. If the New Covenant took the laws of God and internalized them into the minds and hearts of His people so that they would "know the Lord," then what other Scripture would need to be written? The teaching of the arrival of the New Covenant was the ultimate goal of the writers of the New Testament. Once it arrived in its fullness, the whole purpose for writing Scripture ended.

Clement of Alexandria, at the beginning of the third century, made some very interesting comments regarding the cessation of apostolic revelation. Consider the following explanation by Kenneth Gentry where he quotes from Clement's *Miscellanies*:

> In Book 7 of this work Clement deals with the perversion of truth by heretics…Their error is: "They do not make a right but a perverse use of the divine words." He then states that apostolic revelation has ceased: "For the teaching of our Lord at His advent, beginning with Augustus and Tiberius, was completed in the middle of the times of Tiberius. And that of the apostles, embracing the ministry of Paul, *ends with Nero*."[32]

With the Destruction of Jerusalem came the end of new revelation. God did what He promised He would do. That is where Christians should find their assurance rather than in putting our names in the text. And the True Israel continues to live according to the Scriptures that God has already given. Remember, our assurance lies in the fulfilled promises of God, thus making Him the object of our faith, and not in trying to figure out if "I'm personally listed in the Bible." Peter Leithart, pastor of Trinity Reformed Church in Moscow, Idaho, sheds some light on this in his consideration of assurance of salvation:

My axiom here is: There is no "back door" entry to assurance. I want to close the back door, because the effort to enter by the back door doesn't lead to assurance but to the opposite…Entering by the "back door" is any effort to find some alternative way to know that God is gracious to me. God says in His Word, "I forgive you." Trying to get into the back door might take the form of trying to peek over God's shoulder, check the decree and the book of life, and see if "you" includes "me"…that's not a way to assurance because a) we can't peek over God's shoulder at the decree and b) the whole effort to do so betrays a lack of trust in God, in what God has already said to me. God says, "I forgive you," but I'm not sure he really means it, so I have to find some ground of certainty more certain than the promises of God. That is unbelief.[33]

This form of unbelief is the same issue at hand concerning the desire to have new revelation and to date the New Testament books beyond the time that the sign of the fullness of the New Covenant had arrived. If God has spoken to us finally in His Son, and the Spirit of His Son is now among us in the New Covenant, then God had completed His revelation when the sign of that finality was fulfilled.

SUMMARY

The internal evidence of the New Testament Scriptures provides all that is necessary to require their composition prior to 70 AD. Chapter 4 of this book will inherently demonstrate this. But for a more detailed analysis of the argument for a pre-70 AD dating of the New Testament, read appendix A. The pre-70 AD dating of the Scriptures is one of the most important issues confronting the Church today in regards to the poor handling of the Scriptures. People can read a story from start to finish, and with the help of a little context, can understand the straightforward teaching of the story. The Scriptures are no exception. It is the story of God's faithfulness to Israel from start to finish. The final product has arrived—and we get the privilege of presently living in that final product.

Chapter 3:
THE BIBLE WAS WRITTEN…
FOR OUR JOY

GIVING TIME TO GOD

Another reason believers feel overwhelmed with understanding the Bible is because they enter the Scriptures with the mindset of giving time to God. Christianity, somewhere along the line, has been turned into a religion of giving to God. On Sunday mornings, we gather together for worship, and we are told that we are performing before an audience of one. There are many churches that make the claim that their preaching is rooted in the conviction that we were made to glorify God and to enjoy Him forever. But then, those same churches turn around and make the claim that they believe worship is for an audience of one—God Himself.

But how is it that these churches can claim both the conviction that we were made to "…enjoy *Him* forever" and at the same time perform for His enjoyment, since He is the audience. Which is it? Are we performing for God or is He performing for us? Is He enjoying us or are we enjoying Him?[34]

We spend all week giving ourselves to our work, to our spouses, to meet people's needs, and then, when we gather together on Sunday, we are told to give to God, to perform some more for God. It's no wonder people leave our worship gatherings week after week looking for something more. It's because they have already given all they have, and they have nothing left to give. Yet they are told to give more to God. This is not a "come and rest" Gospel, it is a "come and work" Gospel. We are told that we come before an audience of One, and that worship is about performing for God. On the contrary, worship is God performing for us, and us applauding, and crying out for an encore:

> Calvin called worship, as he called creation and redemption, "the marvelous theater" in which God descends to act before a watching world...It is that presence of the Spirit through his ordained means that makes the worship service a theater of grace in which Christ and all his benefits are communicated to those who were once "not a people"— living aimlessly without any definable plot to make sense of or give a sense of significance to their fragmented lives.[35]

We were created to be entertained! This statement will most definitely be received with resistance. Yet, as a result of rejecting this notion, pastors are working overtime to get people to suppress their desires to be entertained. Thus, people are no longer captured by the awe and wonder of God. In essence, we say, "Taste and see that the Lord is good, but make sure you do this out of duty, not because you want to be satisfied by a God who entertains you with His majesty." By contrast, consider the following question: Why is it that the entertainment of our culture has grasped the hearts of its people? It is because the world plays on the fact that God made us to be entertained, whether they formally acknowledge we're made by God or not. So people fill their hearts with any god that they can find to entertain themselves because their desire to be entertained by the true God is suppressed.

Many Christians attend worship gatherings weekly because that's what a good Christian does; they don't really look forward to going. In fact, most people would rather sleep in on Sunday morning if they felt they had the choice. But you see, if they're going to get to heaven, they think that going to church is necessary. Thus, they drag themselves out of bed every Sunday morning to go church so they can perform for God. The sad thing is, they leave every Sunday afternoon feeling the same as when they arrived. They aren't blown away by the majesty of God. The sky doesn't look any grander to them when they leave. During the service, sermons are little more than pep talks on how to be a better Christian: "Read your Bible, pray, serve, because after all that God has done for you, you should at least do that for Him."

So, Christians read their Bible because that's what a good Christian does. Besides, "after all that God did for me, the least I can do is open my Bible and give such a God my time. He's so sad when I don't." So, they read a chapter, or three, or what-have-you, and then close the Bible, not feeling any more satisfied in God than they did before they opened their Bible. Why? Because they were giving to God and not getting from God. The Christian community is told to make God happy by doing what we're told rather than looking to God to make us happy. We are told to stop looking to be so entertained and, instead, to start entertaining, or whatever choice of words we use to communicate that.

It's no wonder the Church is so hypocritical to the world—because while she preaches the message of giving to God, during the rest of the week God's people are entertaining themselves with the world. Who wants a God that requires we start giving to Him? We have better gods than that in the world. Even Baal was good enough for that. No, God says, "Come and get. Come and rest. Come and be satisfied." When we start preaching and teaching that God is calling us to stop giving our best to Him and instead to start being entertained by Him, we'll come to discover that He provides the best entertainment in town. There is no equivalent. Then suddenly, our message to the world is, "Come, for God will satisfy your craving for seeing greatness."

"IT'S ALL ABOUT YOU"

The immediate resistance to this type of talk from scholars and pastors is, "Then it's all about you," or "You make it sound like God's just another drug that they should try out, and luckily they'll discover He's the best one." But that's just a knee-jerk reaction rather than a careful evaluation of what's been said. God is not like another drug that a person should try as though He's next on the stack like the bumper sticker that reads, "Try Jesus! If you don't like Him, Satan will always take you back!" Rather, He is the foundation for all our cravings for pleasure. This calls for putting a stop to piling things on top of God. All that pleasure experiments have ever shown is that they always fail to remain intact as the all-satisfying treasure. But God, being the foundation of why people are trying to seek pleasure, has never changed. He calls us to delight ourselves in Him (Psalm 37:4). This is the Gospel.[36]

Now consider the first argument against this: "It's all about you." Absolutely not! To say that our happiness is the most important thing to us is to say that we want that which can make us the happiest to be center stage. And that can only be God. When a person realizes that God is one and the same as that which makes them the happiest they can be, then to say that their happiness is the most important thing to them is the same as saying that God is the most important thing to them.[37]

Another argument used against this type of thinking is one that says, "You are contradicting yourself: Now you have people reading the Bible because it has to mean something to them." In other words, this book is refuting personal, present-day, situational relevance from the text; but, it is often misunderstood that reading the Bible for our joy suggests that when a person approaches the Scriptures, there has to be something there for *them*, understood to mean, "for them personally, for their present situation." But this misses the point. What is actually there for them is an entertaining, satisfying God in the way He unfolds His plan of redemption through the story of His faithfulness to Israel. Just like when we see part one of a movie we enjoy and can't wait to see part two, we enter the Scriptures anticipating the next part of the drama to unfold before our eyes.

So it is not as though we are looking for some personal relevance to figure out how to handle our bosses at work today. Instead, we are looking for more greatness. We are looking for God. And as God reveals Himself to us in His Word, He also reveals how He works in us through the means of His commandments. We learn the things that we are called to do by observing how God has called other people to do those same things throughout history. The difference between us, and the people of the Old Covenant, is that the New Covenant brought with it the power to obey through Jesus Christ and His Spirit within each of us. All that we need we find in the Scriptures.

SUMMARY

What a tremendous difference it would make in the Church today if we would stop trying to see sufficiency in ourselves by giving to God and started exalting God as the great giver who asks nothing in return. Oh, how worshipping this God would compel our hearts to live out His glorious commands because they are delightful, not burdensome. God has not given us His commandments in order that we might know how to pay Him back for His salvation. No! Rather, He has given us His commandments in order that He might protect our joy in Him by our obedience to them. Our God is faithful; always has been, always will be. See for yourself in the story of His faithfulness to Israel.

PART II:

THE IMPLICATIONS OF READING THE BIBLE THROUGH
NEW COVENANT EYES

Chapter 4:
FULL PRETERISM

ONE MAJOR RESULT

The purpose of this book is to learn how to read the Bible through New Covenant Eyes. Another way of saying that is that the purpose of this book is to learn to read the Bible in its original context. By now, the reader should be keenly aware of the fact that the Scriptures were written to a particular audience, in a particular time. That particular audience is not *us*, and that particular time is not *now*.

The writings of Scripture, however, *were* given to communicate to all generations of all time the faithfulness of God to Israel and the progress of the Gospel from the Jew first and then to the Gentile. All of Scripture tells that story from beginning to end. The Bible starts with creation and death and ends with resurrection and re-creation. It would be next to impossible to deal with all the implications of reading the Bible through New Covenant Eyes for that would require a commentary on every verse in the Bible. But there is one very important and often neglected implication that needs to be addressed because tradition sometimes blinds people to the truth of Scripture.

As was argued in the preface, it is important to understand that the Church that lives today is as capable and Spirit-filled as the Church throughout history. There is absolutely no reason to believe that we in the Church today are unable to uncover some truth in the Scriptures that the Church has missed up to this point. There is no way that every doctrine in the Scriptures has been accurately interpreted and taught already. There is still much to learn. The Bible is unlike any other book in that it is so vast that it will very likely take eternity for the Church to perfectly understand it. Five centuries from now, the Church will yet again rise up and realize that even we today have missed something just like the reformers in the sixteenth century rose up and realized that the Church, up until that point, had missed something, or at the very least, messed something up. This thought frightens a great many people, but the logic is coherent.

Many would argue that the Church Fathers very likely got some minor things wrong, but for some reason, are unwilling to accept that they may have gotten some major things wrong. But who gets to determine what is major and what is minor? Of course, the Church has generally agreed on the doctrines that are considered major, but it's just as likely that the Church does not have every one of those major doctrines correct. Once again, the determining factor as to whether or not these doctrines are correct is not because the church said so, nor is it because it is documented in a creed or a confession. The determining factor is whether or not the Scriptures teach what the Church says it teaches. If we do not follow this reasoning, then the Church has become its own Pope. When the Scriptures contradict the Pope, we must not alter the Scriptures simply because the Pope has said, "Thus says the Lord."

Consider the following words spoken to Martin Luther by the Roman Emperor Charles V: "For it is certain that a single brother is in error if he stands against the opinion of the whole of Christendom, as otherwise Christendom would have erred for a thousand years or more."[38]

And the words of Yohann Eck, also spoken to Martin Luther:

> For what purpose does it serve to raise a new dispute about matters condemned through so many centuries by church and council? Unless perhaps a reason must be given to just anyone about anything whatsoever. But if it were granted that whoever contradicts the councils and the common understanding of the church must be overcome by Scripture passages, we will have nothing in Christianity that is certain or decided.[39]

When a doctrine in the Church is challenged, it is not sufficient to say, "That is heresy because the Church says so." It must be evaluated in light of the Scriptures. Granted, the burden of proof lies on the one who is bringing the challenge, but we must be willing to engage them in the Scriptures to see if, just maybe, there might be something we've missed.

The Church has a history of opposing new or unpopular interpretations. Martin Luther was excommunicated for his belief in justification by faith alone. Galileo was found "vehemently suspect of heresy" due to his view that the earth rotated around the sun. Because of this, he spent the rest of his life under house arrest even after recanting of his heliocentric position. "On 31 October 1992, Pope John Paul II expressed regret for how the Galileo affair was handled, and officially conceded that the Earth was not stationary."[40]

It is not arrogant to challenge the doctrine of the Church. It is arrogant to assume the Church has it right and not be willing to see if the Scriptures indeed say so. It is better to be corrected than to continue in false doctrine simply because we believe certain doctrines have already been dealt with. We should engage any person who raises a challenge against the creeds and confessions by using the Scriptures to refute their arguments after we have given them the opportunity to show us what they believe from the Scriptures. Since the burden of proof lies on them, it is only right that we give them a fair hearing. There is nothing more frustrating than being constantly interrupted when attempting to present an argument or interpretation. Once their presentation is completed, if their interpretation is found to be in error, that person would then not only be shown from the Scriptures where they are wrong, but the Church could also reaffirm her position on the particular doctrine being challenged through the Scriptures rather than through the "Pope." And yes, this must happen every time. This is especially the work of the overseer.

It is very easy to become lazy in our study of Scripture if we cannot or do not determine truth from the Scriptures every time. It is not wrong for any local church to adopt a particular confession or creed, but it is wrong to be unwilling to recognize that everything in that confession or creed needs to be evaluated through the lens of Scripture. If we are willing to say that there are minor doctrines that may be incorrect, then it is inconsistent to say that the major doctrines are absolutely correct. Thus, it is better to stop thinking in terms of major versus minor doctrines and simply start thinking of them as doctrine. If we are certain about what we believe, then we should have no problem demonstrating those beliefs from the Scriptures without resorting to, "The creed says so."

Once again, this does not mean that we should not adopt the creeds and confessions. It simply means that we hold to the statements of the creeds and confessions until those statements are shown to be incorrect through the Scriptures. If and when they are shown to be incorrect, we must change the creeds and confessions.

With that said, there is one particular biblical doctrine that calls for creedal correction. That doctrine is known as full preterism. The word, preterism, means, "pre in fulfillment," or in other words, "past in fulfillment." There are two basic forms of preterism: partial and full. Partial preterists believe that some, if not most, Bible prophecy has already been fulfilled. Full preterists believe that all Bible prophecy has already been fulfilled, although full preterists believe that there is eternal, effectual outworking of these fulfilled prophecies. Proponents of full preterism will sometimes refer to this doctrine simply as preterism because it needs no qualifier since the partial form of preterism already contains the qualifier, *partial*. Other proponents of full preterism refer to this doctrine as consistent preterism because of the consistent hermeneutic that full preterists use in interpreting the Scriptures. This book will use the term full preterism for the sake of clarity.[41]

Adversaries of full preterism tend to call it such names as hyper-preterism (which is intended to be derogatory), unorthodox, and heresy! Is it heresy? Well, according to the confessions and creeds it is unorthodox. Many in the Church at large like to call it heresy because it is outside the bounds of the creeds, but they have no grounds to do so. This creates unwarranted fear in people to the degree that they won't even consider the full preterist position. But what if we were to simply use the Scriptures to determine whether or not it was heresy? If we were to put our creeds and confessions down for a moment and just see what the Scriptures say on the matter, we would all come to a different conclusion than the creeds and confessions. Is full preterism the result of reading the Bible through New Covenant Eyes? You be the judge.

Let us put our contextual lenses on and take a look at the Scriptures. What follows will not be an exhaustive defense of full preterism, but it will be sufficient to get you started. The goal here is to help you see the implications of reading the Bible through New Covenant Eyes, even when it goes against the creeds of the historical Church. You may conclude that the particular doctrine of full preterism does not stand up against the scrutiny of Scripture. Whether that is the end result or not for you, the important thing is that you learn to see the Bible as the sole authority and not allow yourself to be bound by previously determined notions. My prayer for all who read this book is that you will be willing to stand for truth no matter the cost.

As you may have already deduced, this doctrine is costly. But that is to be expected anyway as a follower of Christ. We should not be too naïve as to think that the cost of following Jesus will only be incurred by the world. Martin Luther was condemned as a heretic by the Church. John Huss lost his life at the hands of the Church. Perhaps the Church will learn from her mistakes of the past and deal more kindly with the Martin Luthers and John Husses of our day so that she can benefit in the present and not only in the future.

Sub-Chapter 4A:

THE COMING OF CHRIST

*It is traditionally understood that there will be, in the future, a visible, biological, second coming of Christ to earth. However, this sub-chapter will demonstrate from Scripture that there will be no future, visible, biological second coming of Christ to earth. The Scriptures do teach a coming of Christ that occurred in 70 AD, but that coming was not biological, and therefore, was not a **second** coming of Christ to earth. The coming of Christ was only visible to spiritual eyes, yet was displayed visibly to the biological eyes of all who had faith that the destruction of the Temple in 70 AD was the event that occurred in conjunction with that coming. The coming of Christ was the return of God's presence to mankind that was lost in the sin and death of Adam. This is the Biblical teaching of full preterism.*

THE BIBLICAL CASE FOR FULL PRETERISM

Time dictates nature. We will see throughout chapter 4 that the wrong understanding of the nature of the coming of Christ, the resurrection, and the judgment has caused Christians for centuries to manipulate the biblical time texts concerning these same events. Futurists work overtime trying to fit the time texts of these events into their understanding of their nature. In the end, it is not that the texts regarding the nature of these events actually teach what the traditional view maintains that they teach, but it is blind certainty in the incorrect understanding of the nature of these events that continues to dictate the need to manipulate the clarity of when the Scriptures teach they would occur. Here is basically how this plays out with regards to the coming of Christ:

Matthew 25:31 reads as follows: "But when the Son of Man comes in His glory, and all the angels with Him, then He will sit on His glorious throne." What follows this verse is a discourse on the judgment of the nations at the coming of Christ. Why do we understand passages like Matthew 25 to be talking about a yet future-to-us judgment and coming of Christ? There is no indication in the context that this is the case. We simply assume so because "we are still waiting for the coming of Jesus and the judgment will take place at that time."

As we will soon see, there is nothing in the discourse of Matthew 24-25 that would naturally lead us to this conclusion. The problem is that we wear our magic decoder rings when interpreting texts like this and think to ourselves that since we know that this is talking about the future, then either all of Matthew 24-25 is talking about the future (to us) second coming, or there must be a transition in here somewhere from Jesus' teaching on the destruction of the Temple in Jerusalem. If we didn't use our magic decoder rings, we would not only see that Jesus was talking about events that would happen within one generation of His teaching, but we would never even look for a transition.

Unfortunately, the creeds require that we find a transition because it would be unorthodox to see this passage in context. It, therefore, must be talking about the future (to us) and there must be a transition in there somewhere. Interpreting the Bible that way is called eisegesis (putting ideas into the text). We have been taught that we are not allowed to let texts like this speak for themselves because it has been ingrained in us to be certain about a future (to us) second coming and judgment.

It is very difficult to break with something that you have been taught for so long. In fact, it seems impossible that it could be wrong. So we keep returning to the same texts over and over again trying to figure out how to interpret them in light of a future (to us) second coming and resurrection because we are certain that a full preterist understanding of it cannot be true. Why can't it be true? The typical answer is, "Because there is a future second coming and resurrection." How do you know? "Because the Bible says so." Where? "Right here in these texts like

Matthew 25." And how do you know Matthew 25 is about the future second coming? "Because if it's not, then there is no future second coming and there has to be. There is no way that the Church could be wrong for two thousand years. Thus, I know this is about the future second coming." That is not exegesis. That is not allowing the Scriptures to speak for themselves. That is deciding that no matter what the text says, "it must mean what the Pope and I already believe it means." In this case, the scriptures do not determine what we believe. What we believe determines what the Scriptures say.

But now that we've learned how to read the Bible with audience relevancy in mind, we must begin to come to grips with the fact that the events which the audience alive at that time expected to happen, actually happened according to their expectations. This is where we begin to see that the internal evidence of the Scriptures themselves produces a pre-70 AD completion of the Canon. If the recipients of the New Testament books were told that certain things would happen within their lifetime, then we must believe that they happened within their lifetime. Otherwise, Jesus and apostles were false teachers. And the only event in history that fulfills these things was the destruction of Jerusalem in 70 AD.

Could it be that Matthew 25 is actually teaching about a past event? Let's go back a little bit in Matthew to gain some context.

Matthew 10:16-23

We'll begin with Matthew 10:16-23, since verse 23 is the first place in the New Testament that contains the explicit statement of the Lord's coming:

> [16]Behold, I send you out as sheep in the midst of wolves; so be shrewd as serpents and innocent as doves. [17]But beware of men, for they will hand you over to the courts and scourge you in their synagogues; [18]and you will even be brought before governors and kings for My sake, as a testimony to them and to the Gentiles. [19]But when they

hand you over, do not worry about how or what you are to say; for it will be given you in that hour what you are to say. [20]For it is not you who speak, but it is the Spirit of your Father who speaks in you. [21]Brother will betray brother to death, and a father his child; and children will rise up against parents and cause them to be put to death. [22]You will be hated by all because of My name, but it is the one who has endured to the end who will be saved. [23]But whenever they persecute you in one city, flee to the next; for truly I say to you, you will not finish going through the cities of Israel until the Son of Man comes.

In this passage, Jesus is talking to His twelve disciples. The things that He said would happen to them, in verses 17 and 18, did not happen until after His ascension. Since Jesus is telling His disciples about things that would happen to *them*, how is it possible that Jesus could say, "you will not finish going through the cities of Israel until the Son of Man comes" if we are still waiting for the Son of Man to come? This statement from Jesus makes it abundantly clear that He is not talking to us. Jesus explicitly tells *them* that He would come before *they* finished going through the cities of Israel. It is unmistakable that Jesus is teaching that He would come before all of them died because *they* would be going through the cities of Israel when the Son of Man would come.[42] Matthew 16:27-28 makes this even clearer (as if that's possible).

Matthew 16:27-28

[27]"For the Son of Man is going to come in the glory of His Father with His angels, and will then repay every man according to his deeds. [28]"Truly I say to you, there are some of those who are standing here who will not taste death until they see the Son of Man coming in His kingdom."

Read those verses over and over again until all of it sticks in your head. These same concepts will be seen both explicitly and implicitly many times over as we evaluate other texts. To begin with, we will look at *when* this prophecy would be fulfilled. The words in verse 28 are the important words to notice right away. Jesus is talking to a particular audience, in a particular time. He makes it plain that some of those who were standing there with Him would not die until they would *see* the Son of Man coming in His kingdom. Now, without us even considering when this prophecy would come to pass, if we say that we believe that Jesus tells the truth, then this statement means exactly what it says. Therefore, before all of them died, Jesus came in His kingdom.

There are some who would immediately disagree with the last sentence of the previous paragraph. Notice that the last sentence makes an interpretive switch from *see* the Son of Man coming in His kingdom, which is what verse 28 says, to concluding that Jesus would *actually* come. At first glance, it appears as though they have a case. Why? Immediately following these words from Jesus, Matthew records the event of the transfiguration in chapter 17. Look at what happens in verses 1-3:

> Six days later Jesus took with Him Peter and James and John his brother, and led them up on a high mountain by themselves. And he was transfigured before them; and His face shone like the sun, and His garments became as white as light. And behold, Moses and Elijah appeared to them, talking with Him.

If we compare this with verse 27 of the previous chapter, we see Jesus speaking of Himself coming in "the glory of His Father with His angels." The Greek word, *angelos*, translated as "angels" here can also be translated as "messengers." Thus, putting the two passages together, we see a possible fit: Jesus was seen in the glory of His Father together with His messengers, Moses and Elijah. Yet, expositors that hold to the position that the transfiguration event fulfills this prophecy believe that it can only pertain to the portion in Matthew 16:28 whereas verse 27 is about a yet future second coming for us. The reason for this is because verse 27 tells us that when He comes He will then repay every man according to his deeds. Since that is the case, then it goes without saying that the transfiguration event cannot fulfill verse 27 because Jesus did not repay every man according to his deeds at the transfiguration.

In the transfiguration-fulfillment view, then, there is a division of at least two thousand years between verse 27 and verse 28. It is very unlikely that Jesus would state two different thoughts back to back that would be separated by thousands of years. Without our magic decoder rings, the thought that Jesus was speaking of two different events would never even cross our minds. Where else can we find Jesus stating disconnected thoughts back to back? Apparently, Jesus only likes to do this when He's talking about eschatology.

There are several additional problems with trying to draw a fulfillment in the transfiguration from verse 28. First, in reading the event of the transfiguration, nowhere is it stated that this is in any form a *kingdom* event. This alone, again, does not suffice as a conclusive argument, but it stands as yet another difficulty for the stated position. Continuing on, though, one must ponder how the transfiguration can be considered a "coming" of Jesus. He had been with the disciples all along. The text indicates no departure in order to produce the possibility of a coming.

Further, after the transfiguration event, Jesus tells the disciples who saw the event, "Tell the *vision* to no one until the Son of Man has risen from the dead" (17:9; italics mine). Jesus makes it plain that the disciples saw a vision, not an actual coming of Jesus in His kingdom. In 16:28, Jesus said that they would actually *see* the Son of Man coming in His kingdom. He did not say that they would see a *vision* of the Son of Man coming in His kingdom.

Another problem with the transfiguration-fulfillment is that Matthew tells us that the transfiguration took place six days after Jesus made the prophecy. In essence, to say that the transfiguration fulfilled this prophecy is to say that Jesus believed that many (over against "some") of those who were standing there would be dead within six days. The point of Jesus' statement is that some of them would die before His coming, not simply that some of them would see His coming and some of them wouldn't. To put it another way, if Jesus knew that some of them would see His coming before they died, then the fact that the transfiguration would take place within a week of His statement would relegate the prophecy to absurdity. The prophecy would have to be fulfilled in no less of a time frame than would allow for the ones who would see His coming the probability of death. If not, Jesus would be making a prophecy that would undoubtedly come true since the transfiguration would happen only six days later. It would seem a bit odd for Matthew to place the transfiguration here for the purposes of showing fulfillment since it would hardly require a prophetic statement for such a fulfillment to actually come to pass.

Yet another problem with finding the fulfillment of Matthew 16:28 in the Transfiguration is that verse 27 can in no way, shape, or form be fulfilled by the Transfiguration. Although many translations and commentators would lead you to believe the possibility that verses 27 and 28 might be referring to two different events, verse 27 literally reads as follows: "The Son of Man is *about to come* in the glory of His Father…" (see discussion under "Mello" in this chapter).

Since verse 28 follows immediately on the heels of verse 27, and since the phrase, "some standing here will not taste death" is referring to the coming of the Lord that was about to happen, who could possibly argue logically that verse 27 is speaking of a different event than verse 28? In addition, those who attempt to argue that they are speaking of two different events must argue that verse 27 is about the future (to us) coming of the Lord while verse 28 is speaking of the transfiguration. But one would think that Jesus would prophecy these two events in their proper order, rather than confuse the people.

Let's take a look now at one of the greatest problems with the transfiguration-fulfillment interpretation. To begin with, the response that the disciples had at the transfiguration of Jesus was identical to that of John on the Island of Patmos when He saw Jesus. Take a look at these two passages:

Matthew 17:2, 6-7

…His face shone like the sun, and His garments became as white as light…a voice out of the cloud said, "This is My beloved Son, with whom I am well-pleased; listen to Him!"…When the disciples heard this, they fell face down to the ground and were terrified. And Jesus came to them and touched them and said, "Get up, and do not be afraid."

Revelation 1:16-17

…His face was like the sun shining in its strength. When I saw Him, I fell at His feet like a dead man. And He placed His right hand on me, saying, "Do not be afraid…"

This is what happens when people encounter Christ in the glory of His Father. In other words, Matthew 17 describes a vision of Christ in His heavenly state. So it would appear that the transfiguration is indeed a vision of Christ in His kingdom (cf. 2 Pet. 1:16-18). Thus, the vision of Christ in the transfiguration provides a demonstration of Christ in the glory of His Father. If this is not the same glory as the glory of His Father, then how is it even a vision of the Son of Man in His kingdom where His Father resides? Therefore, to say that the transfiguration fulfilled Matthew 16:28 but did not fulfill Matthew 16:27 is flat-out ridiculous. And since the transfiguration must be the fulfillment of both verses in order for that interpretation to stand, it obviously cannot be the fulfillment of Matthew 16:27-28 because Jesus did not repay every man according to his deeds. To say that the transfiguration was a *vision* of what the Son of Man looks like in the glory of His Father is not the same as saying that they actually saw the Son of Man *coming* in His kingdom.

Finally, let's consider the greatest problem with the transfiguration-fulfillment interpretation. Read the following two texts back to back:

Matthew 16:27-28: [27]For the Son of Man is going to come in the glory of His Father with His angels, and will then repay every man according to his deeds. [28]Truly I say to you, there are some of those who are standing here who will not taste death until they see the Son of Man coming in His kingdom.

Matthew 25:31: But when the Son of Man comes in His glory, and all the angels with Him, then He will sit on His glorious throne.

In both texts, Jesus says that the Son of Man would come in glory with His angels. Notice the identity between these texts: "For the Son of Man is going to come in...glory...with His angels" (Matt. 16). "...when the Son of Man comes in...glory, and all the angels with Him..." (Matt. 25). What is important to notice here is that the teaching of Jesus in Matthew 25 comes after the transfiguration event. If Matthew 16:27-28 was fulfilled in the transfiguration event, then how could Jesus use the same language in Matthew 25 if the event He was teaching about had already occurred? Thus, both Matthew 16:27-28 and Matthew 25 are not only referring to the same event, but there are two things that are inescapable: 1. The fulfillment of this prophecy taught in both passages would occur within one generation of those to whom Jesus was speaking. 2. The transfiguration cannot be the fulfillment of this event. We will deal with the interpretation of Matthew 25 in sub-chapter 4C: The Judgment of the Living and the Dead.

Acts 1:9-11

Another text that is connected to this whole interpretation is Acts 1:9-11:

[9]And after He had said these things, He was lifted up while they were looking on, and a cloud received Him out of their sight. [10]And as they were gazing intently into the sky while He was going, behold, two men in white clothing stood beside them. [11]They also said, "Men of Galilee, why do you stand looking into the sky? This Jesus, who has been

taken up from you into heaven, *will come in just the same way as you have watched Him go into heaven.*"[43]

Strangely, the same interpreters that see the transfiguration as the fulfillment of Matthew 16:28 argue that Acts 1:11 teaches that Jesus has to return visibly, in bodily form, with people staring at Him, in the same way that they watched Him go into heaven. The problem is that if the transfiguration is a fulfillment of *seeing* Jesus coming in His kingdom, then why is it that Jesus looks very different in the transfiguration than He did at His ascension? And since Jesus was as bright as the sun in the transfiguration (just like He was in Revelation), people would hardly be able to stare at Him, whereas it is argued that they were staring at Him in Acts 1:11. It seems as though we have one of two options. Option one is that the statement given by the two men in Acts 1:11 is not referring to the appearance of Jesus' visible biological state nor that people would visibly see *Him* at His coming with biological human eyes.[44] Option two is that the transfiguration is neither a fulfillment, nor a vision, of the Son of Man in His kingdom. It is plain that option 1 is correct: The transfiguration was indeed a vision of the appearance of the Son of Man in His kingdom. It is also plain that the transfiguration cannot be the fulfillment of the prophecy that Jesus made because Jesus had not yet actually come in His kingdom in Matthew 17. Matthew 17 is a *vision* of the appearance of the Son of Man in His kingdom.

Summary of Matthew 10:23, 16:27-28, and Acts 1:9-11

So where are we now?

1. Mathew 10:23 teaches that Jesus would come before his disciples finished going through the cities of Israel.

2. Verses 27 and 28 of Matthew 16 are talking about the same event. That event is not the transfiguration. The transfiguration does, however, provide a glimpse into what the appearance of Jesus would look like when He would come in His kingdom in the glory of His Father.

3. The coming of Jesus in His kingdom would be the time when He would repay every man according to his deeds.

4. There were some people standing there with Jesus that would still be alive at the coming of Jesus in His kingdom to reward every man according to his deeds.

5. Unless some of those people standing there with Jesus are still alive today as you read this book, then this coming of Jesus in His kingdom, in the glory of His father with His angels, to repay every man according to what he has done, has already happened.

6. This coming of Jesus in His kingdom happened in the same way that Jesus departed, according to Acts 1:11. "In the same way" is not referring to the visible biological appearance of Jesus, nor does it mean that people would be staring at him with biological eyes since biological eyes cannot stare at Jesus when He is in the glory of His Father (see endnote 44 of this sub-chapter for an explanation of Acts 1:9-11).

Matthew 24-25

Let's move on to the next passage of Scripture that speaks of the coming of Jesus. At the beginning of Matthew 24, Jesus is exiting the temple when his disciples come up to Him, interested in the temple's buildings. Jesus says to them, "...I tell you the truth, not one stone here will be left on another; every one will be thrown down" (verse 2). The disciples, wanting to know when the temple's buildings would be destroyed ("thrown down"), asked Jesus, "when will this happen, and what will be the sign of your coming and of the end of the age" (verse 3)? So, in verses 4-28, Jesus goes on to tell them all the signs and distresses that must take place before this happens. He then states the following in verses 29-33:

> "*Immediately after the distress of those days* 'the sun will be darkened, and the moon will not give its light; the stars will fall from the sky, and the heavenly bodies will be shaken.' *At that time the sign of the Son of Man will appear in the sky*, and all the nations of the earth will mourn. They will *see* the Son of Man *coming on the clouds of the sky, with power and great glory*. And he will send his angels with a loud trumpet call,

and they will gather his elect from the four winds, from one end of the heavens to the other. Now learn this lesson from the fig tree: As soon as its twigs get tender and its leaves come out, you know that summer is near. Even so, when *you* see all these things, *you know that it is near, right at the door.*"[45]

Jesus is talking to His disciples. He is actually talking to *them* when He says that *they* would see all these things and by that, *they* would know that "it is near, right at the door." Jesus has been answering the disciples' questions. It is noteworthy that Jesus only refers to one "it" in His answer. Which question was Jesus answering? Was it, "when will this happen?" Was it "what will be the sign of your coming?" Or was it, "what will be the sign...of the end of the age?" There are many interpreters who believe that the disciples were asking Jesus questions about two or three different unrelated events. It's almost as though Jesus' comment about the destruction of the Temple gets them all excited for question and answer time and they bombard Him with three unrelated questions. Thus, we are left to figure out which question Jesus has finished answering when He said, "recognize that *it* is near."

But the answer that Jesus gives to His disciples concerns the "when" of the destruction of the Temple, which they understood would happen at the same time as the coming of Christ and the end of the age. The destruction of the Temple was the end of the age; the end of the age happened at the same time as the coming of Christ, which began the *new* age. That is why telling His disciples about when "it" would happen, that is, the destruction of the Temple, answered all three questions.

The Greek word for, "coming," that the disciples used when asking Jesus, "What will be the sign of your *coming*?" is, "parousia." The literal meaning of parousia is, "arrival or presence." This is important because this word helps define the nature of the coming of Christ that the disciples were asking about. They were asking, in essence, "What will be the visible sign that your invisible arrival is near?" They clearly understood that the parousia of Christ would occur in conjunction with the destruction of the Temple, which would end the Old Covenant age.

That is why the issue of the Jesus' comments about destruction of the Temple buildings raised all three questions, the first being, "When will it happen?"

The second set of questions concern the anticipation of this "when" question. "What will be the *sign* of your coming and of the end of the age?" They not only wanted to know *when* these things would happen, but how they could know that the destruction of the Temple, the parousia, and the end of the age were approaching. As you read through Matthew 24-25, you will notice that Jesus never gives them an exact day. In fact, several times throughout the passage, Jesus makes mention of the fact that they had to be alert for they would not know the exact day or hour. Jesus does, however, tell them how they would know that the day and hour was quickly approaching so that they could be alert.

Luke 21 is a parallel passage to Matthew 24. Luke is very helpful in articulating what the final sign was of the impending destruction of Jerusalem that Matthew depicts using Old Testament imagery of war and destruction in Matthew 24:29-33 (cf. Isa. 13). In Luke 21, we read about this same discourse from Luke's perspective:

> [7]They questioned Him, saying, "Teacher, when therefore will these things happen? And what will be the sign when these things are about to take place?" [8]And He said, "See to it that you are not misled; for many will come in My name, saying, 'I am He,' and, 'The time is near ' Do not go after them. [9]"When you hear of wars and disturbances, do not be terrified; for these things must take place first, *but the end does not follow immediately.*"[46]

Luke continues recording some of the things that Jesus states would happen prior to the final sign of the destruction of Jerusalem. After he states these things, Luke explains what that final sign would be in verse 20: "But when you see Jerusalem surrounded by armies, then recognize that her desolation is near." Jesus makes it clear that the Temple would be destroyed by Rome soon after they saw Jerusalem surrounded by Roman armies.

Jesus makes another thing clear to them about the time that these events would take place. In verse 34, Jesus says, "Truly I say to you, this generation will not pass away until all these things take place." C.S. Lewis, the respected Christian apologist and author, said in 1960:

> "Say what you like," we shall be told, "the apocalyptic beliefs of the first Christians have been proved to be false. It is clear from the New Testament that they all expected the Second Coming in their own lifetime. And, worse still, they had a reason, and one which you will find very embarrassing. Their Master had told them so. He shared, and indeed created, their delusion. He said in so many words, 'this generation shall not pass till all these things be done.' And He was wrong. He clearly knew no more about the end of the world than anyone else." It is certainly the most embarrassing verse in the Bible.[47]

On the other hand, if we take Jesus at His word, then this verse is no longer embarrassing. Now, the reader should recall the description of the coming of the Son of Man in His kingdom that was recorded in Matthew 16. You will notice the similarity in both passages (Matthew 16 and Matthew 24) regarding the coming of the Son of Man. They are not carbon copies of each other, but they both indeed speak of seeing the Son of Man coming in glory with His angels.

Mathew 16
[27]"For the Son of Man is going to come in the glory of His Father with His angels, and will then repay every man according to his deeds. [28]"Truly I say to you, there are some of those who are standing here who will not taste death until they see the Son of Man coming in His kingdom."

Matthew 24
[30]"And then the sign of the Son of Man will appear in the sky, and then all the tribes of the earth will mourn, and they will see the Son of Man coming on the clouds of the

sky with power and great glory. [31]"And He will send forth
His angels with a great trumpet and they will gather together
His elect from the four winds, from one end of the sky to
the other.

Either these passages are talking about the same event, or we have
two "comings" of Jesus after His ascension. Matthew 24:30 adds the
phrase, "coming on the clouds of the sky." If you recall from Acts 1:9,
Jesus was lifted up and a *cloud* received Him out of their sight. It appears
that here we have an answer as to what the two men (who were probably
angels) in Acts 1:10-11 meant when they said, "This Jesus, who has been
taken up from you into heaven, will come in just the same way as you
have watched Him go into heaven." John Noë provides some helpful
insight into the "cloud-coming" of Christ:

> The Jews of Jesus' day had studied these "day of the Lord"
> occurrences and were familiar with "cloud-coming"
> phraseology, as well as the application of one with the other.
> The Hebrew scriptures are rich in similes and figurative
> language that poetically portray a heavenly perspective of
> God coming among men in judgment:

> • See, the Lord rides on a swift *cloud* and is coming to
> Egypt (Isa. 19:1). (For the earthly fulfillment, see Isaiah
> 20:1-6)
> • Look! He advances like the *clouds*, his chariots come like
> a whirlwind (Jer. 4:13).
> • For the day is near, the day of the Lord is near—a day
> of *clouds*, a time of doom for the nations (Eze. 30:3).
> • ...He makes the *clouds* his chariots and rides on the wings
> of the wind. He makes winds his messengers, flames of
> fire his servants (Ps. 104:3-4).
> • Also see Eze. 30:18; Ps. 18:9-12; 2 Sa. 22:10-12; Na.
> 1:3; Joel 2:1-2; Zep. 1:14-15).

With familiar cloud-coming imagery Daniel prophesied the coming of the Son of Man (Da. 7:13). Jesus, by deriving his "coming on the clouds" phrase directly from Daniel, was revealing Himself as God and the promised Messiah (Mt. 24:30; 26:64). The high priest Caiaphas immediately understood this claim of Jesus to be Deity and responded, "He has spoken blasphemy!" (Mt. 26:65).[48]

The connection between the cloud imagery and judgment is hard to miss, but this is the imagery in Matthew 24:30. Also notice that in both Matthew 16 and Matthew 24, angels are present with Jesus at His coming. Matthew 24:31 tells us that Jesus sends His angels to gather His elect together and Matthew 16:27 tells us that Jesus would repay every man according to his deeds.

Matthew 25:31

So we return to our text in Matthew 25:31, where we see yet another parallel to these passages: "But when the Son of Man comes in His glory, and all the angels with Him, then He will sit on His glorious throne." This verse adds yet another element: Jesus will sit on His glorious throne when He comes in His glory with the angels. Jesus states in all three passages that He was going to come in glory with angels. So either Jesus is speaking of the same coming (option 1), or Jesus is teaching that He would return twice in exactly the same manner (option 2). No matter which option is chosen, interpreters must define the nature of Christ's coming identically in all the contexts that speak of Him coming in glory with angels. Option two is further from orthodoxy than option one. But there is no third option. And, no matter which option we choose in our interpretation of these passages, one thing is for certain, the orthodox view of *one* future (to us) coming of Jesus is impossible to square with Scripture.

It is interesting to note that those who hold to a double-fulfillment of the comings of Jesus are willing to teach that the first of these two comings (i.e. Matt. 24), which occurred in 70 AD at the destruction of Jerusalem, is described through Old Testament imagery to convey that the coming of Christ in glory with His angels was not visible to biological eyes, except through the events that are described surrounding the destruction of Jerusalem.[49] Yet, when they teach about the *future* (to us) coming of Jesus (i.e. Matt. 25:31), they teach that it will be visible to biological eyes. This, of course, is a double hermeneutic. Either Jesus himself must be literally seen with biological eyes in all the passages that teach of His coming in glory or Jesus is using Old Testament imagery in all of the passages that teach of His coming in glory.

Matthew 26:64

In Matthew 26:64, Jesus says the following to Caiaphas: "It is as you said. Nevertheless, I say to you, hereafter you will see the Son of Man sitting at the right hand of Power, and coming on the clouds of heaven." Regarding the word, *hereafter*, Mathison explains that the "Greek words are, *ar' arti*, and literally mean, 'from now on.' The time element in this text begins in the present and extends into the indefinite future." Mathison is content to interpret this verse in light of Daniel 7:13-14 and Psalm 110:1, which he believes were fulfilled, or at least began to be fulfilled at the ascension of Christ.[50]

The problem here is that Matthew 26:64 contains the Greek word, "horao", which is translated, "see", and is the exact same word that is used in Matthew 16:28 and 24:30. In fact, in both Matthew 24:30 and 26:64, "horao" is in the future, middle, indicative. Jesus uses *horao* to mean, "see with spiritual eyes," in both of these texts. Astonishingly, Mathison seems to recognize this necessary identical understanding of *horao* being used in both contexts, but is unable to recognize that Jesus' "coming in glory with angels" must also, by necessity, produce an identical understanding in each of the passages used.

Is it really all that inconceivable to think that if Caiaphas and the rest of the Jews (the "you" being plural in 26:64) would "see" the Son of Man coming on the clouds of heaven, that the coming of Jesus in glory with the angels to sit on His glorious throne in 25:31 was also "seen" and occurred in the same manner? Jesus is not trying to trick anybody. He is consistently teaching about the same coming throughout these texts, and there is absolutely no reason to believe that this coming did not occur within that generation, before all of those to whom Jesus was talking would die. They saw Jesus do exactly what He said He would within the time frame that He said He would.

So Matthew 10 teaches us that Jesus would come before His disciples finished going through the cities of Israel; Matthew 16 teaches us that Jesus was about to come and would do so before some standing there would die; Matthew 24 teaches us that the coming of Jesus was near and that His coming would occur within that generation; and Matthew 25:31 picks up on that same thought and reads, "When the Son of Man comes in his glory…" When would that be? Jesus has already established that. A further time indicator is unnecessary because He has already said when He would come. He is simply adding further information about what would occur at that coming.

John 14-16

Let us take a look at another text that has posed problems for interpreters for a very long time because of the futurist doctrine of the Church: John 14-16. Jesus is in the upper room with his twelve disciples. After Judas Iscariot has left to betray Jesus, and after Jesus tells Peter that he would deny Him, He begins this next discourse with the remaining eleven disciples by saying the following words:

> [1]"Do not let your heart be troubled; believe in God, believe also in Me. [2]In My Father's house are many dwelling places; if it were not so, I would have told you; for I go to prepare a place for you. [3]If I go and prepare a place for you, I will come again and receive you to Myself, that where I am, there you may be also. [4]And you know the way where I am going."

Jesus then answers Thomas' question by explaining that the way to the Father is through Him. This house is His Father's house and has many dwelling places. Compare this with Paul's teaching in Ephesians 2:19-22:

> [19]So then you are no longer strangers and aliens, but you are fellow citizens with the saints, and are of God's *household,* [20]having been *built on the foundation of the apostles and prophets,* Christ Jesus Himself being the corner stone, [21]in whom *the whole building, being fitted together,* is growing into a holy temple in the Lord, [22]in whom you also are *being built together into a dwelling of God* in the Spirit.

The dwelling places, being fitted together, is the dwelling of God. The goal, then, is to get to the Father, not to a dwelling place. The people *are* the dwelling places, being built upon the foundation of the apostles and prophets, the apostles being the ones to whom Jesus is speaking in John 14.

Thus, the places that Jesus is preparing for them are not rooms for them to be *in,* but for them to *be* the rooms of the Father's house. What is noteworthy here is that Jesus does not say that He will come again to them, but that He would come again and take them to Himself! Jesus is the chief cornerstone of this house, and there are many rooms in this house. This is synonymous with the body illustration of Christ. Christ's body is made up of many parts, Himself being the head. So according to Jesus, He would come again in order to take them to Himself, that where He is, they may be also. He is in the presence of the Father. The Father is not visible on earth to biological eyes. Jesus went to the Father, and He entered into the invisible realm where His Father is. *There* is where Jesus would prepare a place for them, so that where He would be, they would be also.

The way *there* is through Jesus. He says in verses 18-19, "I will not leave you as orphans; I will come to you. Yet a little while and the world will see me *no more,* but you will see me. Because I live, you will also live" (italics mine). Jesus makes it plain here that when He goes to the Father, the world would see Him no more. Period.[51] There are no qualifiers, such as, "no more until I return." He simply says, "no more." But who *would* see Him again? They would!

He goes on to say in verse 20, "In that day you will know that I am in my Father and you in me, and I in you." In what day? When He comes to them to take them to Himself. How will they know that He is in His Father, and they are in Him, and He is in them? Verse 21: "Whoever has my commandments and keeps them, he it is who loves me. And he who loves me will be loved by my Father, and I will love him and manifest myself to him." Will this manifestation be made to biological eyes? Apparently, Judas (not Iscariot) didn't think so. He asks, in verse 22, "Lord, how is it that you will manifest yourself to us, and not to the world?" They would see Him, not with biological eyes, but, as Jesus answered in verses 23-24, "If anyone loves me, he will keep my word, and my Father will love him, and we will come to him and make our home with him. Whoever does not love me does not keep my words. And the word that you hear is not mine but the Father's who sent me." The way the Lord manifested Himself to them and not to the world was by them keeping His Word and thus, loving Him.

Later, in this same discourse, as they traveled together to the Garden of Gethsemene, Jesus continued to discuss things that would happen after He had gone to the Father. We can see this in verses like 15:26: "But when the Helper comes, whom I will send to you from the Father…"; 16:5: "But now I am going to him who sent me…"; 16:10: "…I go to the Father, and you will see me no longer…" After Jesus says, "you will see me no longer" to the twelve disciples, he qualifies this statement in verse 16: "A little while, and you will see me no longer; *and again a little while, and you will see me*" (italics mine). What did the disciples understand Jesus to mean by a little while? Apparently, they didn't understand it at all: "So some of his disciples said to one another, 'What is this that he says to us, "A little while, and you will not see me, and again a little while, and you will see me"; and, "because I am going to the Father"?' So they were saying, 'What does he mean by "a little while"? We do not know what he is talking about'."

There was an important connection that the disciples did make though. When Jesus said, "A little while and you will not see me, and again a little while, and you will see me," the disciples make it clear that they understood that the time between these "little whiles" would occur

91

when Jesus would go to the Father. Whatever else one wishes to make of this text, one thing is for certain, it would be a little while before Jesus would ascend to the Father (when they would see Him no longer), and it would be a little while till He would come again (when they would see Him). Each "a little while" must have a reasonably similar time-ratio for Jesus to be taken seriously. It is hardly conceivable that "a little while" could last two thousand years before He is seen again. It is even less conceivable when compared to "a little while" before He would go to the Father.

In addition, Jesus tells His disciples that in a little while *they* would see Him no longer but *again* in a little while *they* would see Him. How can this apply to both the disciples to whom Jesus was speaking and to us two thousand years later? It cannot. If we take Jesus at His Word, we have seen that He has been utterly consistent in His teaching that His coming again would occur in a little while, within that generation, and before some to whom He was speaking would die.

THE APOSTLES AND TIME REFERENCES

What about the Apostles? Were they as clear as Jesus in teaching the impending coming of Jesus within that generation? Let's take a look at just a few of the time texts that the apostles used and then we'll take a look at some of things that they were expecting to be fulfilled in their generation.

Mello

According to Greek Lexicons, the Greek word mello, has a variety of meanings. Consider the following from *The Greek-English Lexicon of the New Testament and Other Early Christian Literature*, by Bauer, Ardnt, Gingrich, and Danker (BAGD)[52]:

1. when followed by an infinitive—
    a. denotes certainty that an event will occur in the future

    b. with the aorist infinitive—
        i. be on the point of, be about to
        ii. be destined, inevitable
    c. with the present infinitive—
        i. be about to, be on the point of
        ii. a periphrasis [i.e., use of a longer phrasing in place of a possible shorter form of expression] for the future tense
        iii. denoting an intended action: intend, propose, have in mind
        iv. denoting an action that must necessarily follow a divine decree: must, will certainly
2. the participle is used absolute in the meaning: future, to come (as in the expression, "age to come" where mello is translated "to come")
3. delay (as in the question, ti melleis; "Why are you delaying?")

The focus in this section concerns mello when followed by either an aorist or a present infinitive (1b and c above). With such a range of meanings, only the context surrounding the use of the word mello can determine whether mello should be translated as "about to" or "intend" or "will certainly" or any one of these other meanings. It is interesting that mello is never translated as "about to" in any of the contexts speaking about the coming of Jesus in any of our common translations of the Bible. Yet "about to" is not only one possible meaning of mello, but it is the **first** meaning listed by BAGD. The question to ask here is, why is mello *never* translated as "about to" in *any* of the verses discussing eschatology?[53]

The reason translators do not translate mello as "about to" in any of these contexts has everything to do with the fact that they are wearing their magic decoder ring. There is not a single instance of the mello-plus-infinitive construction in the Greek New Testament that does not make perfect sense with the meaning of "about to," unless, of course, we bring into the text our magic decoder ring. It is arguably the case, that all the other possible meanings have become necessary possibilities because the belief in the future (to us) second coming of Jesus requires them. The problem here is that grammarians are using theology to determine the meaning of the word rather than allowing the meaning of the word to determine their theology.

Young's Literal Translation demonstrates this for us. Of the 80 plus places in the New Testament where the combination of mello with the infinitive is used, Young's Literal Translation translates mello as "about to" with only four exceptions: Matthew 24:6, Acts 13:34, Acts 20:13, and 2 Peter 1:12. Both in Mathew 24:6 and in 2 Peter 1:12, mello is conjugated in the future, active indicative. These are the only two verses in the Greek New Testament that contain the combination of mello in its future form together with an infinitive. The translation of the future form of mello as "about to" is very cumbersome to read in English. Yet, the idea of immediacy is still there and should be translated that way.

In Acts 13:34 and 20:13, mello is conjugated as a present, active participle. This conjugation and the present, active indicative conjugation are the most common forms of mello used. So we will look at these two verses below.

> Young translates Acts 13:34 as follows: "And that He did raise him up out of the dead, no more to return to corruption…"

What is interesting about Young's exception in Acts 13:34 is that the word mello is left completely untranslated. *The Interlinear Literal Translation of the Greek New Testament*[54] translates this verse as follows:

> Acts 13:34: "And that he raised him from among the dead, no more to be about to return to corruption…"

> Young translates Acts 20:13 as follows: "And we having gone before unto the ship, did sail to Assos, thence intending to take in Paul, for so he had arranged, intending himself to go on foot."

Young translates the form of mello in this verse as "intending." This is the only time that Young translates mello this way. This seems extremely odd, especially since it is unnecessary. In the end, this particular use of mello does not seem to have any theological implications one way or the other, but for the sake of consistency and accuracy, here is the verse in *The Interlinear Literal Translation of the Greek New Testament*:

> Acts 20:13: "But we having gone before to the ship sailed to Assos, there being about to take in Paul; for so, he appointed, being about himself to go on foot."

So after examining Young's four exceptions, even those four verses make perfect sense when mello is translated to mean "about to." Therefore, every single place in the New Testament containing this combination of mello with the infinitive should be translated as "about to," or at least translated to communicate this concept in the places where the English doesn't lend itself to that exact translation.

Matthew 16:27, which we saw above, is a prime example of this. In Matthew 16:27, mello is indeed followed by the present infinitive form of *erchomai*, which means "to come." Therefore, the word, *mello*, conjugated as a present, active indicative, along with the present infinitive form of *erchomai*, should be translated as, "about to come." This is especially apparent from the fact that in verse 28, Jesus states, "there are some of those who are standing here who will not taste death until they see the Son of Man coming in His kingdom." Context determines the meaning of the word. If the immediate context in these two verses demonstrates that mello should be translated as "about to," then what reason is there to not translate mello as "about to" in the rest of the verses in the New Testament within their contexts of the coming of Christ. Below is a sampling of such verses that deal with the subject at hand, namely, the coming of Christ. In each of these verses, mello will be translated with the words, "about to", as they should be, and will be inserted in brackets.

John 14:22: "Lord, how is it that you are [about to] manifest yourself to us, and not to the world?"

2 Timothy 4:1: "I solemnly charge you in the presence of God and of Christ Jesus, who is [about to] judge the living and the dead, and by His appearing and His kingdom..."

Hebrews 1:14: "Are they not all ministering spirits, sent out to render service for the sake of those who are [about to] inherit salvation?"

Hebrews 10:26-27: "²⁶For if we go on sinning willfully after receiving the knowledge of the truth, there no longer remains a sacrifice for sins, ²⁷but a terrifying expectation of judgment and the fury of a fire which is [about to] consume the adversaries."

James 2:12: "So speak and so act as those who are [about to] be judged by the law of liberty."

1 Peter 5:1-4: "¹Therefore, I exhort the elders among you, as your fellow elder and witness of the sufferings of Christ, and *a partaker also of the glory that is [about to] be revealed,* ²shepherd the flock of God among you, exercising oversight not under compulsion, but voluntarily, according to the will of God; and not for sordid gain, but with eagerness; ³nor yet as lording it over those allotted to your charge, but proving to be examples to the flock. ⁴And *when the Chief Shepherd appears, you will receive the unfading crown of glory.*"⁵⁵

Revelation 3:10-11: "¹⁰Because you have kept the word of My perseverance, I also will keep you from the hour of testing, that hour which is [about to] come upon the whole world, to test those who dwell on the earth. [11]I am coming *quickly*; hold fast what you have, so that no one will take your crown."[56]

Revelation 12:5: "And she gave birth to a son, a male child, who is [about to] rule all the nations with a rod of iron; and her child was caught up to God and to His throne.

Acts 17:30-31: "[30]Therefore having overlooked the times of ignorance, God is now declaring to men that all people everywhere should repent, [31]because He has fixed a day in which He is [about to] judge the world in righteousness through a Man whom He has appointed, having furnished proof to all men by raising Him from the dead."

Acts 24:14-15: "[14]But this I admit to you, that according to the Way which they call a sect I do serve the God of our fathers, believing everything that is in accordance with the Law and that is written in the Prophets; [15]having a hope in God, which these men cherish themselves, that there is [about to] be a resurrection of both the righteous and the wicked.

Above are a number of texts that contain the combination of mello together with an infinitive verb. The texts that follow contain the Greek word mello without the infinitive verb. As you will see, they follow the same line of thinking as the verses with the infinitive. It appears that the apostles used the word, mello, to mean "about to" whether or not they used the infinitive.[57]

Ephesians 1:20-21: "[20]which He brought about in Christ, when He raised Him from the dead and seated Him at His right hand in the heavenly places, [21]far above all rule and authority and power and dominion, and every name that is named, not only in this age but also in the one [about to] come."

Colossians 2:16-17: "[16]Therefore no one is to act as your judge in regard to food or drink or in respect to a festival or a new moon or a Sabbath day—[17]things which are a mere shadow of what is [about to] come; but the substance belongs to Christ."

1 Timothy 4:8:"…for bodily discipline is only of little profit, but godliness is profitable for all things, since it holds promise for the present life and also for the life [about to] come."

1 Timothy 6:18-19: "[18]Instruct them to do good, to be rich in good works, to be generous and ready to share, [19]storing up for themselves the treasure of a good foundation for the future, so that they may take hold of that which is life indeed."

The phrase translated, "for the future," is the Greek word, mello. Literally, verse 19 should be translated as follows: "storing up for themselves the treasure of a good foundation for that which is [about to] come, so that they may take hold of that which is life indeed."

Hebrews 2:5: "For He did not subject to angels the world [about to] come, concerning which we are speaking."

Hebrews 6:4-6: "[4]For in the case of those who have once been enlightened and have tasted of the heavenly gift and have been made partakers of the Holy Spirit, [5]and have tasted the good word of God and the powers of the age [about to] come, [6]and then have fallen away, it is impossible to renew them again to repentance, since they again crucify to themselves the Son of God and put Him to open shame."

Hebrews 9:11: "But when Christ appeared as a high priest of the good things [about to] come, He entered through the greater and more perfect tabernacle, not made with hands, that is to say, not of this creation..."[58]

Hebrews 10:1: "For the Law, since it has only a shadow of the good things [about to] come and not the very form of things, can never, by the same sacrifices which they offer continually year by year, make perfect those who draw near."

Hebrews 13:14: "For here we do not have a lasting city, but we are seeking the city which is [about to] come."

If we put Acts 24:25 in the context where it belongs with Acts 24:14-15, it should become plain that even though verse 25 does not contain the infinitive verb, *mello* should be translated as "about to" since verse 15 does contain the infinitive verb and must be translated as "about to." Here are all three verses together: "[14]But this I admit to you, that according to the Way which they call a sect I do serve the God of our fathers, believing everything that is in accordance with the Law and that is written in the Prophets; [15]having a hope in God, which these men cherish themselves, that there is [about to] be a resurrection of both the righteous and the wicked...[25]But as he was discussing righteousness, self-control and the judgment [about to] come, Felix became frightened and said, 'Go away for the present, and when I find time I will summon you.'"

This is just a tiny sampling of verses in the Bible containing the word mello. Many times, our English translations do translate mello as, "about to." But there is a lack of consistency. Yet, the verses lacking this consistency make complete sense when translated accurately. The real problem has nothing to do with whether or not mello should be translated as "about to." The real problem is that a literal translation of mello in certain verses would force us to reconsider the traditional view of the coming of Christ.

Other Time References

Following is a series of other time references that are also typically either ignored or interpreted in light of traditional presuppositions. These time references must be seen with an impending nature or else they meant nothing to the audiences who received the letters. Audience relevancy must be kept in mind as the Scriptures are read. The following verses are in those very same Scriptures. Important words significant to audience relevancy and time will be placed in italics:

1 Corinthians 10:11: "Now these things happened to them as an example, and they were written for *our* instruction, *upon whom the ends of the ages have come.*

Philippians 4:5: "Let *your* gentle spirit be known to all men. The Lord is *near.*"

1 Thessalonians 5:23: "Now may the God of peace Himself sanctify *you* entirely; and may *your* spirit and soul and body be preserved complete, without blame *at the coming* of our Lord Jesus Christ."

2 Thessalonians 1:6: "For after all it is only just for God to repay with affliction *those* who afflict *you*, 7and to give relief to *you* who are afflicted and to *us* as well when the Lord Jesus will be revealed from heaven with His mighty angels in flaming fire..."

1 Timothy 6:13-14: "13I charge *you* in the presence of God, who gives life to all things, and of Christ Jesus, who testified the good confession before Pontius Pilate, 14that *you* keep the commandment without stain or reproach *until* the appearing of our Lord Jesus Christ..."

When should Timothy expect this appearing and what other instructions does Paul give to him? Once again, let us bring into context verses 18-19 which we saw earlier containing the Greek word, *mello*:

"18Instruct *them* [Timothy's church] to do good, to be rich in good works, to be generous and ready to share, 19storing up for themselves the treasure of a good foundation for that which is [about to] come, so that they may take hold of that which is life indeed."

Of course, Paul has already encouraged Timothy about the life to come in 4:8:

"…godliness is profitable for all things, since it holds promise for the present life and also for the life [about to] come."

Below is the whole chapter of 2 Timothy 3. When read with audience relevancy in mind, this text can be speaking of no other time period than when Paul and Timothy were alive. When verse 1 begins with the phrase, "But realize this," remember that Paul is writing to Timothy. Therefore, this must be understood as, "But Timothy, realize this…" All brackets and italics are mine and are included to bring out the obvious that is frequently ignored:

1But [Timothy,] realize this, that in the *last days* difficult times will come. 2For men will be lovers of self, lovers of money, boastful, arrogant, revilers, disobedient to parents, ungrateful, unholy, 3unloving, irreconcilable, malicious gossips, without self-control, brutal, haters of good, 4treacherous, reckless, conceited, lovers of pleasure rather than lovers of God, 5holding to a form of godliness, although they have denied its power; [Timothy,] Avoid such men as these. 6For among them are those who enter into households and captivate weak women weighed down with sins, led on by various impulses, ⁷always learning and never able to come to the knowledge of the truth. ⁸Just as Jannes and Jambres opposed Moses, so *these* men [who you will know, Timothy,] also oppose the truth, men of depraved mind, rejected in regard to the faith. ⁹But *they* will not make further progress; for *their* folly will be obvious to all, just as Jannes's and Jambres's folly was also. ¹⁰Now *you* [Timothy] followed my teaching, conduct, purpose, faith, patience, love, perseverance, ¹¹persecutions, and sufferings, such as happened to *me* [Paul] at Antioch, at Iconium and at Lystra; what persecutions *I* [Paul] endured, and out of them all the Lord rescued *me* [Paul]! ¹²Indeed, all who desire to live godly in Christ Jesus will be persecuted. ¹³But evil men and impostors will proceed from bad to worse, deceiving and being deceived. ¹⁴*You* [Timothy], however, continue in the things *you* [Timothy] have learned and become convinced of, knowing from whom *you* [Timothy] have learned them, ¹⁵and that from childhood *you* [Timothy] have known the sacred writings which are able to give *you* [Timothy] the wisdom that leads to salvation through faith which is in Christ Jesus. ¹⁶All [Old Testament] Scripture is inspired by God and profitable for teaching, for reproof, for correction, for training in righteousness; ¹⁷so that the man of God may be adequate, equipped for every good work.

It is abundantly clear that the last days that Paul is referring to are the days that Timothy was living in. And the difficult times were going to come upon Timothy. It is further abundantly clear that the particular wicked men that Paul tells Timothy to avoid were going to arise during those difficult times that would come during the last days, in which Timothy was living. And the Scriptures that Paul was referring to are most definitely the Old Testament Scriptures because the New Testament canon had not been completed yet. Does this mean that there is no application that can be made from these verses? Of course there is application. But the application comes from how Paul instructs Timothy, as a believer, to conduct himself against opposition.

In addition, the New Testament canon is inspired by God just as much as the Old Testament canon is inspired by God. But if those were the last days when those particular wicked men would arise, then the days we are living in today are **not** the last days and we do **not** face the particular wicked men that Paul had in mind. This becomes resoundingly clear when we read the very next verse: "I solemnly charge you in the presence of God and of Christ Jesus, who is [about to] judge the living and the dead, and by His appearing and His kingdom" (2 Timothy 4:1). Paul is encouraging Timothy to endure in the faith during this difficult time that was going to come upon *him* and was instructing *him* to "preach the word; be ready in season and out of season; reprove, rebuke, exhort, with great patience and instruction" (v. 2). How would Timothy be able to endure? By the assurance that the appearing of the Lord and His kingdom was about to come. And why was it important for Timothy to preach the word and to be ready in season and out of season? Because the appearing of the Lord and His kingdom was about to come. And Paul told Timothy what would happen to his church before the Lord came:

> "³For the time will come when *they* [Timothy's church] will not endure sound doctrine; but wanting to have *their* ears tickled, *they* will accumulate for themselves teachers in accordance to *their* own desires, ⁴and will turn away *their* ears from the truth and will turn aside to myths. ⁵But *you* [Timothy], be sober in all things, endure hardship, do the work of an evangelist, fulfill *your* ministry."

If Paul is not telling Timothy that these difficult things would occur in his own lifetime, then what use is it for Paul to encourage Timothy by saying, "But *you*..." Paul is contrasting how Timothy should live in a different way than those he is describing in those last days. The reason Timothy is told by Paul to be different than everyone else is because Timothy was to stand in stark contrast to those who would not endure sound doctrine and want their ears tickled. How does Timothy do this if the people Paul is talking about are not the people in Timothy's life? The inescapable fact is that 2 Timothy 4:1 was fulfilled in Timothy's generation just as much as every other verse surrounding it.

This is what it means to read the Bible through New Covenant Eyes. It is recognizing that the Scriptures were written to a particular audience, in a particular time.

First Peter 4 works the same way (italics mine):

> [1]Therefore, since Christ has suffered in the flesh, arm *yourselves* also with the same purpose, because he who has suffered in the flesh has ceased from sin, [2]so as to live the rest of the time in the flesh no longer for the lusts of men, but for the will of God. [3]For the time already past is sufficient for *you* to have carried out the desire of the Gentiles, having pursued a course of sensuality, lusts, drunkenness, carousing, drinking parties and abominable idolatries. [4]In all this, *they* are surprised that *you* do not run with *them* into the same excesses of dissipation, and *they* malign *you*; [5]but *they* will give account to Him who is *ready* to judge the living and the dead. [6]For the gospel has for this purpose been preached even to those who are dead, that though *they* are judged in the flesh as men, *they* may live in the spirit according to the will of God. [7]*The end of all things is near*; therefore, be of sound judgment and sober spirit for the purpose of prayer.

SUMMARY

Reading the Bible through New Covenant Eyes requires that we understand the coming of Jesus to have occurred in 70 AD. The time references given by Jesus and the apostles do not allow for any other possibility. Further, the coming of Jesus was seen through the visible attestation of the destruction of Jerusalem.

Sub-Chapter 4B:

THE RESURRECTION OF THE DEAD

The traditional understanding of the resurrection is stated best by the Westminster Confession of Faith, 32.2 and 33.3:

> *II. At the last day, such as are found alive shall not die, but be changed: and all the dead shall be raised up, with the selfsame bodies, and none other (although with different qualities), which shall be united again to their souls forever.*

> *III. The bodies of the unjust shall, by the power of Christ, be raised to dishonor: the bodies of the just, by His Spirit, unto honor; and be made conformable to His own glorious body.*

The traditional view teaches that the Biblical doctrine of the resurrection of the body refers to individual biological bodies. This sub-chapter will demonstrate from the Scriptures that the Biblical doctrine of the resurrection of the body has nothing to do with individual biological bodies, but has everything to do with the raising of the dead into life, who were in Christ by faith, from their death in the body of Adam.

WHAT WERE THEY EXPECTING TO BE FULFILLED IN THEIR TIME?

It has already been established that the coming of Christ (the parousia) was expected to occur within the very generation of those who were biologically alive while Christ was on earth. The visible event that occurred within that generation which fulfilled all the prophecies regarding the invisible parousia was the destruction of the Temple in 70 AD. It has also been established that the judgment of the nations occurred in 70 AD because Matthew 25:31 is inseparably linked to the parousia. Sub-chapter 4C will explain the judgment of 70 AD.

There is only one parousia taught in Scripture. Therefore, all the events that are linked to the parousia must have, by necessity, occurred in 70 AD as well. Another event that is linked to the parousia is the resurrection. These three events, namely, the parousia, the judgment, and the resurrection, are all taught in Scripture to have occurred in connection with the destruction of the Temple in 70 AD. We can see this in Daniel 12:

> [1]Now at that time Michael, the great prince who stands guard over the sons of your people, will arise and there will be a time of distress such as never occurred since there was a nation until that time; and at that time your people, everyone who is found written in the book, will be rescued. [2]Many of those who sleep in the dust of the ground will awake, these to everlasting life, but the others to disgrace and everlasting contempt. [3]Those who have insight will shine brightly like the brightness of the expanse of heaven, and those who lead the many to righteousness, like the stars forever and ever.

Daniel documents this prophecy given to him by Michael. Here we read about a time of distress that would arise which would be intimately connected to the resurrection. Although the term "resurrection" never actually appears in the Old Testament, the concept is taught in many places, Daniel 12 being one of them. This resurrection would be both a rescuing into eternal life for Daniel's people who have their names written in the book, and a judgment of disgrace and everlasting contempt for the rest. Here we see the connection between a time of distress, the resurrection, and the judgment. When will these three events happen?

[4]"But as for you, Daniel, conceal these words and seal up the book until the end of time; many will go back and forth, and knowledge will increase" (NAS).

"...until the end of time" should be translated, "...until the time of the end."[59] This fits both the Hebrew text and logic. There is no such thing as an end of time. Time will never end, for we will never be infinite beings.

Now, notice what Michael tells Daniel to do: "...conceal these words and seal up the book until the time of the end." When is the time of the end? When would these words be unsealed? The book of Revelation gives us the answer. In Revelation, John unfolds the events that would happen leading up to the destruction of Jerusalem, which occurred in 70 AD.[60] At the end of Revelation, in chapter 22, we read these words:

"[10]And he said to me, "Do not seal up the words of the prophecy of this book, for the time is *near*...[12]"Behold, I am coming *quickly*, and My reward is with Me, to render to every man according to what he has done."[61]

Here in Revelation 22 we see a connection between the parousia of Jesus and the judgment. There is no question that the time texts here match those in the series of verses we saw above. In contrast to what Michael told Daniel, here in Revelation, an angel, probably Michael, tells John *not* to seal up the book, for the time is *near*. So when was the time of the end, recorded in Daniel 12, when the distress, the resurrection, and the judgment would happen? It was the last days that led up to 70 AD, the same last days that Timothy was living in.

Daniel was written approximately 600 years before Revelation. If the time of the end for Daniel was 600 years away, then the nearness of the time of the end for John cannot be *more* than 600 years from the time it was prophesied (see "Nearness Diagram" on the next page). Therefore, even if it is argued that the events that occurred in 70 AD did not fulfill the prophecies of Revelation, at the very most, the prophecies of Revelation were fulfilled within 600 years of its being written. What does that mean for us today? Whether 70 AD fulfilled the prophecies, or some other event within 600 years of Revelation being written, the parousia, the judgment, and the resurrection have already happened! Thus, the issue at hand is not whether or not Jesus is still coming. The issue at hand is when *did* He come? Since there is only one event in history that fulfilled the prophecy of the destruction of the Temple, which is intimately connected to the parousia, the judgment, and the resurrection, the answer is simple: 70 AD.

Nearness Diagram

Can 2000 plus years really be considered near when 600 years was not considered near?

Daniel (530 BC or earlier)	- 600 years pass -	Revelation (65 or 66 AD)	< 600 years
Daniel is told, "seal up the book until the *time of the end*."	The time for the prophecies in the book of Daniel to be fulfilled was obviously not near. Revelation was written 600 years after Daniel was told to seal up the book.	John is told, "Do not seal up the words of the prophecy of this book, for the *time is near*."	The prophecies in the book that were sealed in Daniel were not sealed in Revelation because the time was near. Therefore, "the time of the end" could not be more than 600 years from the time that Revelation was written.

Futurist Time

■ 600 years = not near

■ 2000 years = near

Full Preterist Time

■ 5 years = near

■ 600 years = not near

How Did These Events Occur?

The parousia was not a visible event to biological eyes. That much is evident from the Scriptures we have already seen. This should make us aware that the judgment and the resurrection were also not seen with biological eyes. Or at the very least, the antagonism to this possibility should have been eliminated by now. What remains is a careful look at the Scriptures to determine if this is indeed the case. We'll begin with the resurrection.

THE BODY

In *The Last Days According to Jesus*, RC Sproul states the following: "The great weakness of full preterism—and what I regard to be its fatal flaw—is its treatment of the final resurrection. If full preterism is to gain wide credibility in our time, it must overcome this obstacle."[62] This section on the resurrection will overcome that "fatal flaw."

As we have already seen, it is traditionally understood that at the resurrection, which is believed to be future to us, the biological bodies in the graves will come out of the ground and be reunited to our souls. This is a misunderstanding of both the timing of the resurrection and the word "body" in the contexts dealing with the resurrection, as well as in other contexts.

An immediate verse in Scripture that poses a problem with the view that "body" always means "biological bodies" is Colossians 2:11, which literally reads, "...in Him *you* were also circumcised with a circumcision made without hands, in the removal of *the body of the sins of the flesh* by the circumcision of Christ" (italics mine). In this verse, Paul cannot mean that God removed the biological bodies from the souls of the saints in first century. Thus, the body, in this verse, cannot refer to biological bodies. It must mean something else. And if Paul means something else in Colossians 2 by his use of the singular word, *body*, in connection with his use of the plural word, *you*, it is likely that he means the same thing in the rest of the places where he uses this same combination. In addition, if Paul can use the word, *body* (singular), in Colossians 2, and not mean biological bodies (plural), then this provides for a very strong probability that Paul does not mean biological bodies (plural) in his doctrine of the resurrection of the body (singular), or in any other context where he uses "body" in the singular.[63]

The most well known text on the resurrection is 1 Corinthians 15. Since Paul uses the word "body" (in the Greek, *soma*) throughout the chapter, let us first examine what the traditional view means by "body" in contrast to what the Bible teaches concerning the body of man.

Dr. Douglas Kelly, professor of Theology at Reformed Theological Seminary, in his lectures on Anthropology (the study of man), makes six assertions concerning the body that are commonly held among believers:[64]

1. The body is inherently good.
2. Man is not naturally mortal.
3. Body and soul are not inherently in conflict.
4. The body, though not the seat of sin, does become depraved.
5. The body in the grave is still the body of the person (Westminster Shorter Catechism Q. 37).
6. Resurrection is bodily.

The Body Is Inherently Good

What exactly is meant by the assertion that the body is inherently good? When God formed man from the dust of the earth, that dust sculpture didn't have any moral value to it. It wasn't righteous or unrighteous. It was, however, good, in the same sense that the rest of the creation was good. When God said, "It is good," He didn't mean that the plants were morally good. He meant that the creation was done in excellence. Dr. Kelly states, "The body is not the source of sin. Sin originated in the spirit." Presumably, Dr. Kelly's statement is made in regards to the biological body after it is "animated by the soul." But did the biological body simply become animated by the soul, or did the man that was formed from the dust become a living being? When God breathed the breath of life into the man's nostrils (Gen. 2:7), he became a living being. Adam was a living body.

Scripture does not only speak of man having a body, it speaks of man being a body. Man not only has a body, he is a body within a biological body. This definition of man will become evident as you read through this chapter. The biblical texts that demonstrate this definition of man are the very same texts the traditional view uses to teach a resurrection of biological bodies, especially 1 Corinthians 15. Thus, the reader is asked to hold both definitions side by side as possibilities until these texts have been dealt with throughout the rest of this book. The traditional definition of man is that he is made up of both body *and* soul.[65] The definition of man put forth in this book is that man *is* a body, and he *has* a biological body while he lives on this earth.

If the biological body is meant by Dr. Kelly when he states that "the body is not the source of sin," which would appear to be the case since he is a dichotomist, then what must be meant by his first assertion is that the biological body is good in the sense that it was made with excellence by God. Thus, the biological body is amoral. It is an instrument that man uses for either good or evil, just like a gun can be used for either good or evil. The biological body is a necessary instrument to be able to live in the earthly realm. It does not, however, define man. Man, as a body, can exist without the biological body, but he cannot do so in the earthly realm. Again, this definition of man as a body will become apparent as you read the rest of this book, but especially the arguments set forth in the sixth assertion that "resurrection is bodily."

Man Is Not Naturally Mortal

Where do the Scriptures teach that man is not naturally mortal? It seems an odd assertion to make considering the fact that the man, Adam, died when he sinned. The whole point of being immortal is that you cannot die. Oddly enough, Louis Berkhof, in his *Systematic Theology*, says the following statements in the span of one paragraph:

When the Lord says, 'for in the day that thou eatest thereof that shalt surely die," his statement clearly implies that, if Adam refrains from eating, he will not die, but will be raised above the *possibility of death.* The implied promise certainly cannot mean that, in the case of obedience, Adam would be permitted to live on in the usual way, that is, to continue the ordinary natural life, for that life was his already in virtue of his creation, and therefore could not be held out as a reward for obedience. The implied promise evidently was that of life raised to its highest development of perennial bliss and glory. Adam was indeed created in a state of positive holiness, and was also *immortal* in the sense that *he was not subject to the law of death.*[66]

What!? According to Berkhof (who stands in the traditional view), Adam had to be raised above the possibility of death but he was also immortal in the sense that he was not subject to the law of death. How could Adam be immortal and still have to be raised above the possibility of death? This makes absolutely no sense.[67] And the material between these two sentences is nothing more than an illogical, systematic leap. Why must there be an implied promise of something greater than the ordinary natural life? The problem is that there is an unbiblical presupposition that Adam was tested by God to see whether he would obey or disobey. Dr. Arnold G. Fruchtenbaum, in his teaching outline, "The Fall of Man,"[68] summarizes the traditional view well under the section of the outline entitled, "Man's Probationary Period." In that section, he begins with the following:

> Man, in his state of innocence, was on probation. This probationary period involved three things: the test, the duration, and the goal.
>
> The Test
> There are three things involved in the test itself: the object, the nature, and the purpose of the test.

The Object of the Test

The object of the test was the two trees *in the midst of the garden*. One tree was *the tree of life*, which was the means of imparting eternal life. Had Adam passed his probationary period, he would have been allowed to eat of the Tree of Life and would have eternal life from then on without ever seeing death. The other tree was *the tree of the knowledge of good and evil*. Partaking of this tree meant that it would impart to Adam experiential knowledge of the difference between good and evil. It would be experiential knowledge rather than merely head knowledge. With disobedience, they would know experientially, but also bitterly, what evil was and how it differed from good. Once they partook of this tree, they would have the power to do evil, but not the power to do the good that would commend them before God.

The first question that must be asked is, where is there any mention of a test anywhere in the text? Systematic theology has forced a probationary period into Genesis. While God stated what would happen when Adam ate the fruit, God nowhere stated what would happen if he didn't. And nowhere is it stated that Adam was only allowed to eat of the Tree of Life if he passed this so-called test. In fact, Genesis 2:16-17 explicitly states the exact opposite: "The LORD God commanded the man, saying, 'From *any* tree of the garden you may eat freely; but from the tree of the knowledge of good and evil you shall not eat, for in the day that you eat from it you will surely die'" (italics mine).

The reason that this probationary period is forced upon the text is because it is assumed that God did not create Adam in a mortal state and that God gave Adam the opportunity to earn, as a reward, eternal life for his obedience. In other words, it is assumed that when God told Adam disobedience would result in death that He therefore implied that Adam's obedience would earn him life beyond, and in addition to, the life he already had.

Even Charles Hodge acknowledges that the threat of death for disobeying God's command states, "It is plain that this involved the assurance that he should not die, if he did not eat."[69] That would be the furthest appropriate implication that can be drawn from God's threat of death upon disobedience. It is not a proper implication to say that if Adam did not eat, but obeyed God, that he would gain something greater than not death from the life he already had. Yet, according to the traditional view, Adam had to earn *eternal* life. But to have eternal life is to have immortality. Thus, if Adam had to earn immortality, then he wasn't immortal. And to dig the hole deeper, Paul says that the perishable does not inherit the imperishable (1 Cor. 15:50); the mortal does not inherit immortality. If this is true, then Adam could not inherit immortality by earning it.

Perhaps the traditional view needs some third alternative: Perhaps man was *amortal*, having no mortalness ascribed to him. While this may seem to be a ridiculous possibility, thus the ridiculous term, it is in fact what the traditional view requires in order for a probationary period to have existed before the Fall. According to the traditional view, Adam was created neutral, and was tested by God for x amount of time to see if He would resist eating of the Tree of the Knowledge of Good and Evil. After such a probation, Adam would either become mortal through sin or immortal (i.e. earn eternal life) through obedience. Here is another quote from Berkhof:

> (1) Adam was constituted the representative head of the human race, so that he could act for all his descendants. (2) He was temporarily put on probation, in order to determine whether he would willingly subject his will to the will of God. (3) He was given the promise of eternal life in the way of obedience, and thus by the gracious disposition of God acquired certain conditional rights. This covenant enabled Adam to obtain eternal life for himself and for his descendants in the way of obedience.[70]

The problem here is that in order for man to die, he has to already be mortal. Mortality results in death, not the other way around. But herein lies a giant inconsistency in the traditional view: God said, "In the day you eat of it, you will surely die." If man actually died when he ate the forbidden fruit, then he couldn't become mortal at that point, because he was dead. But if man must become mortal first through sin, then man did not die when he ate the forbidden fruit. But alas, we arrive at the dichotomy of man in Kelly's view. What must be meant by his second assertion is that the biological body of man is not naturally mortal, but became mortal after the Fall. Therefore, according to Kelly and the traditional view, the *soul* of man had to be mortal *before* the Fall while the *biological body* became mortal *after* the Fall. Thus, Adam was both mortal and immortal at the same time! Strangely, it was not the soul that God breathed into the biological body that was immortal, but it was the biological body made from the dust of the ground that was immortal. So the soul of man died when Adam sinned because it was mortal to begin with, but the biological died many years after Adam sinned because it became mortal. You see, according to the traditional view, the penalty for sin causes man to die two deaths, one spiritual and one physical, even though the Scriptures only speak of a second death at the final judgment for those who's names are not written in the Lamb's Book of Life.[71] There is only one death that came as a result of sin in the Garden: sin-death.

Sin-death means separation from God. Man did indeed incur the curse of sin-death when Adam ate the forbidden fruit. Man, defined as a body, died. Adam's biological body did not die until many years later. Consider the following quote from Sam Frost:

> For Paul, man died the day he ate because he was placed under the rule of "the sin" and the sin "reigned in the death." Adam was sentenced the day he ate. He physically died 900 years later. If the sentence of God was "in the day you eat" and it was actually carried out 324,000 (900 years x 360 days a year) days later then what does that say

about the justice of God? How many days did it take for their eyes to be opened? "In the day you eat, your eyes will be opened." The same phrase is used for "in the day you eat, you will surely die." Surely, no one argues that their eyes were opened 324,000 days later.[72]

If they didn't die the sin-death, finally and fully, then neither were their eyes opened, finally and fully, on the day they ate the fruit. In fact, if Adam and Eve did not die, finally and fully, on the day they ate the fruit, then this would demonstrate that the Serpent was telling the truth and God was lying since the text tells us that their eyes were opened immediately after they sinned (Gen. 3:7). In other words, since both God and the Serpent used the same phrase ("in the day you eat from it") to state what would happen when they ate the fruit, the traditional view would teach us that what the Serpent said came true (i.e. their eyes would be opened) but what God said did not (i.e. they would surely die).

This point is made even clearer when we consider that the Serpent said, "You will not surely die!" (Gen. 3:4) Now notice that this statement is immediately followed by, "For God knows that *in the day you eat from it* your eyes will be opened" (v. 5; italics mine). The Serpent told Eve that they would not die on the day they ate the fruit, but rather, that their eyes would be opened on the day they ate the fruit. Since we know from verse 7 that their eyes were opened on the day they ate the fruit, then we also know that Adam, Eve, and the Serpent knew that "on the day you eat of it" did not mean hundreds of years later. The Serpent directly contradicted the words of God by stating that they would not die on the day they ate the fruit. But he did tell them that their eyes would be opened on the day that they ate the fruit. They all knew something would happen immediately, but whether or not they would die was in question as a result of the Serpents lie. The Serpent contradicted God and then manipulated God's words by stating something true, something that sounded good, that would result from eating the fruit. If they did not die the only death that God said they would die, then the Serpent told the truth and God told a lie. The fact is, there was only one death that occurred as a result of eating the fruit, and that death happened immediately just as assuredly as their eyes were opened immediately.

THE CURSE

Before we consider the statement, "for you are dust, and to dust you shall return," let us take a look at the rest of the curse. To the woman, God said, "I will greatly *multiply* your pain in childbirth…" (italics mine). Pain in childbirth was apparently a natural order of things. Sin didn't bring about pain in childbirth, it brought about the *increase* of pain in childbirth. Likewise, to Adam, God says, "By the sweat of your face you will eat bread, till you return to the ground, because from it you were taken; for you are dust, and to dust you shall return." Adam was commanded by God to work the Garden before the Fall. Eating bread was always a result of work, but sin brought about the increase of difficulty in work, because now man was lazy, and would be on his own to make the ground work for Him because now He was separated from God.

The phrase, "till you return to the ground, because from it you were taken," refers to how long Adam would eat bread by the sweat of his face and is therefore stating nothing more than the fact that he was taken from the ground and so he would return to the ground. The ground that Adam would return to was the ground he was created from. If we compare Genesis 2:7-8 with Genesis 3:19, we see these two statements:

> Then the LORD God *formed man of dust from the ground*…The LORD God planted a garden toward the east, in Eden; and *there He placed the man whom He had formed.*[73]

For you are dust, and to dust you shall return.

Adam was created from the dust of the ground outside of the Garden and then he was placed into the Garden. This order is made even clearer when we consider that only after the Garden was completed and the two famous trees were already in the midst of the Garden that Genesis 2:15

tells us, "*Then* the LORD God took the man and put him *into* the garden of Eden to cultivate it and keep it" (italics mine). Now, as a result of his sin, he would return to the dust of the ground outside of the Garden from where he was created. It was to that ground that Adam would return because he would now spend the rest of his days on earth outside the luscious Garden and in the desert (cf. Israel in the wilderness). This is the curse that Adam now faced. That this indeed is what God meant is demonstrated in the fact that God then drove Adam and Eve out of the Garden and made sure they could not return. This whole interpretation is clearly summarized in Genesis 3:23-24:

> [T]herefore the LORD God sent him out from the garden of Eden, to cultivate *the ground* **from which he was taken**. *So He drove the man out*; and at the east of the garden of Eden He *stationed the cherubim* and the flaming sword which turned every direction *to guard the way to the tree of life.*[74]

There are no exegetical grounds to build a case for biological death as a part of the curse. Rather, biological death, as a normal part of life, is assumed. *Where* Adam would die biologically is determined by the curse. The curse was the exodus of Adam from inside the Garden back to the ground outside the Garden that he was created from where he would spend the rest of his days.

It is interesting to note here the relationship between the curse placed upon the man and the woman with the blessing that God gave to them after He created them. In Genesis 1:27-30, we read these words:

> [27]God created man in His own image, in the image of God He created him; (male and female He created them. [28]God blessed them; and God said to them, "Be fruitful and multiply, and fill the earth, and subdue it; and rule over the fish of the sea and over the birds of the sky and over every living thing that moves on the earth." [29]Then God said, "Behold, I have given you every plant yielding seed that is on the surface of all the earth, and every tree which has

fruit yielding seed; it shall be food for you; [30]and to every beast of the earth and to every bird of the sky and to every thing that moves on the earth which has life, I have given every green plant for food"; and it was so.

What does it mean for God to bless someone or something? The Hebrew word, "barak," when used in reference to God giving the blessing, particularly in Genesis, means that God is empowering the object of the blessing to produce that which He blesses them to produce. In Genesis 1:22, God blesses the fish and the birds and tells them to be fruitful and multiply. God is not giving a command here, He is stating a fact that they have been empowered to be fruitful and multiply. According to the *Theological Wordbook of the Old Testament*, "To bless in the OT means 'to endue with power for success, prosperity, fecundity, longevity, etc.'"[75] *The New International Dictionary of Old Testament Theology and Exegesis*, further explains the use of this word:

> 2. The divine blessing over creation. The first thing that God did after creating human life (as well as animal life) was to pronounce his blessing over the work of his hands (cf. Gen 5:2). The emphasis here is on the life-infusing power of the divine word, as God blesses his creation saying...(Gen 1:22, 28; cf. also 9:1). Thus, God's blessing is his formative, empowering word (often, with overtones of appointing destiny). It is not an empty pronouncement or simply an expression of wish or goodwill, nor is it a bare command, although the formula of blessing in 1:28 is couched in the imperative ("Be fruitful...increase in number...fill the earth...subdue it.... Rule..."). Rather, the blessing of God has content; it actualizes and enables. Thus, C. Westermann notes that "the blessing that confers the power of fertility is inseparable from creation where the creator is the one who blesses and the created living being has the power to reproduce itself because of the blessing.... To speak of life and its dynamism is to speak of the effective

action of the creator" (Genesis 1-11, tr. J. J. Scullion, 1984, 140). Moreover, the divine blessing can come on both humans and animals (Gen 1:22, 28; Deut 28:4), as well as on the Sabbath itself (Gen 2:3; Exod 20:11, with no suggestion of the personification of the Sabbath, as is found in later Judaism), or on inanimate objects such as crops, fields and cities, food and drink, kneading troughs, baskets and barns (cf. e.g., Gen 27:27-28; Exod 23:25-26; Deut 28:5, 8; 33:13). What would creation be without the blessing of the creator? That which is blessed functions and produces at the optimum level, fulfilling its divinely designated purpose (contrast, e.g., Gen 3:16-19; Deut 28:15-68).

The blessing that God gave to Adam and Eve was an empowerment to produce two things. First, the blessing that God gave empowered the woman to produce children through whom mankind would multiply and fill the earth and even rule the earth. This implies that childbearing is not the only aspect of producing children that is being blessed, but childrearing is also part of the blessing.[76] While bearing and rearing children would still be difficult and painful at times, the difficulties and pains would be done in the presence of God where sin in the parents and the children was not an obstacle.

These pains and difficulties were the natural issues of (minimal) pain in childbirth and in teaching children how to live as they grow. In addition, sin is not required to have pain when you stub your toe. It brings a certain sadness to parents when their children hurt from such things. These are the natural pains that were part and parcel of the bearing and rearing of children. Sin brought upon the woman the multiplication of pain, not the innovation of pain.

Secondly, the blessing that God gave empowered the producing of every plant and every tree yielding seed for food. Thus, when "the LORD God took the man and put him into the garden of Eden to cultivate it and keep it (Gen. 2:15)," God was present in the Garden to cause every tree to grow (2:9).

Adam was empowered by God to work the Garden before the Fall. Eating bread was always a result of work, but sin brought about the increase of difficulty in work, because now man was lazy, and would be on his own to make the ground work for Him because now He was separated from God. Adam would now have "to cultivate the ground from which he was taken" (Gen. 3:23) rather than the ground in the Garden within the presence of God. Thus, when we look at the curse that God placed upon man and woman, we see a reversal of the blessing that He gave them. Life in the presence of God brought the blessing from God to be fruitful and multiply. Sin brought separation from God, which placed them outside of God's blessing. Now, they were on their own.

There is no indication in the rest of the statements from God regarding biological death that would cause us to think that biological death was not the biological body's original destiny. Consider again the insight from Sam Frost:

> Man *immediately* came under the power of the Sin and the rule and reign of the Death. This had dire consequences on creation itself, but not so much as has been imagined. Where in the narrative of the curses does God punish the whole universe? Does he mention the Sun? The stars? Does God punish the animal kingdom, or the fish? Does he punish the clouds or the trees? The only things mentioned is the "ground" Adam walked on, the heat of his labor (because he was now placed in a desert, not in the cool of the Garden which had a "canopy" over it), and thorns and thistles. Nowhere is the entire creation, or "the whole creation" cursed. At least *not in the text*.[77]

THE POWER OF SIN

Paul teaches us that the power of sin is the law (1 Cor. 15:56). He demonstrates this in Romans 7: "I was once alive apart from the Law; but when the commandment came, sin became alive and I died" (v. 9). Paul is personifying Adam in Romans 7. Adam was the only man that was ever alive apart from the Law and then died. Thus, since God has only one plan for all time, it is obvious that His intention was for Adam to sin.

How did He bring this about? He gave Adam law. He invoked the power of sin. There was no probation period. There was law, sin, and death. Adam had to sin because God's plan was to send Jesus to die for sinners. If there are no sinners, then there is no need for Jesus to die. "For while we were still helpless, at the right time Christ died for the ungodly. For one will hardly die for a righteous man; though perhaps for the good man someone would dare even to die. But God demonstrates His own love toward us, in that while we were yet sinners, Christ died for us" (Rom. 5:6-8). This was not Plan B.

The fact that this was the only plan of God is demonstrated by the Tree of Life. The Tree of Life is intimately connected to the presence of God. It was in middle of the Garden (Gen. 2:9) and Adam and Eve could eat from it and live forever (Gen. 3:22). In Revelation, we learn from John that the Tree of Life is in the holy city, the New Jerusalem, and that it is watered by the river of life coming from the throne of God and of the Lamb. We also learn from John that the Tree of Life is for the healing of nations (Rev. 21:1-2). In both the Garden and the New Jerusalem, the feasting on the Tree of Life represents eternal life because it is intimately connected to the presence of God.

When Adam sinned, he was placed outside the Garden, and God blocked the way to the Tree of Life so that he could no longer have access to it. Sin brought about the judgment of God. Man was no longer permitted to enter into the presence of God because he was dead (i.e. separated from God). The fact that God would no longer permit Man to eat of the Tree of Life shows the eternal plan of God, which is that access to the Tree of Life could only be granted now through Christ. As John tells us in Revelation 2:7, "He who has an ear, let him hear what the Spirit says to the churches. To him who overcomes, I will grant to eat of the tree of life which is in the Paradise of God."

There is also another significant difference between Genesis and Revelation. In Genesis 3:24, we read, "So [God] drove the man out; and at the east of the garden of Eden He stationed the cherubim and the flaming sword which turned every direction to guard the way to the tree of life." In Revelation 22:14, we read, "Blessed are those who wash their robes, so that they may have the right to the tree of life, and may enter by the gates into the city." After Adam sinned, the way to the Tree of Life was blocked. Through Christ, the way to the Tree of Life is accessible through the open gates of the city. The curse of separation from God is removed through Christ. It is only through Christ that man can have immortality and eternal life in the presence of God because this was the eternal plan of God.

So it is incorrect to assert that man is not naturally mortal. He was created mortal because he had to die. The Tree of Life could have sustained him forever in his mortal state (i.e. having the ability to die, but not necessarily experiencing it), but God gave him law so he would sin and, thereby, die. Eternal life in Christ was always the plan of God.[78]

Body and Soul Are Not Inherently in Conflict

Body and soul are both used in Scripture to speak of man. Man is a body; man is a soul. Man is not both a body *and* a soul. Thus, the assertion that body and soul are not inherently in conflict only makes sense if Dr. Kelly means that both biological body *and* soul are not inherently in conflict. That assertion, as it stands, would be correct. However, Dr. Kelly is clearly meaning the dichotomy of body *and* soul, which he defines as man. He argues that the curse announced is that man would return to dust and that this return to dust was in the context of the curse for sin. What Kelly means by this is that biological death was part of the curse. He quotes John Murray for support: "The reason for our return to the dust is not that we are dust, but that we have sinned." Again, Murray's statement would be correct if by it, he didn't mean biological death. To impose biological death as a result of the curse is logically and exegetically flawed. The reasoning of Kelly and Murray is solely based on systematic traditional presuppositions and cannot be supported from the text. The problem with the traditional view put forth here by Kelly has already been dealt with under the previous assertion. But here we can bring to light another problem with the view of man as defined by both his soul and his biological body.

Was Jesus was still a man when His biological body was in the tomb and He was in Hades? (Hades was the location of the biologically dead.)[79] And what about everyone else who has died biologically? Have they ceased to be man? Once again, man is a body/soul within a biological body; he is not a body *and* a soul. Therefore, the best we can make of this assertion is that the soul/body is not inherently in conflict with the biological body because the biological body is the instrument through which the soul/body produces good or evil on the earth.

The Body, Though Not the Seat of Sin, Does Become Depraved

Dr. Kelly's fourth assertion is that the biological body becomes depraved through sin. But as we've already seen, the biological body is the instrument of man just like a gun is an instrument used to produce good or evil. A gun does not become depraved when it is used for evil. It continues to be amoral. In the same way, the biological body does not become depraved when it has been used for evil. As Dr. Kelly states regarding this assertion, "It functions as the agent of sin. Its members are instruments of unrighteousness in the context of the fall." This is an agreeable statement. It is an illogical leap, however, to conclude that, therefore, the biological body becomes depraved.[80] To say that the biological body functions as the agent of sin does not mean that biological body becomes depraved any more than a gun becomes depraved when it is used as an agent of sin.

The Body in the Grave Is Still the Body of the Person (Westminster Shorter Catechism Q. 37)

Question and Answer 37 of the Westminster Shorter Catechism reads as follows:

Q. What benefits do believers receive from Christ at death?
A. The souls of believers are at their death made perfect in holiness, and do immediately pass into glory, and their

bodies, being still united in Christ, do rest in their graves,
till the resurrection.

The Scriptural support for the phrase, "…and their bodies, being still
united to Christ…" is 1 Thessalonians 4:14: "For if we believe that Jesus
died and rose again, even so them also which sleep in Jesus will God bring
with him." It is often assumed that dead corpses will be raised in the
resurrection in the same way that the corpse of Jesus was resurrected. Of
course, this proof text speaks nothing of the resurrection of the corpse
from the grave. And since man is defined as a body (within a body), then
to speak of those who sleep in Jesus has nothing to do with their
biological bodies. This will be dealt with in detail under the final
assertion that "resurrection is bodily." There the doctrine of the
resurrection as it pertains to Paul's use of the term, "body," will be
presented.

The first proof text for the last phrase of the Shorter Catechism's
answer, "and their bodies…do rest in their graves, till the
resurrection…" is Daniel 12:2: "And many of them that sleep in the dust
of the earth shall awake, some to everlasting life, and some to shame and
everlasting contempt." Suffice it to say that even some theologians who
hold to a biological bodily resurrection believe that this text is teaching
the national resurrection of Israel and not the resurrection of biological
bodies. One quote from Kenneth Gentry is sufficient to demonstrate
that Daniel 12:2 is an inadequate proof text for the Shorter Catechism's
statement:

> Dan 12 is not dealing with bodily resurrection but national
> resurrection (as does Eze 37). Dan 12 sees the
> "resurrection" of Israel in the birth of the Christian Church,
> which is the New Israel. Thus, it bears similiarities [sic]
> with Eze 37 and the resurrection of the dry bones of Israel.[81]

The second proof text used is John 5:28-29: "Marvel not at this: for
the hour is coming, in which all that are in the graves shall hear his voice,
and shall come forth; they that have done good, unto the resurrection of

life; and they that have done evil, unto the resurrection of damnation." As we have seen with Daniel 12:2, resurrection from the dust of the earth, or from the graves, as we have here in John 5, does not force a meaning of biological bodily resurrection. We will see later in this sub-chapter why referring to those in the graves cannot mean that the person himself is still in the grave but rather that the corpse in the grave provides a physical location for reference or visitation of the dead who used to live in those biological bodies. Thus, when Jesus teaches that those who are in the graves shall hear his voice and shall come forth unto the resurrection, He is simply speaking of the dead who are identified by the graves where their biological bodies were buried. Does this mean that there were never any biological bodily resurrections? No, for certainly there were: Lazarus, Jesus, and even those referred to in Matthew 27:52-53, among others.

Traditionalists will be quick to point out that 1 Corinthians 15, which we will look at below, teaches that our resurrection follows the same pattern as Jesus. Here we will briefly point out that Paul says in Colossians 1:18, "He is also head of the body, the church; and He is *the beginning, the firstborn from the dead*, so that He Himself will come to have first place in everything." Jesus was not the first one to rise from biological death, yet Paul tells us that He is the beginning, the firstborn from the dead. Jesus *was* the first one to rise from the dead. So Christ did provide the pattern for the resurrection of believers, but the resurrection of His body (i.e. the definition of man) was that pattern. There are significant reasons why Jesus had to resurrect back into His biological body, but we will elaborate more on this later.

The third and final proof text that the Catechism uses to support biological bodily resurrection is Acts 24:15: "And have hope toward God, which they themselves also allow, that there shall be a resurrection of the dead, both of the just and unjust." Here it should be noted that the literal translation is, "…that there is *about to be* a resurrection of the dead, both of the just and unjust" (italics mine). Michael J. Sullivan, in an article entitled, "Kenneth Gentry's Prophetic Confusion and the Analogy of Scripture," is helpful here where he quotes Sam Frost and Kenneth Gentry regarding this verse:

Commenting on the imminent resurrection of Acts 24:15 Sam Frost writes,

"There, the Greek 'mellein esesthai' is rendered "about to be". The two verbs, respectively, are present infinitive active and future infinitive middle (deponent). We only find this particular construction in Luke's Acts of the Apostles three times. The other two spots are Acts 11.28 and 27.10. The first is Agabus' prediction about the coming famine. Certainly something "about to happen" (and did). The final verse is Paul, while on the boat, predicted that their voyage was "about to" end in disaster. Certainly something on the horizon. This construction occurs three times in Acts only. Two times is clearly of events "about to happen" in terms of time. One passage, because it deals with the resurrection (24.15) is not. I have yet to hear any sound answer to what appears to me as arbitrary exegesis on the basis of assumptions. I have studied all occurences [sic] of "mello" in the LXX, the GNT, and the Apos. Fathers. It is a word that sharpens the vague future indicative. It adds to it the certainty of the event from the standpoint of the speaker (hence, it is often translated "certain"). The event in question is certain because it will most certainly happen within the near time of the speaker, without doubt. That is the way this word is used, and particularly this unique construction in Acts. Therefore, I can exegetically conclude that the "resurrection of the just and the unjust" laid for certain in the time of Paul as something that would take place within his own lifetime, and that he based that certainty upon the source that he based all of his assuredness: "the Holy Spirit speaking through the Scriptures" (Westminster Confession)."

And to confirm Sam's support of the Young's Literal Translation of mello in these passages, we need only to quote Gentry himself who supports that imminence should be the primary meaning in Revelation,

"Nevertheless, when used with the aorist infinitive—as in Revelation 1:19—the word's preponderate usage and preferred meaning is: "be on the point of, be about to." The same is true when the word is used with the present infinitive, as in Rev. 3:10. The basic meaning in both Thayer and Abbott-Smith is "to be about to." Mello with the infinitive expresses imminence (like the future)."[82]

We see, then, an imminent expectation of the resurrection in Acts 24:15, the same resurrection that the Westminster Confession of Faith teaches is still future to us. But if the resurrection had an imminent expectation for the readers in the first century, how can we still have that same imminent expectation? How many thousands of years does it take before imminent expectation loses its effect for the readers of such expectation? It is silly to even ponder such a question, considering the readers would have to be alive for thousands of years to even be able to ask them. If they couldn't expect fulfillment in their lifetime, then the fulfillment wasn't about to happen.

A second thing to note is that Acts 24:15 speaks nothing of the resurrection of corpses. Apart from the assumption that the resurrection is for biological corpses, this text does not support such a view. It simply teaches that there would be a resurrection of the dead. Therefore, this verse does not prove anything but that the dead would be raised. Since "the dead" is not referring to biological corpses, then this verse does not really help defend the position that biological corpses will be raised. One must presuppose that "the dead" means "biological corpses" in order to use Acts 24:15 as a proof text for such a position. The meaning of "the dead" will be dealt with in the sixth and final assertion that "resurrection is bodily."

One last thought before we leave this fifth assertion. Dr. Kelly states the following in support of this assertion: "Bodies are still united to Christ. The dust from them still have some sort of union to Christ. 'Come see where He laid.' Not just His body." Did Jesus cease to be a man when His biological body was laying in the tomb? If we push this too far, then in the traditional view, once the soul is separated from the body, man can no longer be man, because man is defined as body *and* soul.[83] It makes more sense to say that the biological body of a person can be spoken of as the person because that is how that person was known on this earth. We cannot seriously think that we literally mean that a person's biological body lying in a grave is the person himself. Consider the following documentation by M.C. Tenney:

> When the body of Roger Williams, founder of the Rhode Island colony, was exhumed for reburial, it was found that the root of an apple tree had penetrated the head of the coffin and had followed down Williams' spine, dividing into a fork at the legs. The tree had absorbed the chemicals of the decaying body and had transmuted them into its wood and fruit. The apples, in turn, had been eaten by people, quite unconscious of the fact that they were indirectly taking into their systems part of the long-dead Williams. The objection may therefore be raised: How, out of the complex sequence of decay, absorption, and new formation, will it be possible to resurrect believers of past ages, and to reconstitute them as separate entities?[84]

If this is what happens to the biological bodies of people in their graves, then how can a family member, who goes to visit a grave, really and literally mean that the person they are visiting is actually laying in the grave? In all likelihood, even the decaying bones that linger could have very well been transferred into the life of a nearby apple tree. In fact, some of the dust of the biological body could even be in the digestive system of another person. At what point do we say that "we're going to see him" and not force the ridiculous concept that the dust from "him" still has some sort of union to Christ, or to the person that lived in that body? The body in the grave cannot be the body of the person for very long because the body in the grave doesn't last very long as a body. It dissolves into dust. Why else do graveyards make so much money? It's because they provide a stone over the hole that the body was placed in so that after the body dissolves, the families and friends still have a memorial to come visit. Without a gravestone or marker, there is no place to visit. The biological body is never to return from the dust again. This leads us to our sixth and final assertion.

Resurrection Is Bodily

Finally, we arrive at an accurate assertion, namely, that resurrection is bodily. Unfortunately, we have two different meanings for the word, "bodily." What Dr. Kelly means is not what the Scriptures teach. We have already seen the traditional view that man is a body *and* a soul. So this assertion is meant to refer to the biological body of man. It will, however, be demonstrated in this section that the bodily resurrection refers to the definition of man that has been proposed throughout this sub-chapter, namely, that man *is* a body. Therefore, resurrection *is* bodily, but this means the resurrection of man, not the resurrection of his biological body.

Dr. Kelly gives the common understanding of the nature of the resurrection: "The resurrection of Christ presents the pattern for *our* resurrection" (italics mine). He gives the following verses in support of this:

> Romans 8:11: But if the Spirit of Him who raised Jesus from the dead dwells in you, He who raised Christ Jesus from the dead will also give life to your mortal bodies through His Spirit who dwells in you.

> Phil. 3:20-21: For our citizenship is in heaven, from which also we eagerly wait for a Savior, the Lord Jesus Christ; 21who will transform the body of our humble state into

conformity with the body of His glory, by the exertion of the power that He has even to subject all things to Himself.

Romans 8:23: And not only this, but also we ourselves, having the first fruits of the Spirit, even we ourselves groan within ourselves, waiting eagerly for our adoption as sons, the redemption of our body.

The resurrection of Christ did indeed provide the pattern for *the* resurrection, but since the resurrection is past, then Christ's resurrection does not provide the pattern for *our* resurrection. This will become more evident as you continue reading this sub-chapter.

In Romans 8:11, Paul speaks of Christ's resurrection, but what it says is that "if the Spirit of Him who raised Jesus…dwells in you…He…will also give life to your mortal bodies." Note that Paul is writing to the Roman church during the first century. Paul is not teaching them about a resurrection that would occur for them after they died. Rather, if we take this verse in its context, we quickly discover that the body was already dead for those who were reading this letter: "But if Christ is in you, although the body is dead because of sin, the Spirit is life because of righteousness" (v. 10).

Note that Paul does not mean, "the body is as good as dead," (which is a necessary interpretation to support the resurrection of our biological bodies) anymore than he means, "the Spirit is as good as life." Paul is using present active indicatives. The body *is* dead; the Spirit *is* life. And although the body is dead, the Spirit of him who raised Jesus from the dead "will also give life to your mortal bodies…"

Following this context comes Romans 8:23, where it is traditionally argued that the "redemption of our body (singular)" means the same thing as the resurrection of our biological bodies (plural). But Paul uses the singular for "body" together with the plural, "our." Paul is teaching about the redemption of their (plural) collective body (singular). The same singular-plural combination is used in Philippians 3:20-21, which speaks of a transformation of the "body" (singular) of "our" (plural) humble state. Again, it is assumed that since "Christ presents the pattern for *our* resurrection" that this transformation "into conformity with the body of His glory" must be speaking of the resurrection of our individual biological bodies.

But Paul's use of the Greek word, "soma," is used in the singular, not in the plural, just like in Romans 8:23. He speaks of the redemption and the transformation of "*our*" (plural) "*body*" (singular). Those of the traditional view will attempt to argue that this is of no consequence, that Paul is using the singular to refer to each of their biological bodies. But this is a forced and illegitimate interpretation of the text. It is their presupposition that requires such an interpretation. Paul used the singular because he meant to use the singular. He used the plural in Romans 8:11 because he meant to use the plural. In Philippians 3:20-21, Paul is teaching about the collective body of Adam being transformed into the collective body of Christ. Again, if we understand Paul to be talking about the body as defining man and not the biological body, then this text provides no problem with a 70 AD, "about to" happen, fulfillment. This understanding will make more sense as we now move into Paul's doctrine of the resurrection.

1 CORINTHIANS 15

Let's take a very brief exegetical look at this passage to see if we can better understand the nature of the resurrection and to whom it applies.

> [1]Now I make known to you, brethren, the gospel which I preached to you, which also you received, in which also you stand, [2]by which also you are saved, if you hold fast the word which I preached to you, unless you believed in vain. [3]For I delivered to you as of first importance what I also received, that Christ died for our sins according to the Scriptures, [4]and that He was buried, and that He was raised on the third day according to the Scriptures, [5]and that He appeared to Cephas, then to the twelve. [6]After that He appeared to more than five hundred brethren at one time, most of whom remain until now, but some have fallen

asleep; [7]then He appeared to James, then to all the apostles; [8]and last of all, as to one untimely born, He appeared to me also. [9]For I am the least of the apostles, and not fit to be called an apostle, because I persecuted the church of God. [10]But by the grace of God I am what I am, and His grace toward me did not prove vain; but I labored even more than all of them, yet not I, but the grace of God with me. [11]Whether then it was I or they, so we preach and so you believed.

Note first of all that Paul explicitly states that the Corinthians received the Gospel, stood in the Gospel, and were saved by the Gospel (v. 1-2). The qualifiers, "if you hold fast" and "unless you believed in vain" do not negate the fact that those who believed the Gospel actually embraced the facts of the Gospel. In fact, his words in verse 11 make this clear: "…so we preach and so *you believed*." Paul lays out the facts of the Gospel and demonstrates that Jesus was raised from the dead (in His biological body) and appeared to many, most of whom were still alive when he wrote, although some had fallen asleep (v. 6). This is very important to observe because it demonstrates that in the verses that follow, Paul is not presenting a proof for the resurrection of Christ. This they already believed. In fact, the argument that Paul puts forward in the verses that follow is built upon their belief that Jesus was raised from the dead. The Corinthians were not questioning the resurrection of Christ, they were questioning the resurrection of "the dead," which is a plural noun (i.e. the dead ones):

[12]Now if Christ is preached, that He has been raised from the dead, how do some among you say that there is no resurrection of the dead? [13]But if there is no resurrection of the dead, not even Christ has been raised; [14]and if Christ has not been raised, then our preaching is vain, your faith also is vain. [15]Moreover we are even found to be false witnesses of God, because we testified against God that He raised Christ, whom He did not raise, if in fact the dead

are not raised. [16]For if the dead are not raised, not even Christ has been raised; [17]and if Christ has not been raised, your faith is worthless; you are still in your sins.

Paul's argument is simple: If Christ was raised from, or out of (Greek, ek), the dead (as was preached and they believed), then how could some of them say that there was no resurrection of the dead ones? In other words, if there is no resurrection of the dead ones, then not even Christ has been raised, because He was a dead one. Thus, the counter thought to this is that if Christ, being a dead one, was raised, which they believed He was, then therefore, the dead ones can be raised. If there is no resurrection of the dead ones, then logic follows that Christ, being a dead one, was also not raised. If this is the case, then their preaching was vain, their faith was vain, and they were still in their sins. But the fact remains that they did believe that Christ was raised from the dead ones, so Paul's argument is strong. The questions that arise are, who are the dead ones that the Corinthians didn't believe would be raised and why did they not believe that they would be raised?

Since the context of Christ's resurrection is the purview of Paul's thought, it is of necessity to recognize that the dead ones refers to Old Covenant Saints, prior to the resurrection of Christ. There were no New Covenant dead ones prior to the resurrection of Christ. With the resurrection of Christ came the establishment of the New Covenant. Thus, any saints after the resurrection of Christ would be New Covenant saints. So the problem that the Corinthians had was with the resurrection of the Old Covenant dead ones. Christ, of course, died under the terms of the Old Covenant, and was raised in order to establish the New Covenant.

What was the issue regarding the Old Covenant saints that the Corinthians were struggling with? Paul was teaching the Law-free Gospel. The Corinthians understood this. The problem had to do with the mixing of the Law with the Gospel. If the Old Covenant saints lived by the Law, then how could they be resurrected in Christ? But Paul taught that apart from Israel, there is no resurrection. The Law-free Gospel was preached to Israel and many of them believed that Gospel. The problem was not with trying to obey the Law, for that was commanded by God. The problem was with placing their hopes in the Law. In fact, if those who obeyed the Law, but lived by the Gospel could not be resurrected, then neither could the Gentiles be resurrected because Christ came to redeem the house of Israel. The Gospel is to the Jew first, and then to the Gentile. After explaining to the Corinthians that if the dead are not raised, then they are still in their sins, he goes on to comment about those that had fallen asleep in Christ (cf. v. 6).

> [18]Then those also who have fallen asleep in Christ have perished. [19]If we have hoped in Christ in this life only, we are of all men most to be pitied. [20]But now Christ has been raised from the dead, the first fruits of those who are asleep. [21]For since by a man came death, by a man also came the resurrection of the dead. [22]For as in Adam all die, so also in Christ all will be made alive.

Christ was the first fruits of those who were asleep. In Colossians 1:18, Paul puts it like this: "He is also head of the body, the church; and He is *the beginning, the firstborn from the dead*, so that He Himself will come to have first place in everything" (italics mine). Christ was not the first person to rise from the visible, earthly grave. He was, however, the first to be raised out of the dead ones. This goes to show that the resurrection that Paul is concerned with is not the resurrection of the biological corpse. It is the invisible body/soul that Paul is concerned with.

But didn't Christ rise from the grave in His biological corpse? Indeed He did. That was made explicit in the first part of 1 Corinthians 15. If Paul is concerned here with the invisible body/soul and not with the biological corpse, then why did Christ resurrect biologically? The answer rests with another question: How else would Christ demonstrate to people in the visible, earthly realm that He did what He said He would do, namely, rise from the dead ones? The only biological body that the Bible promises would not see decay was Christ's. Peter says of David, "he looked ahead and spoke of the resurrection of the Christ, that he was neither abandoned to Hades, nor did his flesh suffer decay" (Acts 2:31).[85]

Jesus Himself responded to the Pharisees' request for a miraculous sign by saying, "A wicked and adulterous generation asks for a miraculous sign! But none will be given it except the sign of the prophet Jonah. For as Jonah was three days and three nights in the belly of a huge fish, so the Son of Man will be three days and three nights in the heart of the earth" (Matt. 12:39-40). The resurrection of Christ's biological body served as a sign of His resurrection from the dead. Thus, the resurrection of the dead is the resurrection of the body/soul, Christ being the first fruits. Here we must remember that the death that came through Adam is not biological death. God told Adam, "In the day you eat of [the fruit], you will surely die." There is only one death spoken of, not two. When Adam ate the fruit, he died, and this resulted in death to all in Adam.

The meaning of death is "separation from God." This separation is displayed in the removal of Adam and Eve from the Garden of Eden. The Law given to Adam guaranteed his fall because the power of sin is the law (1 Cor. 15:56). Why would God give Adam the command to not eat of the Tree of the Knowledge of Good and Evil if He did not intend for Adam to sin? God is sovereign, and this was the eternal plan of God. There is no hint of a so-called "probation period" in the Garden. Heaven was always the ultimate destiny of mankind through Christ. Both the Tree of Life and the Tree of the Knowledge of Good and Evil were placed by God in the Garden to demonstrate the need for Christ.

This often leads people to wonder why we need a biological body. There are a number of reasons. The main reason is that we need biological bodies to live in this earthly realm. You may be asking, "Then why place us here at all? Why not just have us live in Heaven without living on the earth?" This leads to a second reason for biological bodies: Procreation. Invisible souls do not reproduce. Jesus tells the Sadducees that in Heaven, we are like the angels, who neither marry, nor are given in marriage. Procreation is necessary in order to have people to go to Heaven. Without this, everyone's names would be Adam and Eve. In other words, we would have no federal head, and Christ could not be the second Adam to show off the mercy of God by dying for our sins. No sin, no merciful sacrifice of Christ. This is all part of the necessity of a biological body on the earth where man can have the ability to sin *and* be redeemed.

Apparently, living on this earth in these biological bodies is necessary for the redemption of man to be possible. Part of the reason for this seems to be in the necessity of procreation, so that Christ can be the second Adam, our new federal head. And since the Son of God is immortal and cannot die, He had to become a mortal man on the earth in order to die and demonstrate God's mercy for sinners. But beyond all this, God placed us here for the enjoyment of glorifying God in our biological bodies on this earth. These biological bodies are needed as instruments to live on this earth. God again demonstrates how great Heaven will be by placing us here. We get to compare glory with glory. We get to experience something that the angels could never experience. Peter says the following in 1 Peter 1:

> [10]As to this salvation, the prophets who prophesied of the grace that would come to you made careful searches and inquiries, [11]seeking to know what person or time the Spirit of Christ within them was indicating as He predicted the sufferings of Christ and the glories to follow. [12]It was revealed to them that they were not serving themselves, but you, in these things which now have been announced to you through those who preached the gospel to you by the Holy Spirit sent from heaven—*things into which angels long to look.*[86]

Continuing on, in verse 18 of 1 Corinthians 15, the firstfruits that Paul talks about here is rooted in one of the feasts of Israel. The first crop of the barley harvest that was planted in the winter would begin to ripen in the spring. "The first sheaf (Firstfruits) of the harvest is cut and, in a carefully prescribed and meticulous ceremony, presented to the Lord…The firstfruit consecrates the harvest. The word for 'firstfruit' is the Hebrew word re'shiyth, which means: 'the choicest of the choice'."[87] Once the first crop rose forth in its ripened state and was cut and presented to the Lord, the rest would follow soon after. The rest of the wheat did not take thousands of years to rise. And here, Paul uses this feast to demonstrate the nearness of the end (cf. 1 Peter 4:7: The end of all things is near):

> [23]But each in his own order: Christ the first fruits, after that those who are Christ's at His coming, [24]then comes the end, when He hands over the kingdom to the God and Father, when He has abolished all rule and all authority and power. [25]For He must reign until He has put all His enemies under His feet. [26]The last enemy that will be abolished is death. [27]For he has put all things in subjection under his feet. But when He says, "All things are put in subjection," it is evident that He is excepted who put all things in subjection to Him. [28]When all things are subjected to Him, then the Son Himself also will be subjected to the One who subjected all things to Him, so that God may be all in all.

We have already seen that the parousia of Christ took place in 70 AD. We have also already seen that the end of all things (i.e. old mode of existence) came in 70 AD (1 Peter 4:7). The abolishment of all rule and all authority and all power, therefore, occurred in 70 AD. In fact, Paul says, "For our struggle is not against flesh and blood, but against the rulers, against the powers, against the world forces of this darkness, against the spiritual forces of wickedness in the heavenly places" (Eph. 6:12).[88] If our struggle is not against flesh and blood but against invisible rulers and powers, then the struggle that Christ fought and won for us was accomplished in the invisible realm. Therefore, at the parousia of Christ, all of His enemies were put under His feet and the last enemy, death, was abolished.

Now remember, if the death that Paul is concerned with here is the death of Adam, it is not biological death that was abolished, but rather, separation from God. After biological death, the invisible body/soul went to Hades to await the coming Messiah. Hades was the place of the dead, death was the status of the dead. At the parousia of Christ, Death and Hades were thrown into the lake of fire, which is the second death

(Rev. 20). Thus, no more would those who die biologically in the earthly realm go to Hades, the place of Death. Instead, upon biological death, the invisible body/soul goes directly to either Heaven or to the place of the second death, where Death and Hades are.

Paul continues his case for the resurrection of the dead by showing them the logical fallacy of one of the practices of the day if indeed the dead are not raised.

> [29]Otherwise, what will those do who are baptized for the dead? If the dead are not raised at all, why then are they baptized for them?

Baptism was the sign and seal of dying to the Old Covenant mode of existence by being united to the death of Christ (Rom. 6:3-4). It was God's mark upon His people that they belonged to Him, putting to death the body of Adam by being united to the body of Christ. It changed their status from being in Adam to being in Christ. It was a corporate sign and seal. All who were baptized into Christ were joined to the New Covenant body. Thus, even Old Covenant Israel had to be baptized into Christ. Since the Gospel is from Israel, the remnant of Israel that was baptized into Christ was therefore baptized on behalf of Israel. What would be the point of these baptisms if indeed the dead were not raised?

> [30]Why are we also in danger every hour? [31]I affirm, brethren, by the boasting in you which I have in Christ Jesus our Lord, I die daily. [32]If from human motives I fought with wild beasts at Ephesus, what does it profit me? If the dead are not raised, LET US EAT AND DRINK, FOR TOMORROW WE DIE. [33]Do not be deceived: "Bad company corrupts good morals." [34]Become sober-minded as you ought, and stop sinning; for some have no knowledge of God I speak this to your shame.

Paul establishes the final blow against the thinking of the Corinthians that the dead are not raised. The essence of his thoughts here is that if the dead are not raised, then nobody is raised, and they were being persecuted for the sake of the Gospel uselessly. Why live a hard life on this earth for the sake of the Gospel if there is nothing after biological death? But the fact that both Paul and the Corinthians were facing opposition verified the fact that they knew that there was the continuation of life after biological death. What Paul had to correct in their thinking was that if the Old Covenant dead were not raised, then what they knew to be true didn't make any sense at all, since the resurrection of those who had fallen asleep in Christ was contingent upon the resurrection of the dead.

At this point, if Paul was arguing for the resurrection of the biological body, he would have arrived at the end of his discourse. He already established that Christ was raised biologically. And if the point was that the dead are raised biologically following the pattern of Christ, then Paul would have accomplished his purpose and 1 Corinthians 15 would only have 34 verses. But the fact is that the Corinthians understood that the resurrection that Paul was arguing for had nothing to do with the biological body. What they didn't understand yet was what kind of body (singular) the dead (plural) would be raised in.[89]

By following Paul's argument up to this point, it was now clear to them that the dead are indeed raised. But the question remained: Would they be raised in the same body as those who had fallen asleep in Christ or in a different body? The Corinthians didn't yet understand that they would be raised in the same body as the dead, so they wanted to know what kind of body the dead would be raised in:

> [35]But someone will say, "How are the dead raised? And with what kind of body do they come?" [36]You fool! That which you sow does not come to life unless it dies; [37]and that which you sow, you do not sow the body which is to be, but a bare grain, perhaps of wheat or of something else. [38]But God gives it a body just as He wished, and to each of the seeds a body of its own.

Paul begins his explanation with the illustration of a seed. A seed does not come to life into the body that it is designed to become unless it dies. There is a process of simultaneous dying and rising of a seed before it reaches it's full potential. The seed does not die first and then immediately become full blown wheat. While it is dying the wheat is rising. It isn't until the seed has died completely that the wheat has risen completely. This is the way a seed works.

Now each type of seed has its own body. If you have a bag of seeds of the same type, those seeds have one collective body type. Paul is using the singular collective to show that each seed type has a different body, and that each of the individual seeds has the body of its collective type.

Paul goes on in the next couple of verses to demonstrate that everything in the visible realm has it's own type of body. In the seed illustration, he shows that one seed has a certain body, another seed has a different body. But each seed type has a unique body into which all the seeds of that type are raised. It is the same with different types of flesh:

> [39]All flesh is not the same flesh, but there is one flesh of men, and another flesh of beasts, and another flesh of birds, and another of fish. [40]There are also heavenly bodies and earthly bodies, but the glory of the heavenly is one, and the glory of the earthly is another. [41]There is one glory of the sun, and another glory of the moon, and another glory of the stars; for star differs from star in glory.

Each type of flesh is unique. The collective flesh of man is different than the collective flesh of beasts, which is also different than the collective flesh of birds and so on. But men have only one type of flesh while beasts, birds, and fish also have only one type of flesh respectively.

Likewise, there are different bodies on earth than there are in space, which is what Paul means by heavenly bodies; he does not mean the invisible realm. This is clear from the fact that verse 40 is placed between verses 39 and 41 where Paul is distinguishing between types of bodies on earth and types of bodies in space. He is simply continuing his reasoning that even bodies in space have unique bodies and are different than the bodies on earth. And the glory of the bodies on earth are different than the glory of the bodies in space. They are not the same. But the glory of the heavenly is of one type and the glory of the earthly is of another type. And even the bodies in space differ from one another in glory. Each body has its own unique glory. The glory of the sun is different than the glory of the moon. And each of the stars, much like each of the seeds, has its own type of glory.

In each of these illustrations, Paul demonstrates that while there are different types of seeds, flesh, and bodies, each individual seed, flesh, or heavenly body has the same type of body or glory as its collective whole. So it is with the resurrection of the dead. They share in the same body as those who died in Christ, namely, the body of Adam. There is only one body type for mankind. Man is a body, and each individual is in the same collective body as the first man, Adam. Thus, just as Adam was a body of sin, so all who are in Adam have the same body of sin. Therefore, the dead must be raised into the same body of Christ, the second Adam, as those who died after the resurrection of Christ. If we take everything Paul has said here, at the beginning of his explanation of the resurrection, as one unit, we can understand his following dying and rising motif of the one body of Adam:

> [42]So also is the resurrection of the dead. It is sown a perishable body, it is raised an imperishable body; [43]it is sown in dishonor, it is raised in glory; it is sown in weakness, it is raised in power; [44]it is sown a natural body, it is raised a spiritual body. If there is a natural body, there is also a spiritual body. [45]So also it is written, "The first man, Adam, became a living soul." The last Adam became a life-giving spirit. [46]However, the spiritual is not first, but the natural; then the spiritual. [47]The first man is from the earth, earthy; the second man is from heaven. [48]As is the earthy, so also are those who are earthy; and as is the heavenly, so also are those who are heavenly. [49]Just as we have borne the image of the earthy, we will also bear the image of the heavenly.

If we understand that Paul is talking about the collective body of Adam, then we can understand why he uses the singular to refer to the sowing and raising of the dead (plural). Christ took on the body of Adam. All who were baptized into Christ died with Him, thus putting to death the old man, Adam, and were being resurrected into the new man, Christ (cf. Rom. 6:5-6). Since Paul is talking about the collective dead, the natural body of Adam, being raised into the collective spiritual body of Christ, the translation, "it," throughout verses 43-44, would be better translated as "he." *He* is sown in dishonor, *he* is raised in glory, etc. The Greek lends itself to this translation since the pronoun associated with the verbs for "sown" and "raised" can be translated as "he, she, or it," depending on context.

Thus, the dead, like those who had fallen asleep, were united to Christ in His death where He put to death the natural body of Adam and rose a spiritual body. Since Christ was the first fruits of the resurrection, the dying and rising of the rest of the dead were still in the transitional simultaneous dying and rising that was illustrated by the seed illustration. The simultaneous dying and rising of the natural body into the spiritual body began at the death and resurrection of Christ, but it would not be completed until the Old Covenant mode of existence completely died in 70 AD at the destruction of the Temple. It was at that time that the dead who were bound by the Old Covenant were raised out of Hades to complete the resurrection of all the dead in Adam.

The dying and rising of the one collective body of Adam into the body of Christ was only complete when all of the dead were raised. This could only be completed when Christ, the High Priest, exited the most holy place in heaven at His parousia when He completed the atonement for our sins (Heb. 9:23-28). That was the finalization of the New Covenant mode of existence and the complete obliteration of the Old Covenant mode of existence. The Old Covenant was a ministry of death. The New Covenant is a ministry of life. The ministry of death was destroyed in conjunction with the completion of the ministry of life.

It is not the spiritual that is first, but the natural. Both the natural and the spiritual existed in those who were still living biologically. Paul uses these same words in 1 Corinthians 2:12-14:

[12]Now we have received, not the spirit of the world, but the Spirit who is from God, so that we may know the things freely given to us by God, [13]which things we also speak, not in words taught by human wisdom, but in those taught by the Spirit, combining spiritual thoughts with spiritual words. [14]But a natural man does not accept the things of the Spirit of God, for they are foolishness to him; and he cannot understand them, because they are spiritually appraised.

The natural man is the man in Adam. The spiritual man is the man in Christ. Neither of these men in 1 Corinthians 2 was biologically dead. One of them, however, was spiritually dead, that is, separated from God. The only way to move from the natural man to the spiritual man was to die with Christ. Thus, in 1 Corinthians 15, Paul is not talking about biological death (although the dead had died biologically), he is talking about death in the natural man, Adam.

And Paul transitions from speaking about the dead to speaking directly to the biologically living Corinthians when he says, "Just as we have borne the image of the earthy, we will [better: let us; subjunctive mood] also bear the image of the heavenly." We will see, in Paul's next line of thinking, that those who were alive biologically at the parousia of Christ were changed into the same imperishable, immortal body of Christ at the completion of the resurrection of the dead in Christ.

[50]Now I say this, brethren, that flesh and blood cannot inherit the kingdom of God; nor does the perishable inherit the imperishable.

By flesh and blood, Paul does not mean the biological body. He is once again speaking of the natural man. Consider the interaction between Peter and Jesus in Matthew 16:

[15]He said to them, "But who do you say that I am?" [16]Simon Peter answered, "You are the Christ, the Son of the living

God." [17]And Jesus said to him, "Blessed are you, Simon Barjona, because flesh and blood did not reveal this to you, but My Father who is in heaven."

It is obvious from this text that flesh and blood does not refer to the biological body. Jesus is telling Peter that he did not come to grasp that Jesus was the Christ, the Son of the Living God, by human means. It was not the natural man that revealed this to him. Remember 1 Corinthians 2:14: "But a natural man does not accept the things of the Spirit of God, for they are foolishness to him; and he cannot understand them, because they are spiritually appraised." What Paul is teaching in 1 Corinthians 15:50 is that natural man cannot inherit the kingdom of God. Man cannot come into possession of the kingdom as long as he is still in the natural man. The perishable cannot come into possession of the imperishable because it is perishable. A change has to occur. A whole new wardrobe has to be put on to replace the old wardrobe. Once the resurrection was completed, both the living and the dead were then fully transformed, redeemed, and changed through the putting on of immortality and imperishability. Read how Paul puts it:

> [51]Behold, I tell you a mystery; we will not all sleep, but we will all be changed,[90] [52]in a moment, in the twinkling of an eye, at the last trumpet; for the trumpet will sound, and the dead will be raised imperishable, and we will be changed. [53]For this perishable must put on the imperishable, and this mortal must put on immortality.

The resurrection was necessary for the change from the old to the new to be accomplished. Not everyone had to be raised from Hades, for not everyone had died biologically, but everyone in Christ was changed. Upon the completion of the resurrection, the final change from the ministry of death to the ministry of life was instant. The sound of the trumpet here pulls from the imagery of one of the feasts of Israel, called the Feast of Trumpets. David Curtis is helpful here in his explanation of the Feast of Trumpets:

There are several things about this feast which should pique our interest. First, this feast was to be celebrated on the first day of the month. Second, this feast was to be celebrated on the first day of the seventh month. Third, the feast was marked by a blowing of trumpets. The Hebrew word here is teruw'ah, [ter-oo-aw'} which means: "an alarm, a signal, a sound of tempest, a shout, a shout or blast of war or alarm or joy." Why is this significant that this feast was on the first day of the month? The Feast of Trumpets is the only one of the seven feasts which began on the first day of the month.

The Hebrew months each began on the new moon. The other feasts occurred toward the middle of the respective months, when the moon as [sic] at, or near, full. The nights would be filled with moonlight. At the New Moon, the moon is DARK and only a thin crescent.

The beginning of each month was originally dependent upon the sighting of the New Moon when the moon was but a crescent; the nights would be dark, with little moonlight. The precise timing of the New Moon was not always easily determined due to weather conditions and a lack of witnesses.

Two concurring witnesses sighting the first sliver of the new moon determined each new month. The two witnesses see the new moon and attest to it before the Sanhedrin in the Temple. This could happen during either of two days, depending on when the witnesses come. Since no one knew when the witnesses would come, no one knew when the Feast of Trumpets would start. After the appearance of the new moon was confirmed, then the Feast of Trumpets could begin, and the rest of the fall feasts could be accurately calculated from that date. The Feast of Trumpets is also considered a High Sabbath, and no work is to be done. Therefore, all preparations for the Feast of Trumpets had to be made in advance. Since no one knew the exact hour of the new moon's appearance, it kept people in a continual state of alertness.

They knew approximately when the new moon would reveal itself, but they did not know the exact hour of its appearance. I know a lunar calendar seems quite foreign to us living in the west, but we have to understand that the ancients kept track of time in this manner for thousands of years.[91]

So the allusion to the Feast of Trumpets here by Paul is an implied teaching that no one knew exactly when this change would take place. This is in line with the consistent teaching about watchfulness and readiness in the New Testament. It was the day that the saints looked forward to and were excited about. This would be the final change from the old to the new.

> [54]But when this perishable will have put on the imperishable, and this mortal will have put on immortality, then will come about the saying that is written, "Death is swallowed up in victory. [55]"O Death, where is your victory? O Death, where is your sting?" [56]The sting of death is sin, and the power of sin is the law; [57]but thanks be to God, who gives us the victory through our Lord Jesus Christ. [58]Therefore, my beloved brethren, be steadfast, immovable, always abounding in the work of the Lord, knowing that your toil is not in vain in the Lord.

The United Bible Society gives the Greek text in verse 55 a {B} rating. This means that they were pretty sure that this was the original version, but they were not certain. A textual variant that has a lot of great support from several major, trustworthy sources, reads as follows: "Where, O Death, is your sting? Where, O Hades, is your victory?"' This rendering makes far more sense in the context, especially when compared with Revelation 20:14: "Then Death and Hades were thrown into the Lake of Fire. This is the Second Death, the Lake of Fire." In addition, Paul is also referencing Hosea 13:14, which is directly related to Israel: "Shall I ransom them from the power of Sheol? Shall I redeem them from Death? O Death, where are your thorns? O Sheol, where is your sting?"[92]

Both John and Paul are teaching that with the end of the Old Covenant mode of existence came the end of Death and Hades. Death and Hades here refers to the temporal separation from God in which the biologically dead were held. Those who were in the body of Christ by faith were raised from death to life, which brought about the end of separation from God. Those who were not in the body of Christ continued on to eternal death.

With the fullness of the New Covenant, through the resurrection, came the disappearing of the Old Covenant (Heb. 8:13) and the death of Death and Hades. Hebrews 8:8-12 is a quote from Jeremiah 31:27-34, which speaks of God writing the Law on the hearts of those in the New Covenant. When the writing of the Law on the hearts of those in the New Covenant was completed, which coincided with the completion of the resurrection, the Law of the natural man no longer had power over those in Christ.

The resurrected Israel (which is spiritual or true Israel including Jews and Gentiles) consists of the people whom God has redeemed from the rest of mankind, thus changing them from the dead body of Adam to the living body of Christ. No longer do we, who are in Christ, live by law but by grace. Sin, which comes through law, is no longer counted against us because we are in the covenant community where The Law was completely fulfilled in Christ. He made the final atonement in the Holy of Holies to allow us to enter in without our sin being counted against us.

Those who were changed into the body of Christ in the resurrection could no longer die and be separated from God. Since then, those who are born into the body of Christ have the same benefits. Thus, the sting of Death was swallowed up in victory because the power of sin was taken away; the power of sin was taken away because the Law can no longer kill us. We no longer live by the law of the natural man (i.e. living by the flesh), but by the law written on our hearts (i.e. living by the Spirit).

This victory was given to us by God through our Lord Jesus Christ. And that is why Paul says, "Therefore, my beloved brethren, be steadfast, immovable, always abounding in the work of the Lord, knowing that your toil is not in vain in the Lord." The "therefore" told the Corinthians that the motivation for being steadfast, immovable, and always abounding in the work of the Lord is that such toil had an impending goal that was not in vain. This is in contrast to Paul's earlier comments that if the dead are not raised, "let us eat and drink, for tomorrow we die." Instead, abound in the work of the Lord, for tomorrow we will be changed!

SUMMARY

There are other texts concerning the resurrection, which will be dealt with in chapter 5: *Questions and Objections Answered.* This sub-chapter has dealt with Paul's doctrine of the resurrection in 1 Corinthians 15. The resurrection of the body was completed when the resurrection of the dead out of Hades occurred at the parousia of Christ. The resurrection of the body was incomplete until the final resurrection of the Old Covenant saints of Israel. The resurrection was the hope of Israel, and the Gentiles got to share in the resurrection body. Thus, the resurrection for believers was the rising of the new man out of death into life as the body of the old man died in Christ. This is a true and complete rising out of sin-death (i.e. separation from God). Sin-death is not only continued after biological death, it was the state of every person, both the biologically living and dead, before the resurrection of Christ.

So the resurrection of the dead saints out of Hades was a resurrection into eternal life, the same eternal life that the living saints were raised into through the death and resurrection of the body. The Old Covenant saints are not part of a different body. Their resurrection completed the resurrection of the one body of Christ of which Christ was the firstfruits.

Because the parousia brought an end to the death of Adam for those who had faith in Christ, Hades had to be destroyed along with death because Hades kept Old Covenant saints from the presence of God. It was a temporary place of death that believers went to after biological death, and thus had to be destroyed because the end of the temporal covenant had come. Eternal life had finally arrived, and believers could now go to Heaven at biological death.

Not so for the wicked in Hades. They, too, were resurrected out of temporal death, but they remain in the body of Adam. They were raised out of Hades only to continue on in permanent death in the Lake of Fire, the second death. In John 5, Jesus talks about their resurrection in contrast to the resurrection of the saints:

> [28]"Do not marvel at this; for an hour is coming, in which all who are in the tombs will hear His voice, [29]and will come forth; those who did the good deeds to a resurrection of life, those who committed the evil deeds to a resurrection of judgment.[93]

The resurrection of the wicked was not a resurrection of life, but of judgment. They didn't get life, only judgment unto eternal death.

Sub-Chapter 4C:

THE JUDGMENT OF THE LIVING AND THE DEAD

It is traditionally understood that at the visible, future, biological, second coming of Christ, and after the resurrection of the living and the dead, every individual who ever lived will stand before the Judgment Seat of Christ to give an account of their thoughts, words, and deeds. Thus, they will be repaid according to what they have done in their biological bodies, whether good or evil (WCF 33.1). The righteous will enter into everlasting life in the presence of the Lord, but the wicked will be cast into eternal torments, and be punished with everlasting destruction from the presence of the Lord, and from the glory of His power (WCF 33.2).

This sub-chapter will demonstrate from the Scriptures that the Great White Throne Judgment occurred in 70 AD and determined the status of eternal life or eternal death for every person. This brought an end to the Old Covenant temporary mode of existence.

THE JUDGMENT

Our study so far has demonstrated that reading the Bible through New Covenant Eyes requires fulfillment of the parousia and the resurrection in 70 AD. Let us now move into the last sub-chapter of chapter 4, which will deal with the judgment that took place on the final day of the Old Covenant mode of existence. We have already seen that the parousia, the resurrection, and the judgment are synchronous events.

But let's take a look at some of the time texts connected with the judgment to further establish its fulfillment in 70 AD:

> Acts 24:25: But as [Paul] was discussing righteousness, self-control and the *judgment* [lit: about to] come, Felix became frightened and said, 'Go away for the present, and when I find time I will summon you.'"[94]

> 2 Timothy 4:1: "I solemnly charge you in the presence of God and of Christ Jesus, who is [lit: about to] *judge* the living and the dead, and by His appearing and His kingdom..."[95]

> James 5:8-9: "You too be patient; strengthen your hearts, for the coming of the Lord is *near*. Do not complain, brethren, against one another, so that you yourselves may not be judged; behold, the *Judge* is standing *right at the door*."[96]

> 1 Peter 4:5, 7: "but they will give account to Him who is *ready* to judge the living and the dead...The end of all things is *near*..."[97]

Judgment of Every Man According His Deeds

With those texts in mind, we return to Matthew 16:27-28: "For the Son of Man is [about to] come in the glory of His Father with His angels, and will then repay every man according to his deeds. Truly I say to you, there are some of those who are standing here who will not taste death until they see the Son of Man coming in His kingdom." In these verses, Jesus teaches that at the parousia of Christ, which was to happen before some of those who were standing there would die, He would then (i.e. at that time) repay every man according to his deeds. Two points of emphasis here are, "every man" and "according to his deeds."

We see in Matthew 25:31 and following, the description of this judgment "according to his deeds." Notice once again, in verse 31, that

Jesus comes in His glory with the angels, just as was stated in 16:27-28. Matthew 24:31 tells us what the angels did at the parousia: "And He will send forth His angels with a great trumpet and they will gather together His elect from the four winds, from one end of the sky to the other."

The "elect" of Matthew 24 are specifically the elect that were alive during those days. Notice Matthew 24:22 says, "Unless those days had been cut short, no life would have been saved; but for the sake of the elect those days will be cut short." For the sake of the elect, "those days" would be cut short. "Those days" are not cut short for the elect who are *not* living in "those days." That would be useless. In fact, this is further made evident by Matthew 24:24: "For false Christs and false prophets will arise and will show great signs and wonders, so as to mislead, if possible, even the elect." How would false Christs and false prophets mislead people who are not being influenced by their signs and wonders? The point is that the elect that Jesus is referring to are the elect that would be alive during "those days." The days we are living in today are not "those days." "Those days" were the days leading up to the destruction of Jerusalem in 70 AD.

Thus, when we keep Matthew 24:31 in context, the elect that the angels would gather "from the four winds, from one end of the sky to the other" are the elect that were alive during "those days." This gathering of the elect is "a prophecy of the resurrection, taken directly from the Little Apocalypse of Isaiah 24-29, and specifically Isaiah 27:13."[98] But the gathering of the elect at the culmination of the resurrection is not the only gathering that occurs at the parousia of Christ. Matthew 25:32 informs us that all the nations would be gathered for judgment. This is the passage of the well-known sheep and goats judgment. It is the judgment that occurred on the last day of the Old Covenant mode of existence. How were the people of the nations divided? They were divided in the same way that the good fish are put into good containers in order to remove the bad fish that would be thrown away in Matthew 13:47-50.

Thus Matthew 24:31 is about the gathering of the good fish in order to distinguish them from the bad fish. It is in this way that the people of Matthew 25:32 were divided. The good fish were the sheep and the bad fish were the goats. It is commonly believed that this judgment is still future to us because it appears, at first glance, that by the language used, this could not have happened yet. And of course, according to the traditional view, it hasn't. Notice verses 41 and 46: "…'depart from me, you cursed, into the eternal fire prepared for the devil and his angels…' And these will go away into eternal punishment, but the righteous into eternal life." Now there clearly seems to be a final judgment going on here in this passage.

Indeed, there is no doubt that this is speaking of the final judgment for the nations that would be gathered before His throne. We would not think, therefore, based upon the traditional understanding of the final judgment, that there would be any more entering into eternal life after this judgment was completed. Revelation 21-22 describes the New Jerusalem, the place where those whose names are "written in the Lamb's book of life" enter into. This is the "eternal life" that is contrasted with the "second death", the lake of fire, or as Matthew 25:46 puts it, "eternal punishment." Yet, in Revelation 22:22-27, we see something very peculiar happening *after* the great white throne judgment (20:11-15):

> [22]I saw no temple in it, for the Lord God the Almighty and the Lamb are its temple. [23]And the city has no need of the sun or of the moon to shine on it, for the glory of God has illumined it, and its lamp is the Lamb. [24]The *nations will* walk by its light, and the kings of the earth *will* bring their glory into it. [25]In the daytime (for there will be no night there) its gates will never be closed; [26]and they *will bring* the glory and the honor of the *nations into it*; [27]and nothing unclean, and no one who practices abomination and lying, *shall ever come into it*, but only those whose names are written in the Lamb's book of life.[99]

Here we have the glory and the honor of the nations being brought into the New Jerusalem after the judgment has already occurred. In addition, things that are unclean, and people who do what is detestable and false, still exist outside, but are never allowed to enter the holy city.

If the traditional view is correct, it would have been unnecessary to state that those in the lake of fire can never enter the city because the lake of fire is called the second death, or the eternal punishment. Obviously, if it is eternal, and thus permanent, Revelation 21:27 cannot be referring to those in the lake of fire, that is, if we take the traditional view. Yet, after the lake of fire judgment, "the kings of the earth" continue to enter into the city. Furthermore, we see that the leaves of the Tree of Life located in the city are for the "healing of the nations" (22:2). Why do nations need healing if there is no more need for healing?

Now, let's work backwards from here through Revelation 21. We see that the glory and the honor of the nations are being brought into the city (vv. 22-27). The city is made of all sorts of jewels and pearls and measurements symbolic of Israel (vv. 15-21). The names of the twelve tribes and the twelve apostles are inscribed on the gates and walls (vv. 10-14). This city is the Bride, the wife of the Lamb, who is Christ (v. 9). This Bride comes down out of heaven from God adorned for her husband, which happens when John sees a new heaven and new earth (vv. 1-5). And all of this happens after the great white throne judgment (20:11-15).

Why go through all that? To demonstrate that the kings of the earth continue to bring the glory of the nations into this city, the Bride of the Lamb, *after* the final judgment. Thus, the nations in Revelation 21-22 are not the Bride of Christ, but enter into the Bride of Christ. We might say that they are born into the Bride of Christ, thus being the children of the Bride of Christ. If that is true, then that means that Christ is their Father, which brings to mind the prophecy in Isaiah 9:6: "For a child will be born to us, a son will be given to us; And the government will rest on His shoulders; And His name will be called Wonderful Counselor, Mighty God, *Eternal Father*, Prince of Peace" (italics mine).

The Parables of Matthew 25

There are some pertinent questions that must be entertained at this point. If there are nations that are still being healed after the judgment, then who are the nations of Matthew 25? Here we encounter why

155

understanding covenantalism is so important. In Matthew 24-25, Jesus is teaching about the destruction of Jerusalem, the city of His covenant people. The elect of Matthew 24 are gathered together for eternal life, the same eternal life that the kings of the earth from Revelation 21 enter into. They are also the same people that are represented by the five wise virgins in Matthew 25:1-12. There we have a parable of ten virgins preparing to enter the marriage feast with the bridegroom when he arrives. While there is much that can be gleaned from this parable, the main point of it is to teach the disciples to be ready for the coming of the Lord, "for *you* know neither the day nor the hour" (v. 13; italics mine).

Following the parable of the ten virgins comes the parable of the talents. The master entrusts his servants with talents (which were monetary units) according to their ability to multiply money. They all worked for the master and they all had the ability to multiply money. The ability that each of them had did not determine the outcome, nor did the amount given to them. They were simply required to be faithful with what they were given and to use their respective abilities to make more. Two of the servants were faithful and worked hard and one was wicked and lazy. Thus, they were repaid according to what they had done (cf. Matt. 16:27). The two faithful servants were repaid by being given more: "You have been faithful over little; I will set you over much. Enter into the joy of your master" (v. 21, 23). The lazy servant was repaid by losing what he was originally given: "So take the talent from him and give it to him who has the ten talents" (v. 28). In addition, that worthless servant is cast "into the outer darkness. In that place there will be weeping and gnashing of teeth" (v. 30). So the faithful servants enter into the joy of their master (i.e. eternal life); the wicked servant is cast into the outer darkness (i.e. eternal punishment). The main point of this parable is to demonstrate the deeds of the faithful versus the deeds of the wicked who are lazy and do not prepare for the master's return.

Who were the master's servants? Who were the ten virgins? The parousia of Christ was first and foremost a judgment upon Israel. This is the central theme of Matthew 24-25 as Jesus begins by stating that the Temple would be destroyed. Thus, the virgins and the servants are parables about Israel. But the coming of Christ was not simply a local judgment. It was indeed a universal judgment. Notice that in 25:32, that all the nations were gathered before Christ for judgment. The sign of judgment occurring in a local area on earth, in this case, Jerusalem, does not negate the universality of judgment put forth in that sign. Don Preston demonstrates this throughout Isaiah, beginning with Acts 17 as a starting point:

> Acts 17:31—"Because he hath appointed a day, in which he will judge the world in righteousness by that man whom he hath ordained; whereof he hath given assurance unto all men, in that he hath raised him from the dead.":

> Paul was in Athens when he made this prediction. He is not here speaking about the judgment of the dead, nor of Palestine, but the world (Grk. oikoumenen—inhabitable world; viz., the Roman empire). The coming day of judgment would envelope the whole Roman empire, and not just Jerusalem, Judea, and Galilee. We might comment here that in discussing the "little apocalypse" of Isa. 24-29, preterists generally interpret the "earth" that is there made desolate and bare (Isa. 24:12) in terms only of Judah and Israel. However, the fact is often overlooked that in the nine preceding chapters the prophet described God's judgment upon Moab (Isa. 15, 16), Syria and Israel (Isa. 17), Ethiopia (Isa. 18), Egypt (Isa. 19, 20), Babylon, Dumah and Arabia (Isa. 21), Judah (Isa. 22), and Tyre. (Isa. 23) Thus, the judgment spoken of in the little apocalypse was world-wide; chapter twenty-four merely summarizes the judgments that overtook the ancient world in the preceding chapters.

> The ax in God's hand and razor by which he would shave the world of its inhabitants was Assyria. (Isa. 7:20; 10:12, 15) Assyria was like a rending storm and overwhelming scourge that would pass through the land, leveling all in its

path. The Jews thought they would escape; they thought they had a covenant with death (Assyria) and with hell were in agreement. (Isa. 28:15) Ahaz had taken the gold and silver found in the temple and the treasures of the king's house, and sent them for a present to the king of Assyria (II Kng. 16); Hezekiah paid the king of Assyria three hundred talents of silver and thirty talents of gold; he even stripped off the gold from the doors of the temple, and from the pillars, to pay to the king of Assyria to conclude a treaty of peace. (II Kng. 18:13-16) The Jews thought that they would thus escape God's judgment by the Assyrians. But God said he would annul their agreement with Assyria and they would be trodden down when the overwhelming scourge passed through the land; as in fact came to pass. (Isa. 28:18) Furthermore, what the Assyrians failed to accomplish, the Babylonians would complete.

God's judgment in carrying the nation into captivity under the Assyrians and Babylonians was typical of the eschatological judgment under Rome when the nation would suffer ultimate and irrevocable destruction. Hence, prophecies of the coming salvation in Jesus are interwoven throughout the little apocalypse, showing it has another, plenary application that would be fulfilled in the days of the Messiah. (Isa. 25:8; 26:19; 28:16) But the point we want to make here is that, just as the judgment of the little apocalypse by Assyria brought within its sweep the whole world of ancient man, so the eschatological judgment would not be limited to Jerusalem and Palestine. All men would feel the rod of Christ's correction.[100]

The Kingdom of Heaven

While the eschatological judgment would come upon the whole world, we must understand that this means "the whole world at that time." And the phrase, "all the nations," often means the nations that were around at that time. This is evident from a multitude of texts from the Old Testament. Here are few:

> Deuteronomy 2:25
> This very day I will begin to put the terror and fear of you on all the nations under heaven. They will hear reports of you and will tremble and be in anguish because of you."

Here, He's talking to Israel. The nations today don't presently have the terror of Israel.

> Deuteronomy 29:24
> All the nations will ask: "Why has the LORD done this to this land? Why this fierce, burning anger?"

Have all the nations today asked this?

> 1 Chronicles 14:17
> So David's fame spread throughout every land, and the LORD made all the nations fear him.

Do all the nations fear David today? No, because contextually, "all the nations" means the nations at that time.

When the Old Testament was being written, the writers were chiefly concerned with the nations of the known world in existence at that time. The New Testament is the same. The writers of the New Testament were concerned with the known world throughout which the Gospel would travel from Jerusalem to the furthest reaches of the Roman Empire. The judgment in Matthew 25:31 and following would come upon that generation who heard the Gospel and rejected it. Consider the woes that Jesus gives to the scribes and Pharisees in Matthew 23. Jesus tells the crowds and his disciples to "practice and observe whatever they tell you—but not what they do. For they preach, but do not practice" (v. 3). The scribes and Pharisees did the opposite of what they preached. The

Jews followed the scribes and Pharisees, who represented Israel as their leaders. All the things they did, therefore, would, in turn, come upon them: "Truly, I say to you, all these things will come upon this generation" (v. 36). But by way of contrast, consider the dialogue between Jesus and his disciples in Mark 9:38-41:

> [38]John said to Him, "Teacher, we saw someone casting out demons in Your name, and we tried to prevent him because he was not following us." [39]But Jesus said, "Do not hinder him, for there is no one who will perform a miracle in My name, and be able soon afterward to speak evil of Me. [40]"For he who is not against us is for us. [41]"For whoever gives you a cup of water to drink because of your name as followers of Christ, truly I say to you, he will not lose his reward.

Let's take at look what Jesus teaches will happen at the judgment:

> Matthew 13:41-43: [41]"The Son of Man will send forth His angels, and they will gather out of His kingdom all stumbling blocks, and those who commit lawlessness, [42]and will throw them into the furnace of fire; in that place there will be weeping and gnashing of teeth. [43]"Then the righteous will shine forth as the sun in the kingdom of their Father He who has ears, let him hear.

> Matthew 13:47-50: [47]"Again, the kingdom of heaven is like a dragnet cast into the sea, and gathering fish of every kind; [48]and when it was filled, they drew it up on the beach; and they sat down and gathered the good fish into containers, but the bad they threw away. [49]"So it will be at the end of the age; the angels will come forth and take out the wicked from among the righteous, [50]and will throw them into the furnace of fire; in that place there will be weeping and gnashing of teeth.

The wicked and the stumbling blocks are actually gathered out of the kingdom, taken out from among the righteous, and thrown away into the furnace of fire. Notice that it is the ones who remain that enter into eternal life. Just like in the days of Noah, when the floods came and the door was shut, it was those who were unaware and unprepared that were taken away (Matt. 24:37-39). Following the illustration of Noah, the man in the field and the woman grinding at the mill that are taken are the ones who are not prepared and ready for the coming of the Lord.

The kingdom of heaven was coming to earth. Those who were ready would get to enter the kingdom and have eternal life. Those who were not ready like the wicked in the days of Noah, and in the parables of Matthew 24 and 25, would likewise be taken out from the kingdom and thrown into eternal punishment. The New Israel *is* the kingdom of heaven. This is what is meant by, "repent, for the kingdom of heaven is at hand."

Christ, the King of the kingdom of heaven came to earth. He is also the Israelite that came to redeem His people. The Jews who were of the faith of Abraham were the remnant that God promised to save. The kingdom was growing as the Gospel spread. And Gentiles who embraced the Gospel by faith entered into the kingdom as well. They were part of the New Israel, the kingdom of heaven. As long as the Old Covenant, the kingdom of the flesh, still remained, there was overlap. The Old Covenant was putting on the New Covenant. The old fleshly kingdom was dying as the new spiritual kingdom was rising. This is the same dying and rising motif of the resurrection of 1 Corinthians 15. So until the fleshy kingdom completely died and gave rise to the fullness of the spiritual kingdom, there existed both wheat and tares in the one kingdom that was being changed from death to life. In the parable of the wheat and the tares (Matt. 13), Jesus tells his angels not to gather the tares until the harvest because otherwise, they might uproot the wheat too.

Eternal Life and Eternal Death

Thus, returning to Matthew 25:31 and following, we arrive at the harvest. The angels have gathered together all the nations and the people are separated into the categories of sheep and goats, just like the wheat and the tares are separated and the good fish and the bad fish are separated. In addition, we must keep in mind that these verses follow on the heels of two parables with no indication that Jesus has transitioned out of parabolic language.

There were not ten literal virgins waiting for a literal bridegroom; the servants were not literally making money for a literal master; nor are the nations literally standing before a literal throne. The spiritual meaning behind these parables is literal, but the actual illustrations were not to literally take place. Thus, the spiritual meaning behind the Great White Throne judgment is that the nations of that generation were actually judged, but were not literally standing before a literal throne. The parable illustrates the point perfectly. They were judged for their deeds, just as Jesus told His disciples that anyone who gave them a glass of water in His name would by no means lose their reward. The eternal life and eternal punishment that all of these parables speak of did not begin after biological death, but actually began while the people were still biologically alive on the earth.[101]

Those who entered the kingdom of heaven (i.e. the New Jerusalem) by faith had eternal life that began immediately. Those who were not written in the Lamb's book of life would never enter and their eternal punishment began here as well. If we keep in mind that the judgment of the sheep and the goats was restricted to that generation, then we can realize that there were specific people who were alive at that time that could know their eternal destiny. They either embraced the Gospel or abandoned it at the time of the judgment, which took place at the destruction of Jerusalem (the point of reference) in 70 AD.

Does all of this mean that those who had died before 70 AD, including the Old Covenant nations were not judged? On the contrary, they, too, entered into eternal life or death respectively. But all who died before 70 AD were already divided in Hades. Their eternal destinies were secured, but they were held in the temporal location of Hades until that final day of the Old Covenant mode of existence. As we have already seen, there are several places that teach about the judgment of the final day, and they all provide various perspectives. It isn't as though there were several different consecutive times when each of the judgments took place. Rather, the various perspectives provided, which would all take place at the time of the judgment, demonstrate that a judgment would definitively take place, and that all would be judged at that time, both the living and the dead.

> Second Timothy 4:1: "I solemnly charge you in the presence of God and of Christ Jesus, who is [about to] judge the living and the dead, and by His appearing and His kingdom..."

> First Peter 4:3, 5: "³For the time already past is sufficient for you to have carried out the desire of the Gentiles...⁵but they will give account to Him who is [about to] judge the living and the dead."

Notice how Revelation describes the judgment:

> 19:20-21: "²⁰And the beast was seized, and with him the false prophet who performed the signs in his presence, by which he deceived those who had received the mark of the beast and those who worshiped his image; these two were thrown alive into the lake of fire which burns with brimstone. ²¹And the rest were killed with the sword which came from the mouth of Him who sat on the horse, and all the birds were filled with their flesh."

All of this is symbolic language of eternal judgment. The beast and the false prophet are thrown *alive* into the Lake of Fire. The Lake of Fire cannot be describing the actual placement of these two people (who are symbolically described) into a location *before* their biological deaths anymore than there can be an actual sword coming out of the mouth of Him who sat on the horse. (And why would Jesus be literally sitting on an actual horse? Is the horse His throne from which He executes judgment?) The point is that their eternal punishment, which is eternal death (i.e. permanent separation from God), had been secured before they died biologically. They entered into eternal death while still alive biologically. Yet we must remember that there is most definitely a place of eternal punishment that the soul continues onto after biological death.

Thus, while the eternal destiny of people alive on earth is secured, those who die biologically apart from Christ continue on into that same eternal punishment where Satan is now located: "And the devil who deceived them was thrown into the lake of fire and brimstone, where the beast and the false prophet are also; and they will be tormented day and night forever and ever" (v. 10). The torment of separation from God is not because of a place. It is because of a status. The place simply provides a location for the eternally dead to exist after they leave the location of the visible realm. The torment, however, begins here. Those whose names are not written in the Lamb's book of life just don't recognize it because they do not yet see with spiritual eyes the fullness of God's wrath. Again, we see the judgment in Revelation 20:11-14:

> [11]Then I saw a great white throne and Him who sat upon it, from whose presence earth and heaven fled away, and no place was found for them. [12]And I saw the dead, the great and the small, standing before the throne, and books were opened; and another book was opened, which is the book of life; and the dead were judged from the things which were written in the books, according to their deeds. [13]And the sea gave up the dead which were in it, and death and Hades gave up the dead which were in them; and they were judged, every one of them according to their deeds. [14]Then death and Hades were thrown into the lake of fire This is the second death, the lake of fire. [15]And if anyone's name was not found written in the book of life, he was thrown into the lake of fire.

Notice that earth and heaven fled away (cf. 2 Peter 3). This is the end of the Old Covenant. Is there a literal book of life that contains hand-written names of all God's people? Certainly not. Were there dead people in the sea that somehow escaped Hades? Certainly not. When we compare this with Revelation 21:1, we see that in the New Heavens and New Earth (i.e. the New Covenant; cf. 2 Peter 3), there is no sea. Seas divide nations. The point is that spiritually, there is no more sea that can keep the nations divided. And the death of Death and Hades demonstrates the end of the temporal order of things. No more are people who are in Christ kept separated from God, but now enter into their final destiny of being in the presence of God. No more do those who are apart from Christ await their final destiny, but are cast into the lake of fire (i.e. eternal death and punishment). Consider again Don Preston on the matter of the lake of fire:

> The claim that if the fire of hell is literal, that it must therefore be yet future, is a non-sequitor (It does not follow). For instance, the land of Edom, destroyed long, long ago, was to be set on fire and burn forever (Isaiah 34). Edom was destroyed, and does not exist today. Yet, there is no literal fire burning in the region where Edom once existed. There is no literal fire, yet, her punishment was fulfilled. Does the fact that the fire was not literal say that she was not destroyed? No, for Malachi 1:1-3.[102]

Relief From Affliction

In addition to the eternal punishment that the final judgment brought upon the wicked of that generation, the final judgment also destroyed the spiritual influence that the wicked had during that time. Much of the affliction that is described in the texts that discuss the signs leading up to the destruction of Jerusalem has to do with false prophets, antichrists, and deception (cf. Matt. 24:5, 10, 11; 2 Tim. 2:16-18; 2 Pet. 2; Jude). 2 Thessalonians especially deals with this. The relief that the

Thessalonians were to receive would come by means of the judgment. Once the Temple was destroyed, the influence of the enemies of the cross would fall with the Temple, for Christ would be revealed in the saints when the Old Covenant finally and fully disappeared. Once that event happened, it would become evident that the wicked would then "pay the penalty of eternal destruction, away from the presence of the Lord and from the glory of His power" (2 Thess. 1:9). Paul encourages them to stand firm in their faith, in chapter 2, in the following way:

> ¹Now we request you, brethren, with regard to the coming of our Lord Jesus Christ and our gathering together to Him, ²that you not be quickly shaken from your composure or be disturbed either by a spirit or a message or a letter as if from us, to the effect that the day of the Lord has come. ³Let no one in any way deceive you, for it will not come unless the apostasy comes first, and the man of lawlessness is revealed, the son of destruction, ⁴who opposes and exalts himself above every so-called god or object of worship, so that he takes his seat in the temple of God, displaying himself as being God.

Notice that the affliction, carrying over from chapter 1, would even be brought on by the man of lawlessness.[103] The affliction here specifically regards spiritual deception. At the coming of the Lord (2:1, 8), when the lawless one "is taken out of the away" and revealed (2:7-8), "God will send upon them a deluding influence so that they will believe what is false, in order that they all may be judged who did not believe the truth, but took pleasure in wickedness" (2:11-12). This is in line with the permanence of the eternal punishment that took place at the judgment. These would never turn to the truth for they entered into the lake of fire (i.e. eternal punishment) at the coming of Christ, before their biological death.

SUMMARY

The time of the judgment was 70 AD. The destruction of Jerusalem was a local event, but had universal consequences. Everyone who ever existed up until that point was judged in 70 AD. Some passages describe the judgment of those who were in Hades, who had died biologically. Other passages describe the judgment of those were alive biologically at the parousia of Christ. The Great White Throne Judgment was not about biologically sending people to either heaven or hell. It was about determining the final eternal status of every person. Those who were alive biologically entered into either eternal life or eternal death while remaining on earth and continued on in their eternal status when they died biologically. Those who were dead biologically, also entered into that same eternal life or eternal death, but either in heaven or in the final location of eternal death. As has been demonstrated, location does not determine status. Status determines location. Therefore, whether alive biologically, or dead biologically, the judgment brought about the final status of eternal life or eternal death for everyone.

Conclusion of Chapter 4:

FULL PRETERISM

The Scriptures speak clearly concerning the time of the parousia, the resurrection, and the judgment. The impending nature of these events was communicated to the audience in the first century. Most believers today take the verses about the impending coming of Christ to mean soon for us. If they mean soon for us, then wouldn't they have meant soon for the original audience? If we believe that Jesus is coming soon, then on what grounds did the apostles have to state that Jesus was coming soon when they wrote in the first century? One answer that is frequently given is "the signs of the times."[104] But the fact of the matter is, the signs of the times occurred in the events leading up to the destruction of Jerusalem in 70 AD, and many of them have appeared cyclically throughout history since then. There is no reason to believe that at least some of those "signs" cannot occur more than once, but the fulfillment of what those signs predicted could only occur "soon" once.

Thus, if the fulfillment did not occur in 70 AD, then neither can we be confident today, or in any generation, that the fulfillment of the signs we see around us will occur soon for us. The fact of the matter is that soon means soon no matter what generation you live in. That is why today, people still believe Jesus is coming soon, because people today understand "soon" to mean the same thing that people in the first century understood "soon" to mean.

Therefore, Christianity must abandon the doctrine of a future-to-us parousia and embrace the clear teaching of Scripture that Jesus did indeed come soon, within that generation, before some of those to whom He was speaking during His life on earth, had died. History demonstrates to us that the event which finally and fully fulfilled the prophecies linked to the *invisible* parousia, the *invisible* resurrection, and the *invisible* judgment was the *visible* destruction of Jerusalem in 70 AD.

Chapter 5:
QUESTIONS AND OBJECTIONS ANSWERED

INTRODUCTION

This chapter will answer some common questions and objections about full preterism. Every question you may have about full preterism may not be answered here, but you are welcome to go to www.newcovenanteyes.com and ask additional questions and request for additional information there. Please be aware that the scope of this book is simply to provide the reader with a basic primer on reading the Bible contextually and understanding the basics of full preterism as a necessary implication. This book is mostly dealing with the eschatological aspect of full preterism. If the Lord permits, there will be a sequel to this book called, *Living Our Lives With New Covenant Eyes*, which will provide a far more detailed analysis regarding the soteriological aspect of full preterism. Thus, the answers to the questions that follow will have a focus on eschatology and not on soteriology.

HOW COULD THE CHURCH GET THIS WRONG FOR TWO THOUSAND YEARS?

Part of the reason that the Church may have missed this for two thousand years is due to the fact that some of the texts were modified in the second century to fit the futurist interpretation. For example, in the second century, 1 Corinthians 15:51 was tampered with because Paul and all his correspondents had died prior to the resurrection, that is, according to their understanding of the resurrection. There are five textual variants on 1 Corinthians 15:51 (see sub-chapter 4B, endnote 32). Bruce Metzger makes the following comment regarding the reason for the variants: "Because Paul and his correspondents had died, the statement 'we shall not all sleep' seemed to call for correction."[105]

If the text was altered because correction to the Word of God was needed, is it any wonder that people in the second century thought that the resurrection was still future to them? Once that happened, the pattern was set. How long was it before this problem was realized? Metzger included this comment in his third edition of *A Textual Commentary On The Greek New Testament* in 1971. Who knows how long before 1971 anybody realized that this text was tampered with, but it most certainly wasn't two thousand years ago. How did the Church miss *that*? Add to this the fact that the word, "mello", is rarely translated in our English texts (as we have seen) due to the same misunderstanding that they had in the second century, and we wonder how the Church got this wrong for 2000 years. If modern translations were not effected by the creeds, nobody would be a futurist.

Further, how many times throughout Scripture did God's people, Israel, go astray from truth and God brought them back? A lot. Consider just one example from 2 Kings 22. Josiah became king when he was eight years old. In the eighteenth year of his reign (v. 3), they find the book of the Law. This book of the Law had been lost for at least eighteen years. There are all sorts of possible reasons why the book had been lost, but the point is, the people did not have the Law of God for at least eighteen years. Consider what Matthew Henry has to say about this:

> Whether this was the only authentic copy in being or no, it seems the things contained in it were *new* both to the king himself and to the high priest; for the king, upon the reading of it, rent his clothes. We have reason to think that neither the command for the king's writing a copy of the law, nor that for the public reading of the law every seventh year (Deut. 17:18; 31:10, 11), had been *observed for a long time*; and when the instituted means of keeping up religion are

neglected religion itself will soon go to decay. Yet, on the other hand, if the book of the law was lost, it seems difficult to determine what rule Josiah went by in doing that which was right in the sight of the Lord, and how the priests and people kept up the rites of their religion. I am apt to think that the people generally took up with abstracts of the law, like our abridgements of the statutes, which the priests, to save themselves the trouble of writing and the people of reading the book at large, had furnished them with—a sort of ritual, directing them in the observances of their religion, but *leaving out what they thought fit*, and particularly the promises and threatenings (Lev. 26 and Deut. 28, etc.), for I observe that these were the portions of the law which Josiah was so much affected with (v. 13), for these were *new* to him.[106]

Here's what's important for us to realize: They were practicing things wrong for a long time, partly because the book of the Law had been lost and partly because they were living according to the abstracts of the Law that the priests put together according to what they saw fit. When they finally looked into the Law and saw that the observances of their religion were not in line with the Law, they had to correct the abstracts they had put together. This sounds a lot like our situation today. Has the Word of God ever been fully lost? No, but as we saw earlier, it was tampered with. Now that we have a full Greek Manuscript that clearly contradicts the creeds in their doctrine of eschatology, it's time that we correct our "abstracts."

What about the fact that so many divisions in the Church exist today over truth? Are we to say that God has failed in protecting truth? No, the truth is clear. It's us that mess it up. If we argue that the Church has to be right in the area of eschatology because God was working in the Church, then you have to take that to its logical extent and say that God is failing everywhere. It is inconsistent to say that, while the Church may have erred in a bunch of other doctrines, she most certainly didn't err in the creeds just because the Church has believed them for so long. The truth is not determined by how long the Church believes something or how many people believe it. It isn't about majority rules.

Whatever reason God has to allow for wrong doctrine in the Church, we must not say that if the Church got anything "major" wrong throughout history that, therefore, God failed or wasn't providentially working in the Church. The content in the Word of God will take eternity to fully understand because they communicate about an infinite God. So we mustn't for a moment think that the Church will ever arrive at full comprehensive truth from the Scriptures. She will always be learning and developing her doctrine for eternity because it will take that long to scratch the surface of the infinite God. One reason why we have the Word of God is so that we can always be learning the truth, and when we discover where we are wrong, we can correct it.

IF THE COMING OF JESUS OCCURRED IN 70 AD, WHY DIDN'T ANYBODY DOCUMENT IT? WOULDN'T THIS SOLVE THE DEBATE?

One of the most difficult obstacles to overcome in conversing with futurists about full preterism is that futurists attempt to seek answers to questions based upon their own framework. In other words, futurists believe that the parousia of Jesus will be visible to biological eyes where the world will visibly see a man in a biological body descending out of the sky. Thus, because of this misunderstanding of the parousia of Jesus, futurists insist that full preterists explain how this could have occurred in 70 AD and it not be documented.

The problem, therefore, is that futurists fail to understand that the parousia of Jesus had everything to do with a change in our spiritual status from death to life in relation to God. It had everything to do with restoring our relationship to God and nothing to do with a biological descent of Jesus. This restoring of our relationship to God was not visible. What was visible was the end of the Old Covenant mode of existence by means of the destruction of Jerusalem.

The destruction of Jerusalem was documented and that is why there is no debate over whether or not Jerusalem was destroyed in 70 AD. The

Scriptures teach persistently that all of the invisible realities of the New Covenant mode of existence were to occur in conjunction with the visible destruction of Jerusalem. Invisible things cannot be documented apart from the revelation of God. Visible things can be documented. That is why we have the destruction of Jerusalem documented and not the parousia of Christ. In order for the invisible parousia to be documented, God would have to continue revealing new things through inspiration. That would mean that our Scriptures would not have ended with the book of Revelation. To argue that full preterists should have documentation to prove that the parousia of Christ occurred in 70 AD is to argue that more Scripture should have been written.

Granted, someone could have documented that they *believed* that the parousia of Jesus occurred in conjunction with the destruction of Jerusalem, but such documentation would be based on faith and not sight. Therefore, even if such documentation were written, futurists would still find it insufficient because they have an incorrect understanding of the parousia of Christ. With that said, who's to say that people didn't document the parousia of Christ based on their faith? Just because we don't have it doesn't mean it wasn't written. Such documentation can only be argued for from Scripture, not from eyewitnesses. So it would serve as more of a commentary than a historical document. As such, full preterists are searching the Scriptures and producing faith-based documentation.

The problem isn't with the lack of documentation or a lack of clarity in the Scriptures on the matter; the problem is with trusting the creeds and tradition over the Word of God. Jesus and the apostles couldn't be any clearer about the impending fulfillment of the prophecies.

In addition, consider the following answer from Dr. Kelly Nelson Birks regarding the documentation problem:

> Ah, the "documentation problem." I have always wondered why some Christians find such a thing necessary to be addressed. Personally, I could care less because i [sic] am convinced by the scriptures alone and that is sufficient for me. But I think folks who are not so convinced need

"something" in addition to that. Now, don't take me wrong on this. I'm not saying that you or any other Christian believes the bible [sic] to be insufficient relative to what it says. But i [sic] do think that we end up falling into a very subtle trap when we feel that in order to receive something to be true biblically, that it must be "historically corroborated" by others outside of the biblical text. This is Interesting [sic] regarding the AD 70 parousia because...

The fact that God personally created the universe cannot be corroborated "historically," but we believe it because scripture says so. (No one was around to see Him do it, so why do Christians take THAT on faith but not the first century parousia of Christ?)

-There exists no "historical" documentation as provided by those "outside" of the scriptures that verifies that Christ was "seen" rising from the dead and actually "coming out" of the tomb. And yet, we take that on faith, and we take on faith the testimony in scripture of those who saw him post-crucifixion?

-No one "saw" Jonah come out of the whale's belly and documented it, and yet....

Keep in mind to [sic] that the so called lack of historical documentation works in two directions: On the one hand you ask "why weren't some at least aware of the parousia when it happened?"...But who's to say they weren't aware that it DID happen and it just did not get recorded? Or, it did get recorded but it has not survived in antiquity. (Isn't that at least a "possibility"? In a court of law it's called "reasonable doubt.") As opposed to the unbelieving idea that if it did not get recorded, then this "proves" that it did not happen!?! The last being the classic "argument from silence" and a true double edged sword that cuts both ways. After all, God promised to preserve His Word, but there exists no promise to preserve any non-inspired historical documentation. Actually, there exists more inspired "proof" (the Bible) that the Parousia did happen right on time at the destruction of Jerusalem and the Temple, right up until the mid-second century. Up until that time, the only real writings that spoke of the timing of the Parousia was the scriptures themselves. There was no "real" competing theorem on the subject until the alternative "futurist" view (mid-second century) of Christ coming at the end of history which began to be postulated by the writings of Justin Martyr, and the authors of 2nd Clement and The Shepherd of Hermas. (The so-called "Postponement Theory.") Please see J.N.D. Kelly's book "Early Christian Doctrines," Pg.'s 459-61...Aland's "A History of Christianity," Vol. 1, Pg.'s 87-102...and Torrance's "The Evangelical Theology of the Ancient Catholic Church," Pg.'s 222-300.

The funny thing about the so called "no documentation problem" as to the parousia of AD 70 is that: (1) It survives on simply not believing the scriptural testimony as to it's veracity that it would occur at the fall of Jerusalem (Olivette [sic] Discourse, et al). (2) It makes a slave of the veracity and sufficiency of the scriptures to non-inspired sources. (3) It exists on the "Thomas Philosophy" of Christianity: "Unless I 'see with my eyes,' and put my fingers into his wounds, I will not, not believe." (Double negative in Greek). So the Christian who says "unless I can verify the parousia of AD 70 with something that is tangible (like an independent source verification), then I will not, not believe." But what did Jesus say to Thomas on the night he appeared to him?..."Thomas, you believe because you have SEEN. But blessed are those who have NOT SEEN and yet have believed." (John 20:29!) Clearly, the greater blessing is available for those who believe in the scriptural testimony of the coming of Christ at AD 70 alone, without any need for further outside verification. So Thomas missed the blessing didn't he? And so do unbelievers in Christ's specifically prophesied AD 70 Parousia. (Why do you think it is that they simply cannot grasp the significance of the AD 70 parousia? Approaching the scriptures and not believing what they say, cuts one off from further revelation therein.—"Therefore take care HOW you listen; for whoever has—because they have listened—to him shall more be given—further understanding—and whoever does not have, even what he thinks he has shall be taken away from him."—Lk 8:18…Mk. 8:38, Mk. 4:24-25!) I fear that Christians who do not believe in the veracity of Christ's own teaching concerning his AD 70 parousia must also join Thomas in his unbelief as to his own failure to believe what others, outside of an independent corroboration, have testified to. When it comes to the AD 70 parousia, men who doubt it or say "no" to it are no better than Thomas was.

In Lk. 17:20-21, Jesus said that when the kingdom of God appeared, it would not be "seen" with the physical earthly eye. He said, "The kingdom of God does not come with an outward (visible) sign. (So much for the 6 foot tall Carpenter being "seen" in the sky…You can't historically "document" what was not seen!) Neither will men say, 'It's over here, or over there,' for behold, the kingdom of God is among you."…The kingdom of God IS among you, whether you see it or not. Do we as "believers", BELIEVE that or not, and if not, how can we rightly refer to ourselves as "believers"? Same thing holds true to the AD 70 parousia. Are we "bible believers" period, or believers in the bible [sic] ONLY if it can be independently corroborated through a non-inspired source? The fact is that those who doubt an AD 70 parousia are exercising a secularist mindset that is devoid of the influence of the Holy Spirit speaking in the scriptures.[107]

So as you can see, the "documentation problem" isn't a problem at all when the parousia of Christ is properly understood.

I'VE HEARD THAT FULL PRETERISM ROBS PEOPLE OF THEIR HOPE IN THE RESURRECTION. IS THAT TRUE?

Once again, the problem with this objection is that futurists are demanding that full preterists answer according to the futurist framework. The majority of futurists are hoping for a resurrection of the biological body. They completely misinterpret the doctrine of the resurrection. The correct interpretation was presented in sub-chapter 4B of this book. For our purposes here, we must understand that once we shed these biologically bodies, we go to heaven. Biological bodies cannot exist in Heaven. They are designed for earth.

But even before we shed our biological bodies, since we are presently in the New Heavens and New Earth (i.e. the Eternal Kingdom), then we no longer need to hope that we will someday be in the presence of God, for we already are in His presence. Therefore, we do not need to hope for a resurrection of our biological bodies, for our restoration back into the presence of God is what the resurrection brought about.

If you were offered a million dollars, would you rather hope for it or have it? Would having it rob you of your hope? No, because who cares about the hope you once had at that point. Fulfillment is greater than hope. Full preterism doesn't rob anybody of their hope, it helps open their eyes to false hope in exchange for reality.

IS FULL PRETERISM A THREAT TO THE GOSPEL?

Since it is incorrectly believed that full preterism takes away the "hope of the resurrection," then therefore, it is also incorrectly believed that full preterism is a threat to the Gospel. Full preterism is not a threat to the Gospel. In fact, full preterism is the only eschatology that is consistent with the teaching of Scripture that our salvation is complete.

Do we have assurance that our sins are forgiven? How? In the Old Covenant, once a year, the high priest would enter the Most Holy place twice to make atonement for sins. The first time was for himself; the second time was for the sins of the people. The Jews would eagerly wait outside for the high priest to exit the Most Holy place. Only if the high priest came out the second time could they have assurance that their sins were atoned for. Hebrews makes it abundantly clear that Jesus fulfilled all the copies and shadows of the Old Covenant through heavenly realities. Consider the following from Hebrews 8:

> [1]Now the main point in what has been said is this: we have such a high priest, who has taken His seat at the right hand of the throne of the Majesty in the heavens, [2]a minister in the sanctuary and in the true tabernacle, which the Lord pitched, not man. [3]For every high priest is appointed to offer both gifts and sacrifices; so it is necessary that this high priest also have something to offer. [4]Now if He were on earth, He would not be a priest at all, since there are those who offer the gifts according to the Law; [5]*who serve a copy and shadow of the heavenly things...*"[108]

Just one chapter later, the writer of Hebrews speaks of the purification rites under the Old Covenant and goes on to explain how they were copies and shadows of the heavenly realities:

> [9:23]Therefore it was necessary for the copies of the things in the heavens to be cleansed with these, but the heavenly things themselves with better sacrifices than these. [24]For Christ did not enter a holy place made with hands, a mere copy of the true one, but into heaven itself, now to appear in the presence of God for us; [25]nor was it that He would offer Himself often, as the high priest enters the holy place year by year with blood that is not his own. [26]Otherwise, He would have needed to suffer often since the foundation

of the world; but now once at the consummation of the ages He has been manifested to put away sin by the sacrifice of Himself. [27]And inasmuch as it is appointed for men to die once and after this comes judgment, [28]so Christ also, having been offered once to bear the sins of many, *will appear a second time for salvation* without reference to sin, to those who eagerly await Him.[109]

Notice the connection that the writer of Hebrews makes between the high priest of the Old Covenant and Jesus. The writer is teaching his audience that in the same way that the high priest under the Old Covenant had to appear a second time, so Christ had to appear a second time in order to guarantee that His sacrifice was accepted by God and salvation could be brought to the people. The only reason that we, today, can know that God no longer counts our sins against us and that our salvation is guaranteed is if Jesus, our High Priest, has appeared a second time without reference to sin.

Incidentally, this is also the means by which the New Covenant was inaugurated, just as it was with the first covenant (9:18). Christ Himself was the sacrifice that inaugurated the New Covenant. But the only way that we can know that the New Covenant was inaugurated is by the appearing of Christ a second time.

So full preterism is not a threat to the Gospel; it is actually necessary for the Gospel to be able to produce what it promises. One of the problems with the futurist position is that it has created a dichotomy between soteriology (the study of salvation) and eschatology (the study of last things). But the Scriptures don't distinguish the two. Biblical eschatology is the foundation for the salvation of God's people. Pardon for sins is impossible until the second appearing of Christ. Therefore, we must either embrace full preterism, or abandon the Biblical teaching that our salvation is complete.

IF ALL THE PROPHECIES HAVE BEEN FULFILLED, WHY DO WE STILL NEED OUR BIBLES?

The application of God's Word to our lives does not end just because the prophecies have been fulfilled. The better we understand God's faithfulness to Israel, the better we will understand His faithfulness towards us. God is a promise keeping God, and our faith rests not in how He speaks to "me personally" through texts we rip out of context, but in what He has already accomplished for His people in the New Covenant. And the only way that we can fully understand the New Covenant is by understanding the Old Covenant.

The writings of the apostles in the New Testament are not about some new thing that God all of a sudden decided to do because He didn't like the way things were going. The writings of the apostles in the New Testament were a proclamation that the fulfillment of the promises given in the Old Testament had finally arrived. Their announcement essentially was: "It's finally here!" Reading the Bible through New Covenant Eyes helps us to know God better. And there is no greater thing than that!

How do we come to know God better? By learning about how He works for His people. It is not enough to say, "All things are fulfilled so there is no need to read our Bibles anymore." To the contrary, the only way that we can know that the parousia, the resurrection, and the judgment have already happened is through the God-inspired Scriptures. Without the Scriptures, the destruction of Jerusalem in 70 AD would just be another event in history. It's the Scriptures that teach us about the invisible realities that are connected to visible signs. Without the Scriptures, how would we know today the meaning of a rainbow?

Even beyond the Scriptural doctrine of full preterism, the Scriptures teach us many other doctrines that we could not understand without them. There is more to the Scriptures than full preterism. The Scriptures provide our doctrine of God, Christ, and the Holy Spirit, as well as many other doctrines. To say that all prophecies have been fulfilled is different than saying that all things are already known. There are many things that the Scriptures have yet to teach us.

DOESN'T THE BIBLE TEACH THAT WE WILL LIVE ON A NEW EARTH?

No. There is a grave misunderstanding that Scripture teaches that this earth will be fixed and we will eventually live on this newly fixed earth. The Scriptures, however, do not teach anything about God fixing this earth. They do teach that God restored our relationship back into His presence so that we could go to Heaven and no longer to Hades. Plus, there are several Scriptural texts that point to the fact that the inheritance of the saints is in Heaven:

Philippians 3:20: For our citizenship is in heaven...

Colossians 3:1-2: ¹Therefore if you have been raised up with Christ, keep seeking the things above, where Christ is, seated at the right hand of God. ²Set your mind on the things above, not on the things that are on earth.

I Timothy 6:7: For we have brought nothing into the world, so we cannot take anything out of it either.

Hebrews 11:13, 16: ¹³All these died in faith, without receiving the promises, but having seen them and having welcomed them from a distance, and having confessed that they were strangers and exiles on the earth...¹⁶But as it is, they desire a better country, that is, a heavenly one. Therefore God is not ashamed to be called their God; for He has prepared a city for them.

I Peter 1:3-4: ³Blessed be the God and Father of our Lord Jesus Christ, who according to His great mercy has caused us to be born again to a living hope through the resurrection of Jesus Christ from the dead, ⁴to obtain an inheritance which is imperishable and undefiled and will not fade away, reserved in heaven for you...

The Scriptures teach us that the ultimate location of God's people is heaven, not some new earth.

WILL THIS EARTH EVER COME TO AN END?

There is no reason to believe it will. In fact, there is Biblical evidence that suggests otherwise:

> Ecclesiastes 1:4: A generation goes and a generation comes, but the earth remains forever.

> Psalm 78:69: And He built His sanctuary like the heights, like the earth which He has founded forever.

> Ephesians 3:20-21: [20]Now to Him who is able to do far more abundantly beyond all that we ask or think, according to the power that works within us, [21]to Him be the glory in the church and in Christ Jesus to all generations forever and ever. Amen.

Is there any reason why this earth should come to an end? Is there any reason to think that God will not have generations come and go for all eternity? Consider the words of the Psalmist in Psalm 148:

> [1]Praise the LORD! Praise the LORD from the heavens; Praise Him in the heights! [2]Praise Him, all His angels; Praise Him, all His hosts! [3]Praise Him, sun and moon; Praise Him, all stars of light! [4]Praise Him, highest heavens, and the waters that are above the heavens! [5]Let them praise the name of the LORD, For He commanded and they were created. [6]*He has also established them forever and ever; He has made a decree which will not pass away.*[110]

What did the LORD establish forever and ever? Angels, sun, moon, stars, highest heavens (or skies), and the waters above the skies. Will the angels ever come to an end? Then neither will the universe, including the earth. What came to an end, however, was the old age (known as "the present age" when the Scriptures were written). Do you recall what Jesus taught in Matthew 24? He said the Temple would be destroyed within their generation. The disciples came to Jesus and said, "Tell us, when will these things happen, and what will be the sign of Your coming, and of *the end of the age*" (italics mine)? The end of that present age came with the destruction of Jerusalem in 70 AD when "the age to come" began. The Bible talks a lot about the end of the age and the passing of "the heavens and the earth" (which speak of the Old Covenant mode of existence), but never the end of the actual earth that we live on.

DOESN'T ROMANS 8 TEACH THAT THE CREATION ITSELF WILL BE SET FREE FROM ITS BONDAGE TO CORRUPTION?

Romans 8 does teach that creation itself will be set free from its bondage to corruption, but it is important to understand that what Paul means by "the creation" is Israel, not the irrational creation that God made in Genesis 1. (Irrational in this context means non-human creation.) This is the first misconception that must be overcome in the traditional interpretation of Romans 8. While the Greek word, "ktisis," is sometimes used in Scripture to speak of physical creation, it is also used in the limited sense of mankind and/or society. Here are some examples (brackets and italics mine):

Mark 16:15: And He said to them, "Go into all the world and preach the gospel to all *creation*."

2 Corinthians 5:17: Therefore if anyone is in Christ, he is a new *creature* [ktisis]; the old things passed away; behold, new things have come.

Galatians 6:15: For neither is circumcision anything, nor uncircumcision, but a new *creation*.

Colossians 1:15, 23: He is the image of the invisible God, the firstborn of all *creation*...if indeed you continue in the faith firmly established and steadfast, and not moved away from the hope of the gospel that you have heard, which was proclaimed in all *creation* under heaven, and of which I, Paul, was made a minister.

The fact that Paul is referring to Israel in Romans 8 when he speaks of "the creation" being subjected to futility can be seen from a number of observations.

The first observation is that Israel is said to have been created by God in Isaiah 43:

> [1]But now thus says the LORD, he who created you, O Jacob, he who formed you, O Israel: "Fear not, for I have redeemed you; I have called you by name, you are mine...[15]I am the LORD, your Holy One, the Creator of Israel, your King."

The second observation is stated well by Max King:

> In the New Testament Scripture we read of a **new creation** that is identified with the community of believers in Christ. Paul wrote, "Therefore if any man be in Christ, he is a new creature: old things are passed away; behold, all things are become new" (2 Cor. 5:17). A *new creation* implies the existence of a previous creation, made old by reason of that which is new. What is the identity of the *old creation*? What determines the creation that precedes the new in Christ? This question is answered by observing what

determines the *new creation*. Who would deny that the new creation in Christ is the community of the New Covenant mode of existence? The new creation in Christ, therefore, stands over against not the irrational material creation of Gen. 1, but the Old Covenant creation of the Exodus/Sinai founding events. The new creation is to be seen in view of the "weakness and unprofitableness" of the old. "For if that first covenant had been faultless, then should no place have been sought for a second. For finding fault with them, he saith, Behold, the days come, saith the Lord, when I will make a new covenant with the house of Israel and with the house of Judah" (Heb. 8:7,8). According to Scripture, God determined to make the house of Israel and of Judah a *new creation* by means of a *New Covenant*. It can be seen, therefore, that Israel, in having the promise of a New Covenant which was productive of a new creation in Christ, logically answers to the old creation of salvation-history.[111]

The third observation comes from verses 20-21 of Romans 8:

> [20]For the creation was subjected to futility, not willingly, but because of Him who subjected it, in hope [21]that the creation itself also will be set free from its slavery to corruption into the freedom of the glory of the children of God.

Why would Paul use the words, "not willingly," if he were referring to irrational creation? This would seem an obvious thing if he were referring to irrational creation, would it not?[112] In addition, consider some of Paul's thoughts in Romans leading up to this point that demonstrates that he is talking about God's creation of Israel at Mount Sinai through the giving of the Mosaic Covenant:

Romans 5:20-21: [20]The Law came in so that the transgression would increase; but where sin increased, grace abounded all the more, [21]so that, as sin reigned in death, even so grace would reign through righteousness to eternal life through Jesus Christ our Lord.

Here we see what is meant by "subjection to futility." God placed Israel under the futility of the Law where sin would abound in order that, through Christ, they would be set free from their slavery to corruption into the freedom of the glory of God. Look at what Paul refers to regarding bondage and slavery versus freedom (italics mine):

Romans 7-8: [7:14]For we know that the Law is spiritual, but I am of flesh, sold into *bondage* to sin. [24]Wretched man that I am! Who will set me *free* from the body of this death? [8:1]Therefore there is now no condemnation for those who are in Christ Jesus. [2]For the law of the Spirit of life in Christ Jesus has set you *free* from the law of sin and of death. [15]For you have not received a spirit of *slavery* leading to fear again, but you have received a spirit of adoption as sons by which we cry out, "Abba! Father!" [20]For the creation was *subjected to futility*, not willingly, but because of Him who *subjected* it, in hope [21]that the creation itself also will be set *free* from its *slavery to corruption* into the *freedom* of the glory of the children of God.

Paul is talking about the bondage of sin that comes through the Law versus the freedom that comes through Christ. That freedom would come when the Son of God would be revealed: "For the anxious longing of the creation waits eagerly for the revealing of the sons of God" (8:19). At that time, the creation, that is, Israel, would be "set free from its slavery to corruption into the freedom of the glory of the children of God" (v. 21).

Paul then states that the "whole" creation "groans and suffers the pains of childbirth together until now" (v. 22). It was not only Israel that groaned and suffered, but the Gentiles as well. Paul is expanding on the groaning of Israel to also include the groaning of the Gentiles who were under the same futility (cf. Rom. 2:12-16). The groaning of Israel can be seen in Paul's Old Testament allusion found in Isaiah 26:16-18:

> [16]O LORD, they sought You in distress; they could only whisper a prayer, Your chastening was upon them. [17]As the pregnant woman approaches the time to give birth, she writhes and cries out in her labor pains, thus were we before You, O LORD. [18]We were pregnant, we writhed in labor, we gave birth, as it seems, only to wind. We could not accomplish deliverance for the earth, nor were inhabitants of the world born.

Isaiah 26 is unmistakably the text that Paul is drawing from. The language is the same. But Paul takes this idea and applies it to all mankind. Look at how Paul states it in Romans 8:22: "For we know that the whole creation groans and suffers the pains of childbirth together until now." So the subjection of creation to futility is referring to the giving of the Law to Israel at Sinai.

The fourth observation is a recognition that the "whole creation" expands upon the "creation." In what way can the irrational creation be expanded upon? In other words, if Paul is talking about the entire creation that God created in Genesis 1 by his initial reference to the "creation," how could he go any further to include the "whole creation?"

The fifth observation comes from Don Preston:

> If "creation" in Romans 8 is the physical creation, then, are we willing to argue/accept that mosquitos [sic], slugs, and bugs, will one day become "Sons of God"? (a bit of argumentum ad absurdum to be sure, but, a valid question nonetheless!)[113]

The sixth observation has to do with context. Romans 8 comes between Romans 7 and 9. In Romans 7, Paul is discussing the bondage of sin through the Law. Which law? The Law given to Israel:

> [5]For while we were in the flesh, the sinful passions, which were aroused by the Law, were at work in the members of our body to bear fruit for death. [6]But now we have been released from the Law, having died to that by which we were bound, so that we serve in newness of the Spirit and not in *oldness of the letter*.[114]

In Romans 9, Paul is speaking about Israel. It is commonly thought that Paul suddenly switches to a discourse about Israel to make a point, but the fact is, Israel has been Paul's point throughout Romans. It is because of Israel that the Gospel has come to the Gentiles.

So Romans 8 does indeed teach that the creation itself would be set free from its bondage to corruption. But the creation that was set free from its bondage to corruption was Israel.[115]

HOW DO YOU EXPLAIN SIN REMAINING ON THE EARTH?

The issue of sin remaining on the earth is a common criticism of full preterism. But this criticism has no biblical support. There is no question that Christ put away sin by the sacrifice of Himself since he was offered once to bear the sins of *many* (Heb. 9:26, 28). It is one thing to have our sins put away by Christ so that they are no longer counted against us. It is an entirely different thing to have sin remaining on the earth. If there is no sin that remains on the earth, then in what way could Christ have died for all of our sins, past, present, and future? Whether or not you believe that the parousia already happened or is yet to happen in the future, both positions have the same issue to contend with: Sin still exists on the earth after Christ's death and resurrection. The fact that the resurrection of the body has already occurred in no way causes a problem with sin remaining on the earth. The resurrection had nothing to do with the end of sin on the earth. It had everything to do with the change from being dead in sin to being eternally alive in Christ, no matter how much we sin.

Those who wish to take issue with the full preterist position (argued for in this book) that sin will continue on this earth for eternity fail to realize that this isn't a problem at all. Whether sin remains on the earth after the death and resurrection of Christ for two thousand years or an eternal amount of years, sin is still here. Once again, that's the whole point of Christ dying for people who would be born after His resurrection. He paid for the sins of His people in future generations just as much as in past generations. What difference does it make whether that includes generations for two thousand years or an eternal amount of years? It seems a better tribute to God's *eternal* power and love to have saved people from their sins on the earth for all eternity rather than simply a couple thousand years. This whole "problem" with sin remaining on the earth for eternity is quite baffling, for the idea that sin would be removed after the parousia of Christ is completely based on the systematic implications of the traditional view, but actually has no biblical support.

WHAT ABOUT SIN REMAINING IN BELIEVERS?

Another way of asking this question is if we are immortal and glorified already, then why do we still sin? The answer to this question is that being immortal and glorified has nothing to do with whether or not you can sin. It has everything to do with whether or not you can die. The rule in the Garden was sin *once* and die. But because God has made us immortal and does not count our sins against us through Christ, we can no longer die because of sin. In the New Covenant, we live under the seventy times seven principle (cf. Matt. 18:21-22).

The righteous are freed from sin when our biological bodies die and we go to heaven. As long as we live on this earth, we will have to battle sin. The issue isn't whether or not we have the ability to sin. The issue has to do with the fact that temptation is still present. Temptation does not exist in Heaven.

HOW DO YOU EXPLAIN DEMONIC ACTIVITY TODAY?

There is no demonic activity today. The mind is a powerful thing. Those who are thought to be demon possessed are no different than those who are "healed" by faith healers today. "Demon possession" today can be very easily explained scientifically. Nobody today has a clue what demon possession was really like before Satan and his demons were thrown into the final location of eternal death.

DO FULL PRETERISTS BELIEVE THAT WE ARE IN THE ETERNAL STATE NOW?

Yes, but that doesn't mean that there isn't a place we go to after biological death. It simply means that eternal life and eternal death begin here.

IF CHRIST AROSE IN THE SAME BODY THAT WAS CRUCIFIED, WHERE IS THAT BODY NOW?

The Scriptures do not tell us the answer to this. What we do know, however, is that He most certainly does not have His biological body anymore. Jesus returned to being omnipresent, not limited by a biological body, but remains 100% God and 100% man forever. Remember, man is not defined by his biological body.

WHAT DO YOU DO WITH THE THOUSAND-YEAR REIGN OF REVELATION 20?

There is no escaping the fact that the thousand-year reign had to take place before the Great White Throne judgment, which came after the binding of Satan for a thousand years. This means that the literal period of time of the thousand years of Revelation 20 took place between the biological coming of Christ to earth and the parousia of our Lord in 70 AD. Mathison, in *Postmillennialism: An Eschatology of Hope*, attempts to point out what he believes is a weakness of full preterism in its doctrine of the Millennium:

The most serious problem is that their 'Millennium' is too short…Full preterists chide futurists for not taking seriously biblical language that denotes a short period of time. But in this case full preterists are not taking seriously biblical language that indicates a long period of time…We must take all time indicators seriously—those which indicate short periods of time and those which indicate long periods of time.[116]

Is Mathison's criticism valid? While he and others may think so, to the contrary, the interpretation proposed below takes seriously the "biblical language that indicates a long period of time." First, consider the following explanation of the thousand-year time frame presented by Kenneth Gentry:

The proper understanding of the thousand-year time frame in Revelation 20 is that it represents a long and glorious era and is not limited to a literal 365,000 days. The figure represents *a perfect cube of ten*, which is the number of quantitative perfection. The thousand here is no more literal than that which affirms God's ownership of the cattle on a thousand hills (Psa. 50:10), or promises Israel will be a thousand times more numerous (Deut. 1:11), or measures God's love to a thousand generations (Deut. 7:9), or expresses the desire for a thousand years in God's courts (Psa. 84:10), or compares a thousand years of our time to one day of God's days (Psa. 90:40).[117]

Question: If "a thousand" is to be taken figuratively, then why must the word "years" be taken literally? In other words, couldn't it be just as well that John is not defining a literal period of time at all, whether it is actually one thousand exactly or a longer period of time? John could just as well be figuratively describing the perfect accomplishments of Christ that no earthly king could possibly accomplish. In fact, if "the figure…is the number of quantitative perfection," then John is figuratively defining the perfect reign rather then a length of time.

It interesting to note the length of time that Saul, David, Solomon, and Jehoash (Joash) each reigned. All of these kings reigned for forty years (Acts 13:21; 2 Sam. 5:4; 1 Kings 11:42; 2 Kings 12:1). It is not a coincidence that the thousand-year reign of Christ was forty years as well. It is also interesting to note that Israel wandered in the wilderness for forty years before entering the promise land (Num. 14:33-34). This, too, is not a coincidence. The transition period of the dying to the Old Covenant mode of existence and rising to the New Covenant mode of existence was a forty-year period, the same forty-year period of the reign of Christ with His saints.

The reign of Christ with his saints did not come to an end after that forty-year period. Christ reigns with His saints forever (Luke 1:33; Rev. 11:15; 22:5). The thousand-year reign of Revelation 20 is not about how long Christ would reign with His saints. The thousand-year reign of Revelation 20 is about what would perfectly be accomplished during those forty years. This doesn't mean that Christ could not accomplish all that He did in less than forty years. The point is that Old Testament types and shadows had to precisely be fulfilled by heavenly realities. Time is significant for humanity. A wilderness wandering in the twinkling of an eye would not be much of a wilderness wandering. And so even though Christ could easily accomplish whatever He wanted to in the twinkling of an eye, such a feat would fail to incorporate humanity into the process. God displays His glory and power by accomplishing things in human time.

Thus, the transitional process of bringing the Old Covenant mode of existence to an end and the New Covenant mode of existence to its fullness had to take time. And that amount of time could be no longer and no shorter than forty years in order to fulfill the Old Testament types and shadows. Christ brought about all that He promised He would, through the spread of the Gospel by humans, within the amount of time that He promised He would, which displays the glory of God to humanity in the greatest possible way. Another way of saying this is that Christ reigned with His saints for a thousand years, which occurred in a forty-year period of time.

WHAT ABOUT THE OLD TESTAMENT TEXTS THAT TEACH CERTAIN THINGS WOULD HAPPEN "SOON" THAT DIDN'T HAPPEN UNTIL HUNDREDS OF YEARS LATER?

The Old Testament texts that teach that certain things would happen "soon," actually happened soon for the intended audiences. Each of these prophecies in the Old Testament have actually been shown (by non-preterists) to have been fulfilled within the very generation to whom the prophecies were spoken.[118] Some of these texts include Isaiah 51:5; Ezekiel 7:7, 30:3; Jeremiah 48:16; Joel 1:15, 2:1, 3:14; Obadiah 1:15; Zephaniah. 1:7, 14.

One example is Isaiah 13:6: "Wail, for the day of the LORD is near!" It is sometimes claimed that this prophecy was not fulfilled for 142 years from the time it was prophesied. But the Bible Knowledge Commentary shows that Babylon was destroyed within fifteen years after the prophecy.[119] Don Preston remarks:

> The point is that it is irresponsible to claim that the prophecy entailed a period of 142 years. While that argument "sounds good" to those unfamiliar with the issues, it shows a lack of scholarship and study to make the arguments...[120]

The Bible itself actually confirms that all of the Old Testament texts teaching impending things actually occurred within forty years of their being prophesied.

As a side note, we must not miss something crucial here. The prophecy in Isaiah 13 is a prophecy about the destruction of Babylon (v. 1). In verses 9-10 we read these words:

> [9]Behold, the day of the LORD is coming, cruel, with fury and burning anger, to make the land a desolation; and He will exterminate its sinners from it. [10]For the stars of heaven

and their constellations will not flash forth their light; the sun will be dark when it rises and the moon will not shed its light.

This is the same prophetic language used in Matthew 24:29, right before the prophecy of the coming of the Son of Man:

> [29]"But immediately after the tribulation of those days the sun will be darkened, and the moon will not give its light, and the stars will fall from the sky, and the powers of the heavens will be shaken. [30]"And then the sign of the Son of Man will appear in the sky, and then all the tribes of the earth will mourn, and they will see the Son of Man coming on the clouds of the sky with power and great glory. [31]"And He will send forth His angels with a great trumpet and they will gather together His elect from the four winds, from one end of the sky to the other.

The language employed by Jesus here in Matthew 24 is the same prophetic language used throughout the Old Testament to prophecy judgment upon various nations and even the end of political systems.[121] It is nowhere used in the Bible to speak literally of the end of the world. In fact, look at the verses that follow Isaiah 13:9-10 and see how Isaiah describes the destruction of Babylon:

> [11]Thus I will punish the world for its evil and the wicked for their iniquity; I will also put an end to the arrogance of the proud and abase the haughtiness of the ruthless. [12]I will make mortal man scarcer than pure gold and mankind than the gold of Ophir. [13]Therefore I will make the heavens tremble, and the earth will be shaken from its place at the fury of the LORD of hosts in the day of His burning anger.

We must be careful not to bring into the New Testament our modern thinking about prophetic language, but rather, we must understand them the same way those in the first century would have understood them—the way they understood prophetic language in the Old Testament.

2 PETER 1:20 TEACHES THAT PROPHECY IS NOT A MATTER OF ONE'S OWN INTERPRETATION. ISN'T FULL PRETERISM ONE'S OWN INTERPRETATION SINCE IT GOES AGAINST THE HISTORY OF THE CHURCH?

Full preterism is not one's own interpretation, but is based on what the Scriptures teach. 2 Peter 1:20-21 reads as follows: "[20]But know this first of all, that no prophecy of Scripture is a matter of one's own interpretation, [21]for no prophecy was ever made by an act of human will, but men moved by the Holy Spirit spoke from God." This text does not teach anything regarding the interpretation of Scripture. The English Standard Version brings out the meaning of this text nicely: "...[20]knowing this first of all, that no prophecy of Scripture comes from someone's own interpretation. [21]For no prophecy was ever produced by the will of man, but men spoke from God as they were carried along by the Holy Spirit."

When verse 20 is taken in context with verse 21, we see that Peter was teaching that the men who prophesied did not interpret the prophecy, but just spoke directly from God, being moved by the Spirit. Men in the Church in the new age do not produce new prophecies from God in this way. Interpreting the prophecies recorded in the Scriptures is a totally different thing. If men in the Church today did produce new prophecies from God, then the Scriptures would be ever expanding. Therefore, no generation of the church from 70 AD onward can claim to have any such spoken word from God, other than the Bible itself. Since that is the case, then any and every generation could have erred on the doctrine of eschatology, even if they are all stacked together as a united front.

HOW DO YOU RESPOND TO THE ACCUSATION THAT FULL PRETERISM IS THE HERESY OF HYMENAEUS AND PHILETUS?

First of all, at the time that Paul was writing, Hymenaeus and Philetus were heretics because the resurrection was not past. In order to put full preterists in the same camp with Hymenaeus and Philetus, it would have to be demonstrated from Scripture that the resurrection is still future. The creeds don't count, for they were not inspired by God. 2 Timothy 2:16-18, however, was inspired by God, and was written by Paul to refute this heresy because the resurrection was still future to his audience.

The problem with Hymenaeus and Philetus is that they were teaching that the resurrection had already happened before it did. If the traditional view of the resurrection is correct, then how could these men overthrow the faith of some of the people in Timothy's church? In other words, if the resurrection is about biological bodies coming out of the graves and no more biological death occurring after that, how could they possibly overthrow the faith of some when all that the people would have to do is go check the graves or go see that believers were still walking around, particularly Timothy, their own pastor?

Plus, people were still dying from day to day, so how would this heresy even take root? It couldn't take root if the traditional view was right! The point is that the resurrection had nothing to do with biological bodies, but rather, it had to do with the resurrection of the body of Adam in the body of Christ. See the interpretation of 1 Corinthians 15 in sub-chapter 4B of this book.

In summary, the reason that Hymenaeus and Philetus had any sway at all is because Paul was teaching a law-free Gospel, and if the resurrection had already taken place while the Temple was still standing, then salvation came through the Old Covenant mode of existence. That is what caused some people's faith to be overthrown. They learned from Paul that salvation in Christ comes outside of the Old Covenant mode of existence, apart from circumcision. But if the resurrection had already occurred and the Old Covenant was still in existence (i.e. The Temple still standing), then obviously, the Gospel isn't law-free. To attach the heresy of Hymenaeus and Philetus to full preterists won't fly because the context won't allow it. What was future to them is not future to us.

HOW IS THIS VIEW OF THE BODY WITHIN A BODY DIFFERENT FROM GNOSTIC DUALISM?

This is an interesting question, and often a criticism, because the view proposed in this book is not dualism of any sort. Full preterists are not arguing that the biological body is evil or good. We are arguing that the biological body is amoral. Ironically, it is the futurist position that has the leanings of Gnostic dualism. According to the traditional view, the inner man of 2 Corinthians 4 is being renewed and no longer has to die because it goes immediately to be with the Lord upon the death of the biological body. But why does the biological body still have to die? According to the traditional view it is because it is so tainted with sin that it has to die before it can be redeemed and glorified. So according to the traditional view, in its body *and* soul dualism, the soul is being changed into holiness, but the body still has to die because it is still evil. You may try to manipulate this as much as you would like, but the bottom line is, it's the traditional view that has the "spirit is good, matter is evil" tendency. While the traditional view would not argue that all matter is evil, they do, however, implicitly teach that the matter of the human body is evil. Max King explains it this way:

> This kind of outward-inward dualism opens the door for an unbiblical dichotomous redemption—the spirit or soul **now** *versus* the physical body **later** by means of physical death and resurrection. Presumably this delivers Paul from Greek anthropological dualism because, for Paul, the body eventually is redeemed through resurrection, whereas in Greek thought, redemption means merely the escape of the soul from the body of death.[122]

But does the eventual redemption of the biological body through resurrection really save the traditional view from Greek dualism? In the traditional view, the biological body is raised and then changed into a body of non-death (i.e. life). So the eventual fix for this Greek dualism isn't resolved at all because once the body is raised it is no longer a body of sin and death. Thus, in the traditional view, the soul does indeed escape from the body of sin and death. This is Gnostic dualism in sheep's clothing.

What has been argued for in this book is that "the body" that is raised, redeemed, and changed, is not the biological body. Instead, "the body" is the definition of man. And that body lives on this earth in a visible biological instrument called "a body." That biological instrument is neither good, nor evil, but is used for good or evil by "the body," which is who we are. The biological instrument eventually dies and decays in the ground. It is the body, which defines who we are, that was raised, redeemed, and changed. Full preterists are not proposing any escape from the body of sin of any sort. We are arguing for a complete change from a body of death to a body of life. And there is no separation between the soul and the body of sin and death because they are one and the same. The soul/body is redeemed without any sort of separation. In fact, it was even changed and redeemed while still living in these biological bodies.

ARE YOU SAYING THAT WE ARE ALREADY SANCTIFIED?

Yes, because the meaning of sanctification in Scripture is not about being freed from our individual sins. The meaning of sanctification in Scripture is about being freed from the body of sin and death in Adam and being changed into the resurrected body of life in Christ. Sanctification was the process of dying and rising that Paul taught in 1 Corinthians 15.

DON'T JOHN 5:25-29 AND REVELATION 20:5 TEACH TWO RESURRECTIONS, ONE SPIRITUAL AND ONE PHYSICAL?

These texts do not teach two resurrections. Both John 5:25-29 and Revelation 20:5 teach the gradual, transitional outworking of the *one* resurrection that Paul taught in 1 Corinthians 15. The resurrection of the body of Adam, dying and rising in Christ, is *the* resurrection that fully occurred by way of the dead resurrecting from Hades. Scripture makes a distinction between the dead who are still living biologically and the dead who have died biologically. Both had to be resurrected. The difference is that those who had died biologically actually had to be resurrected from Death (the temporary status) and Hades (the temporary location) while those who were still living biologically had to be changed by way of the resurrection of the body. Thus, those who were living biologically were not resurrected from the place of the dead. Yet their death was a death united to Christ and their resurrection was a resurrection united to Christ, just like those who were raised out of Hades. The collective dead was the body that was dying and rising in 1 Corinthians 15. The body could not be completely resurrected, though, without the completion of the promised resurrection of Israel (i.e. the dead ones). That was part and parcel of the resurrection body.

The change that both the biologically living and dead would incur came about through the final and permanent death of the Old Covenant ministry of death and the rising to fullness of the New Covenant ministry of life. When the Old Covenant ministry of death was gone, the Old Covenant saints were released from its captivity and resurrected into the New Covenant ministry of life. That was the moment when the resurrection of the body was completed. As demonstrated in sub-chapter 4B, If Old Covenant saints were not raised, then neither was the rest of the body of Adam that was in Christ, for salvation is of the Jews (cf. Romans 11).

Between the time of Christ's resurrection and 70 AD, those who died biologically went to Hades, but were not held there. They were able to pass through Hades and go to the outer courts in the New Jerusalem to await the second coming of Christ (the High Priest) out of the most holy place.[123] These are the ones that shared in the first resurrection (Rev. 20:5-6). They were the firstfruits of Christ, the first stalk. These are the ones that God brought with Christ at the parousia (1 Thess. 4:14). They reigned with Christ for a thousand years (not a length of time but a perfect reign).

Why would they go to Hades before going to heaven? Hades was located between earth and heaven as well as between earth and the final location of eternal death (see 2 Cor. 12:1-4). We usually tend to think of heaven and hell in terms of up and down. But the invisible realm should not be thought of as directional for it is not like the visible realm. Hades was where the dead were held until the final judgment. Thus, Hades prevented the dead from passing on to their eternal destinies until Christ provided the necessary means for believers to enter the presence of God. Since Hades was not yet cast into the Lake of Fire prior to the final judgment, those who were alive in Christ had to pass through Hades on their way to the New Jerusalem, which was still in heaven at that time.[124]

So how many resurrections do John 5 and Revelation 20 teach? Only one: the resurrection of the body of which both the living and the dead were a part. Let's take a look at John 5:24-29:

> [24]"Truly, truly, I say to you, he who hears My word, and believes Him who sent Me, has eternal life, and does not come into judgment, but has passed out of death into life. [25]Truly, truly, I say to you, an hour is coming and now is, when the dead will hear the voice of the Son of God, and those who hear will live. [26]For just as the Father has life in Himself, even so He gave to the Son also to have life in Himself; [27]and He gave Him authority to execute judgment, because He is the Son of Man. [28]Do not marvel at this; for an hour is coming, in which all who are in the tombs will hear His voice, [29]and will come forth; those who did the good deeds to a resurrection of life, those who committed the evil deeds to a resurrection of judgment."

In verses 24-27, Jesus is talking about people who are biologically alive. Jesus states that those who hear His word, and believe God, pass out of death into life. He further states that a time is coming *and now is* when this would happen. So "the dead" in verse 25 is referring to those who are in sin-death but are still biologically alive. We must remember that being part of "the dead" did not begin at biological death. It began at biological birth. We are able to determine that "the dead" refers to Old Covenant saints in some of Paul's texts, such as 1 Corinthians 15, because the context demands it. Here, the context demands that Jesus is talking about the dead who are living.[125]

Notice that in this passage, judgment is not neutral. It is contrasted with life. It is used negatively to mean eternal death. In verses 28-29, He is talking about the dead who are in Hades. This is clear by the fact that He refers to them as being in the tombs. In these verses, He states that a time is coming, but does not add the phrase, "and now is." There seems to be a distinction between the present and future passing from death to life for those who are alive biologically versus the future-only resurrecting of the dead in Hades. That is, the passing from death to life began during Jesus' first coming and would continue into the future whereas the resurrection of the dead in Hades was only future. At what point in Jesus' first coming does the "hour that now is" refer to? John 12:23-33 helps us here:

> [23]And Jesus answered them, saying, "The *hour has come* for the Son of Man to be glorified. [24]Truly, truly, I say to you, unless a grain of wheat falls into the earth and dies, it remains alone; but if it dies, it bears much fruit. [25]He who loves his life loses it, and he who hates his life in this world will keep it to life eternal. [26]If anyone serves Me, he must follow Me; and where I am, there My servant will be also; if anyone serves Me, the Father will honor him. [27]Now My soul has become troubled; and what shall I say, 'Father, save Me from *this hour*'? But for this purpose I came to this hour. [28]Father, glorify Your name." Then a voice came out of heaven: "I have both glorified it, and will glorify it again." [29]So the crowd of people who stood by and heard it were saying that it had thundered; others were saying, "An angel has spoken to Him." [30]Jesus answered and said, "This voice has not come for My sake, but for your sakes. [31]Now judgment is upon this world; now the ruler of this world will be cast out. [32]And I, if I am lifted up from the earth, will draw all men to Myself." [33]*But He was saying this to indicate the kind of death by which He was to die.*[126]

Jesus is clear here that the hour had come for Him to die. But His actual death didn't occur on the exact day that He said this. It wasn't until some time later that He died, yet Jesus refers to His death as the hour that had already come. The point is that His death was to occur sometime during the hour that was "now here."

Thus, in John 5:25, when Jesus says that an hour is coming and is now here, He means two things: 1. The time period when the dead who would hear the voice of the Son of God and live would occur at some point during the hour that began while He was on earth. The actual time period of "living" would not begin until His resurrection. 2. The hour, in which the dead hearing the voice of the Son of God and being brought to life, that was "coming" is the same hour in which those who were in the tombs would hear His voice and come forth to a resurrection of life or of judgment. In other words, an hour was coming when all the dead (both alive biologically and dead biologically) would come to life and never die again (cf. 11:25-26). But for those who were living biologically, the coming to life from being dead would begin at the resurrection of Christ and would continue on through to the resurrection of the body (which was consummated by the resurrection of the Old Covenant dead from Hades).

We must remember that the resurrection of the body was consummated by the resurrection of the dead from Hades. We also must remember that THE Death and THE Life refer to the death of the body of Adam versus the life of the body of Christ. In verse 24, the phrase, "has passed out of death into life" is literally, "has passed out of *the* Death into *the* Life." Jesus is teaching that those who believed were going to pass out of the Death of the body of Adam into the Life of the body of Christ. Being united to Christ, they would no longer be in *the* Death. Thus, they would be placed into the body of Christ that died in the flesh and came to life in the Spirit (cf. Rom. 6:3-10; 1 Pet. 3:18).

Dying with Christ is not the same as being in the Death. Dying with Christ is life because it means conquering the Death. Therefore, whoever believes in Jesus will never die even if he dies! This is how Jesus states it in John 11:25-26 in discussing the resurrection of Lazarus with Martha:

"²⁵Jesus said to her, 'I am the resurrection and the life; he who believes in Me will live even if he dies, ²⁶and everyone who lives and believes in Me will never die. Do you believe this?'"

Christ is the resurrection and the life! Thus, believing in Him brought eternal life at the resurrection even if they died biologically. And whoever lived biologically and believed in Him would never die. So those who believed were taken out of the Death of Adam and placed into the Life of Christ so that they would never die again. Therefore, Jesus is speaking of those who would take part in the death and resurrection of Christ through the death and resurrection of the body.

One last thought regarding John 5. This is a text that provides one perspective of the judgment. Remember from our study of the judgment that there are different texts that speak of the different aspects of the judgment even though they aren't consecutive judgments that occur one after the other. There is just one judgment, though different ways of describing the judgment. In John 5:29, there is no separation of sheep and goats because the dead who are in their tombs (which is a point of reference for those in Hades) were already separated based upon their deeds.

DOESN'T JOB 19:25-27 TEACH A RESURRECTION OF THE BIOLOGICAL BODY?

Job 19:25-27 does not teach a resurrection of the biological body. Young's Literal Translation translates these verses as follows:

> ²⁵That—I have known my Redeemer, The Living and the Last, For the dust he doth rise. ²⁶And after my skin hath compassed this [body], Then from my flesh I see God: ²⁷Whom I—I see on my side, And mine eyes have beheld, and not a stranger, Consumed have been my reins in my bosom.

Job is talking about his own skin being destroyed by boils. He isn't being prophetic in verse 25, he is saying that the Lord is the one who rises the dust (and makes the skin that Job was suffering in). In verse 26 he is saying that even after God destroys his skin with boils, he will still be alive in the flesh to see that God is on his side (vv. 26b-27a). This is the most straight-forward reading of that text, especially if you read it in Young's Literal Translation.

WHAT ABOUT THE RAPTURE TEXT: 1 THESSALONIANS 4:13-18?

First Thessalonians 4:13-18 is not teaching about the rapture of biological bodies meeting the Lord in the sky. This passage does, however, teach the same gathering together of the elect into the presence of God as Matthew 24.

In 1 Thessalonians 4:15, Paul tells the Thessalonians, "For this we say to you *by the word of the Lord*" (italics mine). Is there a place where Paul is pulling this from? Where did Jesus teach what Paul taught in this passage? Take a look at the side by side comparison with the Lord's words in Matthew 24:29-34:

Matthew 24:29-34	1 Thessalonians 4:13-18
Words of Jesus	"by the word of the Lord"
The coming of the Lord Jesus	The coming of the Lord Jesus
On the clouds	In the air
With the angels	With the angels
With the sound of a trumpet	With the sound of a trumpet
The gathering of the elect	The gathering of the elect
This generation shall not pass until it is all fulfilled	"We who are alive and remain until the coming of the Lord."

But that's not all. The parallels go further than our present set of verses. Paul parallels the words of Jesus throughout Matthew 24 as he writes 1 Thessalonians 4-5:

1. Christ Himself returns	Matt. 24:30	I Thess. 4:16
2. From Heaven	Matt. 24:30	I Thess. 4:16
3. With a shout	Matt. 24:30 (in power)	I Thess. 4:16
4. Accompanied by angels	Matt. 24:31	I Thess. 4:16
5. With trumpet of God	Matt. 24:31	I Thess. 4:16
6. Believers gathered	Matt. 24:31	I Thess. 4:17
7. In clouds	Matt. 24:30	I Thess. 4:17
8. Time unknown	Matt. 24:36	I Thess. 5:1-2
9. Will come as a thief	Matt. 24:43	I Thess. 5:2,4
10. Believers unaware of impending judgment	Matt. 24:37-39	I Thess. 5:3
11. Judgment comes like sudden labor pains	Matt. 24:8	I Thess. 5:3
12. Believers to be watchful	Matt. 24:42	I Thess. 5:4
13. Warning against drunkenness	Matt. 24:49	I Thess. 5:7

The first observance that we should make is that since Jesus was teaching about His coming at the destruction of Jerusalem in Matthew 24, that, therefore, Paul was teaching about the same thing in 1 Thessalonians. In his book, *The Last Days According to Jesus*, RC Sproul makes the following comments regarding these two texts:

> One can legitimately take the descriptive language of the Olivet Discourse in a figurative way, because the language is so similar to Old Testament prophetic imagery. But Paul's language in 1 Thessalonians 4 is clearly of a different sort. Here the genre of the text makes it highly unlikely that Paul was describing an event hidden from earthly view.

But the language is of the exact same genre. Is this good exegesis on Sproul's part, or simply his presupposition that demands it? In both texts, both Paul and Jesus predicted the coming of the Lord to gather together the saints. Jesus says this will happen in their generation. Paul says, "*we* who are alive and remain." How many "comings" of the Lord are taught in Scripture to occur with His angels, in fire, in power and glory, to gather the saints? It is a dual hermeneutic that concludes that there is more than one and that they actually look different. It is not the full preterist who has a problem with eisegesis, it is the futurist. Let's take an exegetical look at our text.

Context demands that Paul was speaking *to* the Thessalonians, not to us. We can see this clearly in the verses leading up to our text:

> [9]Now as to the love of the brethren, *you* have no need for anyone to *write to you*, for *you yourselves* are taught by God to love one another; [10]for indeed *you* do practice it toward all the brethren who are in all Macedonia. But we urge *you*, brethren, to excel still more…[127]

Are we to practice love for one another with the brethren who are in Macedonia? Perhaps if we lived with the Thessalonians. But we don't. So once again, audience relevancy matters. The "we's" and "you's" in our passage, then, are referring to those particular people, in that particular time.

> [13]But we do not want you to be uninformed, brethren, about those who are asleep, so that you will not grieve as do the rest who have no hope. [14]For if we believe that Jesus died and rose again, even so God will bring with Him those who have fallen asleep in Jesus.

The ones who had fallen asleep in Jesus here are those who were reigning with Him for a thousand years.[128] They were not coming back to get their biological bodies. They were coming with Jesus to bring salvation to the body of Christ. They were part of the firstfruits. All believers had to be gathered together into the resurrected body before any believers could enter the presence of God. This included those who were waiting in the outer courts of the New Jerusalem for Christ to come out a second time.

> [15]For this we say to you by the word of the Lord, that we who are alive and remain until the coming of the Lord, will not precede those who have fallen asleep.

It is important to notice that those who had fallen asleep here are not said to have fallen asleep *in Jesus*. Rather, these are the ones who were asleep in 1 Corinthians 15:20: "But now Christ has been raised from the dead, the first fruits of those who are *asleep*" (italics mine). Contextually speaking, these are the dead in Christ in 1 Thessalonians 4:16:

> [16]For the Lord Himself will descend from heaven with a shout, with the voice of the archangel and with the trumpet of God, and the dead in Christ will rise first. [17]Then we who are alive and remain will be caught up together with them in the clouds to meet the Lord in the air, and so we shall always be with the Lord. [18]Therefore comfort one another with these words.

The language used in this text is Old Testament language. The use of Old Testament language in the New Testament has been demonstrated throughout this book and only one comment from Don Preston is necessary here: "...the word "descend" was commonly used with priest's decent [sic] out of the temple to announce that atonement had been completed."[129] This is synonymous with Christ exiting the Most Holy Place a second time where He brings with Him those who have fallen asleep in Jesus in verse 14.

The dead in Christ are the Old Covenant saints who are united to Christ through covenantal incorporation by way of baptism.[130] The first thing that happened at Christ's descent was the resurrection of the dead to complete the resurrection of the body. Then, in verse 17, the catching together of those who are alive and remain is the same gathering as Matthew 24:31. The Greek word that is translated "caught up" in most English translations does not actually contain any directional value to it. The word "up" is inserted because of the traditional presupposition that we will literally fly into the sky in our biological bodies to meet Christ.

The proper translation here is simply, "caught together." This sounds exactly like "gather together." Where were they caught together? With the dead in the resurrection body in the clouds. Once again, as we have seen numerous times, clouds are not literal clouds. This is Old Covenant imagery used to describe the presence of God. Why were they caught or gathered together in the clouds of the Lord's coming? "To meet the Lord in the air." This word, "air," is often thought to mean the sky up above. But it is the same Greek word used by Paul in 1 Corinthians 9:26b: "I box in such a way, as not beating the *air*" (italics mine). Does Paul mean by this that he boxes in such a way, as not beating the sky above? Is he aiming to hit something in the sky? Of course not. He's using a boxing analogy where a boxer aims for the target right in front of him, within his immediate vicinity in such a way, as not missing the target and hitting air in that same immediate vicinity. So what would make us think that Paul would use this word any differently in 1 Thessalonians 4:17? Only traditional presuppositions.

So what does Paul mean in 1 Thessalonians 4:17? Recall that "parousia" means arrival or presence, and remember that the difference between the Old Covenant and the New Covenant has everything to do with God's permanent presence with us now. With those things in mind, the explanation of what Paul means is very simple: At the descent of Christ, the whole resurrected body was gathered together into the presence of God, "and so we shall always be with the Lord." The emphasis here is that now the resurrected body of Christ, which is all of His people changed, redeemed, and transformed by faith into immortality, will always be in the presence of the Lord (i.e. with the Lord) because they have overcome death in Christ. Death equals separation from God. There was no more death for those who believed, only life in the permanent presence of God.

HOW DO YOU EXPLAIN 2 CORINTHIANS 5?

It is traditionally understood that 2 Corinthians 5:1-10 is teaching that when we die biologically, we go to Heaven to be with Lord and that we will be reunited with our biological bodies in order to appear before the judgment seat of Christ to be recompensed for our deeds "in the body." Part of the reason why it is believed that this text is about the biological body is because of verses 16-18 of chapter 4:

[16]Therefore we do not lose heart, but though our outer man is decaying, yet our inner man is being renewed day by day. [17]For momentary, light affliction is producing for us an eternal weight of glory far beyond all comparison, [18]while we look not at the things which are seen, but at the things which are not seen; for the things which are seen are temporal, but the things which are not seen are eternal.

It is believed that the outer man that is decaying is the biological body, while the inner man that is being renewed day by day is the soul. Therefore, in this view, it follows that the contrast between the houses in chapter 5 must be talking about our biological bodies. The immediate problem with this is that 5:1 says that the earthly tent is torn down. In what sense is our biological body torn down? Some may argue that Paul says, "…*if* the earthly tent is torn down…," attempting to make a case that while the body is decaying, for some, it will be torn down by persecution or death. But if we read the rest of the sentence, we see that Paul said, "…if the earthly tent…is torn down, we have a building from God…" Do those who's biological bodies only decay, and are not torn down, not have a building from God? This is just the beginning of the problems that this passage poses to the traditional view.

The traditional interpretation is actually wrought with problems contextually. But before we look at those problems, consider this question: What sense does it make to come back and get our biological bodies after we go to heaven? If we are in the presence of God, how can we be incomplete? Yet the traditional view teaches that even though we are in the very presence of God, which is the greatest possible thing, we are still incomplete and look forward to something more, namely, being in the presence of God *with our biological bodies*. But once we are in heaven, what need do we have for our biological bodies?

Some actually say that we don't need them, or that it isn't that we are longing for them, but that God is just giving us something more. But how can God give us anything more than Himself? There is nothing more that He can give us. Plus, if this passage is talking about biological bodies, then Paul certainly does say that we are longing for them (v. 2-3). So let's look at the problems with the traditional view in this text and then learn what the text actually teaches. Read the first four verses carefully:

> ¹For we know that if the earthly tent which is our house is torn down, we have a building from God, a house not made with hands, eternal in the heavens. ²For indeed in this house we groan, longing to be clothed with our dwelling from heaven, ³inasmuch as we, having put it on, will not be found naked. ⁴For indeed while we are in this tent, we groan, being burdened, because we do not want to be unclothed but to be clothed, so that what is mortal will be swallowed up by life.

The first thing that Paul states is that if the earthly tent is torn down, we *have* (present, active, indicative) a building from God, a house not made with hands. If the earthly tent is referring to our biological bodies, then the house not made with hands must also be another body that our soul enters into that is presently waiting for us in Heaven. And this building or house from God is contrasted with the earthly tent that is torn down. This is a completely different house. It is not the first tent rebuilt into a better house. This house from God is not made with hands, which brings us to another problem: The biological body was not made with hands either.

Whatever the difference is between these two "bodies," Paul is teaching that the first one was made with hands, while the second one is not. This is clearly implied in the text. Therefore, the house not made with hands cannot be made from the same tent that was torn down (which was made with hands), especially since the house not made with hands is already made (i.e. we *have*).

To drive this point home, Paul teaches that in this present house, we groan, longing to be clothed with our dwelling from, or out of, heaven. So this new dwelling is not only a completely different house, but it is from heaven, not from earth. The biological body was made from, or out of, the dust of the earth (made with hands?). The new house is made without hands and is from, or out of, heaven. In addition, Paul says that they longed to be clothed with this dwelling from Heaven so that they would not be found naked. So Paul is teaching that there is no state of nakedness, but that they would move from one house to the next, because "while we are in this tent, we groan, being burdened, because we do not want to be unclothed but to be clothed."

If this passage is teaching that the houses are our biological bodies, then we actually have one body before we die, another body that we receive in Heaven, and then we get the old body back just to have it changed into a glorified body. The problem gets worse when we consider that the house made without hands is eternal in the heavens. So now the body that we put on after we die biologically is an eternal body, which means that the old body that we get back has to be put back on over the eternal body. Therefore, man will have two bodies on top of each other for all eternity. Is that really necessary? Or to ask a better question, is this taught anywhere else in Scripture? The answer is a resounding, "no!"

Then what does this passage teach? Let's go back a little in 2 Corinthians and get a little more context. Paul makes a series of contrasts between the Old Covenant and the New Covenant. Consider the following:

> The letter of Christ written not with ink but with the Spirit of the living God (3:3).
>
> The letter of Christ written not on tablets of stone, but on tablets of human hearts (3:3).
>
> Servants of a new covenant, not of the letter, but of the Spirit (3:6).
>
> The letter kills, but the Spirit gives life (3:6).
>
> The ministry of death, in letters engraved on stones, came with glory but the ministry of the Spirit even more glory (3:7-8).
>
> The ministry of condemnation has glory, but much more does the ministry of righteousness abound in glory (3:9).

For indeed what had glory, in this case, has no glory because of the glory that surpasses it (3:10).

For if that which fades away was with glory, much more that which remains is in glory (3:11).

Moses wore the veil and their minds were hardened, but whenever a person turns to the Lord, the veil is taken away (3:13-16).

No liberty under Moses, but where the Spirit of the Lord is, there is liberty (3:17).

The god of this world has blinded the minds of the unbelieving, but God has shone in our hearts to give the Light of the knowledge of the glory of God in the face of Christ (4:3-6).

Carrying about in the body (singular) the dying of Jesus, so that the life of Jesus also may be manifested in our (plural) body (singular; 4:10).

Constantly being delivered over to death for Jesus' sake, so that the life of Jesus also may be manifested in our mortal flesh (4:11).

Death works in us, but life in you (4:12).

The outer man decaying, but the inner man being renewed day by day (4:16).

Things which are seen are temporal, but things which are unseen are eternal (4:18).

The earthly tent/house, which is made with hands, is torn down, but we have a building from God, a house not made with hands (5:1).

The earthly house is temporal, but the house not made with hands is eternal (5:1).

We do not want to be unclothed, but clothed (5:4).

What is mortal is swallowed up by life (5:4).

At home in the body, absent from the Lord (5:6).

We walk by faith, not by sight (5:7).

We prefer to be absent from the body and at home with the Lord (5:8).

Paul is consistent. Starting from the beginning, the contrast is between the Old Covenant and the New Covenant. He is not talking about biological bodies at all. In Chapter 3, Paul is teaching how much better the New Covenant is compared to the Old Covenant. For those who turn to the Lord, the veil that kept Israel from seeing the fading away of the glory of the Old Covenant, would then have the veil taken away because the glory of the Lord never fades away. This is the ministry of the New Covenant. Paul says, "Therefore, since we have this ministry, as we received mercy, we do not lose heart" (4:1). The proclamation of the Gospel is the ministry of the New Covenant. Notice how Paul ties the Old Covenant veil from chapter 3 to the blinding of minds from seeing the light of the Gospel: "And even if our gospel is veiled, it is veiled to those who are perishing, in whose case the god of this world has blinded the minds of the unbelieving so that they might not see the light of the gospel of the glory of Christ, who is the image of God" (5:3-4).

This blinding through the veil is directly related to the Old Covenant. It was the Old Covenant mode of existence that was used to blind the minds of the unbelieving from seeing the light of the Gospel because they embraced the glory of the Old Covenant. This was the reason why Paul and Timothy (who were Jews) faced such persecution in proclaiming the Gospel. They were preaching a Law-free Gospel. So they were "afflicted in every way, but not crushed; perplexed, but not despairing; persecuted, but not forsaken; struck down, but not destroyed; always carrying about in the body the dying of Jesus, so that the life of Jesus also may be manifested in our body" (5:8-10).

In order to understand all of this better, it is important to note the distinction between the "we's" and the "you's" through these chapters. Paul starts off chapter 3 by distinguishing he and Timothy from the recipients of the letter: "Are *we* beginning to commend ourselves again? Or do *we* need, as some, letters of commendation to *you* or from *you*? *You* are our letter, written in *our* hearts, known and read by all men" (vv. 1-2; italics mine). Now, pay close attention to this distinction throughout 2 Corinthians 3 and 4:

3:3being manifested that *you* are a letter of Christ, cared for by *us*...4Such confidence *we* have through Christ toward God. 5Not that *we* are adequate in *ourselves* to consider anything as coming from *ourselves*, but our adequacy is from God, 6who also made *us* adequate as servants of a new covenant...12Therefore having such a hope, *we* use great boldness in *our* speech, 13and are not like Moses, who used to put a veil over his face so that the sons of Israel would not look intently at the end of what was fading away...18But *we all* [Paul, Timothy, and the recipients of the letter], with unveiled face, beholding as in a mirror the glory of the Lord, are being transformed into the same image from glory to glory, just as from the Lord, the Spirit. 4:1Therefore, since *we* [not we *all*] have this ministry, as *we* received mercy, *we* do not lose heart, 2but *we* have renounced the things hidden because of shame, not walking in craftiness or adulterating the word of God, but by the manifestation of truth commending *ourselves* to every man's conscience in the sight of God. 3And even if *our* gospel is veiled, it is veiled to those who are perishing...5For *we* do not preach ourselves but Christ Jesus as Lord, and *ourselves* as *your* bond-servants for Jesus' sake. 6For God, who said, "Light shall shine out of darkness," is the One who has shone in *our* hearts to give the Light of the knowledge of the glory of God in the face of Christ. 7But *we* have this treasure in earthen vessels, so that the surpassing greatness of the power will be of God and not from *ourselves*; 8*we* are afflicted in every way, but not crushed; perplexed, but not despairing; 9persecuted, but not forsaken; struck down, but not destroyed; 10always carrying about in the body the dying of Jesus, so that the life of Jesus also may be manifested in *our* [plural] body [singular]. 11For *we* who live are constantly being delivered over to death for Jesus' sake, so that the life of Jesus also may be manifested in *our* mortal flesh. [12]So death works in *us*, but life in *you*. [13]But having the same spirit of faith, according to what is written, "I believed, therefore I spoke," *we* also believe, therefore *we* also speak, [14]knowing that He who raised the Lord Jesus will raise *us* also with Jesus and will present *us* with *you*. [15]For all things are for *your* sakes, so that the grace which is spreading to more and more people may cause the giving of thanks to abound to the glory of God. [16]Therefore *we* do not lose heart, but though *our* outer man is decaying, yet *our* inner man is being renewed day by day. [17]For momentary, light affliction is producing for *us* an eternal weight of glory far beyond all comparison, [18]while *we* look not at the things which are seen, but at the things which are not seen; for the things which are seen are temporal, but the things which are not seen are eternal.

Paul is clearly drawing a distinctive line here in these verses. There is no question that Paul is referring to he and Timothy when he uses "we, us, our, and ourselves," and he is referring to the Corinthians when he uses "you and your." There is also no question that he is referring to himself, Timothy, and the Corinthians when he uses "we all" because "we all" includes more than then just he and Timothy. Thus, Paul and Timothy were carrying about in the Old Covenant body the dying of Jesus so that the life of Jesus would also be manifested in that body.

Remember, Paul and Timothy were Jews and were part of that Old Covenant body that was dying while the New Covenant body was resurrecting. Thus, through all the persecution, they were going about their business while in the Old Covenant body that was dying so that the life of Jesus would be manifested, or seen, in that Old Covenant body through their ministry. They were constantly being delivered over to this death of the Old Covenant for Jesus' sake, so that the life of Jesus would also be seen in their mortal flesh.

Paul has already taught them about the resurrection of the body of Adam in 1 Corinthians 15. The body of Old Covenant Israel is a microcosm of that body. They are not disconnected; rather, the Old

Covenant mode of existence followed the pattern of Adam. Living in the flesh is living according to the Adamic order. It is doing things according to earthly means. This is why following the Old Covenant mode of existence is called living according to the flesh as opposed to living according to the Spirit, which is the New Covenant mode of existence (cf. Rom. 8:1-11). So Paul and Timothy had the ministry of suffering in that body for the sake of the Gentiles, in this case, specifically the Corinthians, in order that the Gospel would produce life in them: "So death is at work in us, but life in you" (2 Cor. 4:12).

It is in this way that Paul knows that "he who raised the Lord Jesus will raise us also with Jesus and bring us *with you* into his presence" (v. 14). So in verses 16-18, the outer man equals the fleshly or natural man of the Old Covenant mode of existence and the inner man equals the spiritual man of the New Covenant mode of existence. The Old Covenant was temporal and was decaying (cf. Heb. 8:13). The New Covenant is permanent and eternal. The Old Covenant was seen in the earthly tabernacle made with hands while the New Covenant is unseen in the heavenly tabernacle. These are the buildings that Paul is contrasting in 2 Corinthians 5:

> [1]For we know that if the earthly tent which is our house is torn down, we have a building from God, a house not made with hands, eternal in the heavens.

Compare verse 1 above with Hebrews 9:11-12:

> [11]But when Christ appeared as a high priest of the good things to come, He entered through the greater and more perfect tabernacle, not made with hands, that is to say, not of this creation; [12]and not through the blood of goats and calves, but through His own blood, He entered the holy place once for all, having obtained eternal redemption.

Back to 2 Corinthians 5:

> [2]For indeed in this house we groan, longing to be clothed with our dwelling from heaven, [3]inasmuch as we, having put it on, will not be found naked. [4]For indeed while we are in this tent, we groan, being burdened, because we do not want to be unclothed but to be clothed, so that what is mortal will be swallowed up by life. [5]Now He who prepared us for this very purpose is God, who gave to us the Spirit as a pledge. [6]Therefore, being always of good courage, and knowing that while we are at home in the body we are absent from the Lord—[7]for we walk by faith, not by sight—[8]we are of good courage, I say, and prefer rather to be absent from the body and to be at home with the Lord.

Verses 6-8 are literally translated as follows:

> [6]having courage, then, at all times, and knowing that being at home in the body, we are away from home from the Lord,—[7]for through faith we walk, not through sight—[8]we have courage, and are well pleased rather to be away from the home of the body, and to be at home with the Lord.[131]

Paul is telling them that as long as the Old Covenant mode of existence was still in effect, then he and Timothy were still not in the new home with the Lord. Until the resurrection of the Jews was completed by way of the Old Covenant dead rising at the destruction of the Temple, the Gentiles could not be in their new home either. That is why Paul and Timothy are writing in this way.

> [9]Therefore we also have as our ambition, whether at home or absent, to be pleasing to Him. [10]For we must all appear before the judgment seat of Christ, so that each one may be recompensed for his deeds in the body, according to what he has done, whether good or bad.

It was Paul and Timothy's ambition that whether they were in the resurrected New Covenant body or in the dying of the Old Covenant body, it was their aim to please God. Why? Because at the completion of the resurrected body, Paul, Timothy, and the Corinthians would appear before the judgment seat of Christ.

RICHARD PRATT ARGUES THAT BIBLICAL PROPHECIES ARE SELDOM FULFILLED EXACTLY AS THEY ARE STATED. IF THAT IS TRUE, THEN HOW CAN YOU BE CERTAIN THAT FULL PRETERISM IS AS CLEAR AS YOU SAY IT IS?

Richard Pratt, professor of Old Testament at Reformed Theological Seminary, wrote a chapter in, *When Shall These Things Be?*, called, "Hyper-Preterism and Unfolding Biblical Eschatology," which was published again in *Reformed Perspectives Magazine* in 2005. In this article, he begins by summarizing the prophetic argument for full preterism, which he calls, Hyper-Preterism:

> Biblical prophecies predict an imminent return of Christ.
> All biblical prophecies must be fulfilled as predicted.
> Therefore, the imminent return of Christ was fulfilled.[132]

So far so good. But then Pratt goes on to reveal the desperation that futurists feel in being able to show full preterism to be false. In fact, as Pratt states, "For the most part, opponents of hyper-preterism have argued against the first premise. They have challenged the idea that the Scriptures speak of Christ's imminent return."[133] Have they been successful? No, because the Scriptures *do* speak of Christ's imminent return! So Pratt, recognizing this, attempts to come at full preterism from a different angle:

> ...to my knowledge no critiques of hyper-preterism have focused on the second premise. No one has challenged the idea that biblical prophecies must be fulfilled just as they

predict future events to be...In contrast to the hyper-preterist proposal, we will argue that biblical prophecies are seldom fulfilled exactly as they are stated. Therefore, even if the Scriptures did predict that Jesus' return would take place within a few years, his return could still be in our future, even more than two thousand years later.[134]

Really? Pratt's premise for his article should concern us. Furthermore, his use of Old Testament prophecies throughout his chapter do not support his attack on what he calls "hyper-preterism." Pratt would have been better off to leave well enough alone. His desperate attempt to find something, anything, that would show full preterism to be false has led him down the path to open theism, which is a view that believes that human decisions and actions can alter the plan of God because God's foreknowledge of future events is limited. Although Pratt attempts to distance himself from open theism, he ends up embracing it in his arguments as is demonstrated by Edward Hassertt in *House Divided: Bridging the Gap in Reformed Eschatology. A Preterist Response to When Shall These Things Be?* The irony is, Pratt calls full preterists the heretics. Since Pratt's chapter has been dealt with in detail in *House Divided*, and would require a lengthy chapter in this book to show all the problems with his arguments, we will only briefly work through his chapter to see if any of his arguments have any weight to them. Pratt begins his critique as follows:

From the start, we should acknowledge that many Christians endorse the view on the fulfillment of prophecy taken by hyper-preterists. Their outlook on prophetic fulfillment is largely based on Deuteronomy 18:22, where Moses warns against false prophets:

If what a prophet proclaims in the name of the Lord does not take place or come true, that is a message the Lord has not spoken. That prophet has spoken presumptuously. Do not be afraid of him.

It is quite common on a popular level for evangelicals to understand this passage to teach that everything a true prophet says about the future will come to pass. Many evangelical scholars have been subtler in their interpretations of the verse, but little effort has been put into adjusting general perceptions of prophecy to account for these more subtle understandings. As a result many evangelicals do not dispute the hyper-preterist interpretation of this passage.[135]

Yet Pratt never states, nor engages, the "hyper-preterist" view on the fulfillment of prophecy. He simply states that many Christians endorse the view that many *evangelicals* understand. So who is Pratt arguing against in his chapter? Is it the full preterists who hold to a view of Deuteronomy 18:22 that he never actually deals with, or is he arguing against the view that many evangelicals believe about this verse? Pratt produces a subtle level of literary trickery here to get his readers to believe that full preterists have the same view of Deuteronomy 18:22 that many evangelicals do. Thus, he believes that in defeating the popular view of this verse, he has somehow defeated the full preterist view. The various types of prophecies that he puts forth in the rest of the chapter actually support his opposition to the popular view. The whole problem with his argument throughout his chapter, however, is that he never actually effectively demonstrates a fault with the full preterist view!

Pratt shows that there are prophetic utterances that contain contingencies. Thus, for example, if those who are prophesied against repent, then the curse against them would not come to pass. There is no problem here because the prophetic utterances contained the contingencies when they were uttered.

Moving on, Pratt then shows that there are levels of divine determination: (1) conditional predictions, (2) unqualified predictions, (3) confirmed predictions, and (4) sworn predictions.[136] Level one is no problem because those prophetic utterances had conditions attached to them. Concerning level two predictions, Pratt states the following:

"We have already seen one example of this kind of prediction in Jonah 3:4, where the prophet says, 'Forty more days and Nineveh will be overturned.' There are no explicit conditions in this prophecy, and the prophet Jonah makes it clear that God was determined to destroy the city. This was no mere possibility; it was a serious threat. Even so, the widespread repentance within the city of Nineveh caused God to delay his judgment against that city.[137]

Granting Pratt's argument for implicit conditions in unqualified predictions, this argument is invalid because Pratt would have to demonstrate that Israel repented before the destruction of Jerusalem in order to apply this level of divine determination to the prophecies against Jerusalem in the New Testament. This applies to level three determinations as well. Concerning the fourth level of divine determination, here is what Pratt explains:

While it is true that God is utterly determined to carry out predictions qualified by oaths, there is still some latitude for God to react to intervening historical contingencies, because predictions never cover every detail of future events. First, the question of *when* often remains in the balance; timing can be influenced by reactions of people who hear a prediction. Second, precisely *who* will experience what is predicted often remains flexible. Third, the *means* by which a prediction will come true is often left unspecified. Fourth, to *what degree* a prediction will be fulfilled always remains an open question.[138]

Pratt unwittingly helps the full preterist here. He first states the obvious that "predictions never cover every detail of future events." Then, his following comments demonstrate the types of things that give

God latitude in fulfilling the prophecies if those things were not covered in the details. If they were covered in the details, then they would have to come to pass exactly as predicted.

The New Testament prophecies regarding the coming of the Lord lack no details regarding the *timing* of their predictions. Nor do they lack details regarding *who* was to experience the predictions. Nor do they lack the *means* by which the predictions would come true. This isn't rocket science. When the details are in the prediction, and the prediction is a sworn prediction, then those details must come to pass exactly as they are predicted. Mr. Pratt has done nothing but demonstrate that full preterism must be true.

Although Pratt spends a few pages attempting to demonstrate reasons for the delay of Christ's return, he fails to do so because he cannot contend with the details regarding the prophecies in the New Testament about the coming of the Lord. He even admits, "It would appear that in the early years after Christ's ascension, the Christian community had high hopes for an imminent return of Christ. It is not surprising then that discouragement set in when years passed by without his appearance."[139] This comment is revealing in a couple of ways. First, the audience that received the predictions had hopes for an immanent return. Why? Because that's what Jesus and the apostles predicted in the details! Second, Pratt speaks of discouragement that set in as years passed by without his appearance. If the first century Christians were discouraged because they clearly understood that Jesus would return soon, then people in the Church today, two thousand years later, ought to be depressed all the time rather than hopeful.

CONCLUSION

This chapter has answered the most common questions and objections that people have with full preterism. There are certainly many questions and objections that have yet to be answered regarding soteriology. Since the scope of this book has been to provide a primer on reading the Bible contextually and the eschatological implications of doing so, if the Lord permits, there will be a sequel to this book called,

Living Our Lives With New Covenant Eyes, which will provide a detailed study of soteriology in light of full preterism.

There is one more common question, which deserves an answer in this book that is asked by almost everyone who encounters full preterism. That question is asked in a variety of ways: "What does this mean for us today?" "Why are we still here?" "What's in it for me?" Since this question is the most important question that a person can ask, the final chapter will be devoted to answering that question.

Chapter 6:

WHAT'S IN IT FOR ~~ME~~ US?

Contrary to popular belief, the Bible is not a book that teaches about the end of God's dealings with mankind on earth as we know it. It is a book that teaches about how God restored His relationship with mankind on earth as we know it. That restored relationship was completed in 70 AD and will continue with mankind forever on this earth as generations come, and generations go. A common question that is often posed by people who are faced with full preterism is, "What do we do now?" It is a great question that is worthy of an answer. It makes sense to wonder what's in it for us if all the prophecies in the Bible have been fulfilled. To begin with, if the resurrection is behind us, what does that mean for us today?

Well, if the resurrection hasn't happened, then we are still under the Old Covenant mode of existence, which means that all we get is death. Many skeptics think that full preterism robs them of their hope that they will be resurrected. But the problem is that a hope in the resurrection demands a need for it. If we want the resurrection to still be future, then we have to be willing to lose our eternal life that God has given to us because in order for there to be a resurrection, there has to be a Hades for us to go to after biological death. Who wants that?

The fact is that now, as a result of the resurrection and the eternal death of Death and Hades, all whose names are written in the Lamb's book of life have eternal life already and get to go to heaven immediately after the death of their biological bodies. This really is no different than the traditional view on this matter, except that the traditional view is inconsistent as to why we *can* go to Heaven after biological death. So the Biblical doctrine of full preterism teaches that we have been freed from the sin and death of Adam and have been given the eternal life that comes to us *because* the resurrection has already taken place. So what's in it for us? Eternal life now!

How are people saved today? Well, since the resurrection has already taken place, those whose names are written in the Lamb's book of life have eternal life at birth. The temporal death under the Old Covenant mode of existence was cast into the eternal death at the parousia of Christ. Thus, all who are not in the Lamb's book of life remain under the curse of the sin of Adam, which is the death that was cast into *eternal* death (i.e. The Second Death). When the temporal death died, the eternal death took over. Another way of saying this is that the temporal death was swallowed up by the eternal death. The whole point of eternal death is that there is no escape from it or resurrection out of it.

Therefore, those whose names are written in the Lamb's book of life must have eternal life at birth. Are we to continue to evangelize? Absolutely. The reason is because we are compelled to bring to light the glory of Christ to those who do not know that they have eternal life.[140] Remember, as long as we are in these biological bodies, we cannot see the invisible reality of God's glory or His wrath. Faith embraces the truth. We don't know that truth until we are faced with it. It is only then that we can believe it. And this makes sense because if you think about it, even after we come to faith, we continue to sin and not trust God. If we who do know the truth and have faith still sin, is it any wonder that those who have eternal life and have not yet embraced the truth are still living in sin?

How many times have Christians questioned their eternal life? Why, then, would we expect those who have not yet believed the Gospel to be aware of their eternal life? But as generations come and generations go, the Gospel will continue to be the power of salvation for all who believe. Since the earth will remain forever, there will be eternal generations of people that will join us in Heaven. It is also true that people in these eternal generations will also enter into the Lake of Fire.[141]

But if this is true, then does that mean that it doesn't matter how we live? Can we just "live it up?" Yes and no. Yes, because our sins are no longer counted against us. God cannot love you any more or any less then He already does. No, because those who recognize the glory of God have a desire to live for His glory. So if we claim to believe the Gospel, then how can we who have died to sin through the death and resurrection of the body still live in it? It isn't a matter of how we are required to live; it is a matter of how we desire to live. There is far greater joy for the one who lives for the glory of God than for the one who does not.

It is on this point we see that sin still has consequences. We must not forget that just because our sin no longer affects our relationship with God, it does indeed negatively affect our lives on earth. Sin can produce serious negative consequences to us and to those around us. If a man commits adultery, he will face consequences for his actions. If a person gets drunk and kills somebody while driving, their sin of drunkenness has produced a consequence that will have painfully affected many lives, including their own. Yet, we have the freedom to live for God's glory and the freedom to fail without the fear of *God's* wrath:

> Romans 8:15: For you have not received a spirit of slavery leading to fear again, but you have received a spirit of adoption as sons by which we cry out, "Abba! Father!"

God, our Father, wants the things of this earth to grow strangely dim in the light of His glory and grace. This has always been the goal of God in creating this earth and placing man here. The glories of this earth are magnificent. But He has given us a weight of glory way beyond anything that this world has to offer. Of all the things on this earth, sin offers and succeeds in giving us the greatest pleasure possible short of God. God loves us so much and wants us to understand so much how great the glory of heaven will be that He is willing to do what is necessary for us to recognize this to the extent of even allowing sin to remain in this world. For those who understand how much greater the glory of God is compared to our sin comes inexplicable joy through His Son taking upon His wrath for us. The goal of God in the death of Christ is the glory of

God for sinners that could never see that glory without the death of Christ for the payment of their sins. Therefore, since we cannot yet see the full glory of God while we are in these biological bodies on the earth, we have the continuation of sin to help us grasp that glory through the pleasure of God over the pleasure of sin. And it is a glorious thing not to have our sins counted against us! So live for the glory of God and love one another.

WHAT THEN SHALL WE DO NOW?

What can the Church do? What should the Church do? How does the Church revise the creeds and begin to change her doctrine without disrupting the faith of its people? We do it slowly. We must teach our people gently. We mustn't expect them to suddenly change. Each local church must, however, begin this change. There is a strong probability that local churches that embrace full preterism will be removed from the denominations that they are a part of. These local churches should move forward. Any local church that remains convinced of the futurist position, but is willing to continue in conversation within the Church are welcomed to converse with us at any time.

Full preterism is the truth of Scripture. We are not the heretics, but we are willing to converse with anyone who holds to a view that isn't Biblical. The Church should remain united, but it must not remain unbiblical. Therefore, the Church is moving forward with full preterism, but we should be patient with denominations and local churches who wish to deny the truth of Scripture regarding this doctrine because of tradition. The Church will change, but it will take time. The important thing is that we do not allow for the clear truth of full preterism to become simply an acceptable doctrine in the Church. It must become the only accepted eschatology in the Church.

What can individuals do who embrace this view but have no local church nearby that embraces full preterism or that is willing to change? There are several options here: (1) If you are a man called by God to be a pastor, then consider planting a church. This is never easy, but it very well may be the best option for the Church to move forward in the truth.

(2) If this is not you, then begin to pray that God will raise up a man that will plant a church where you are. And never cease to pray for this. God will provide. (3) If there is a full preterist church that is close enough to attend, then join that church. This is especially important in a church-planting situation. It is difficult enough to plant a church. Add full preterism to the mix, and you can imagine the challenge. Be a part of the building process for the sake of truth. This may require some sacrifice on your part because planting a church takes sacrifice, sometimes small, sometimes large. But if you want the truth of full preterism to spread, you have to be willing to do your part. (4) If there are no full preterist churches near you, as you pray for one, continue to worship with a local church that holds to the futurist position. This will be very frustrating at times and you will very likely receive a lot of criticism. But we must demonstrate the love of Christ to all of our Christian brothers and sisters whether they are futurists or full preterists. One thing you can do is give people a copy of this book. It was written for the very purpose of helping people to understand full preterism rather than going on hearsay.

Above all, always remember that this change in doctrine will most definitely happen in the Church, but it will take time. We shouldn't expect it to happen overnight. We must be patient and endure for the sake of future generations. Never forget that our Father will always take care us. Stand for the truth of Scripture no matter the cost. It is worth it in the end!

May all who have read this book be driven to see the Church and the world around them through New Covenant Eyes. And may this ultimately be the result of reading the Bible through New Covenant Eyes.

Afterword

J. Jeremiah Thompson

The book that you now have in your hands is the result of applying the principle from its title, *Reading the Bible Through New Covenant Eyes*. Over the past five years, Alan and I have been on an amazing and challenging journey in our quest to understand the Word of God. God has blessed Alan with the gift, opportunity, and determination to write this book. In it he argues for a consistent application of the historical-grammatical hermeneutic, which is generally held to and taught in most evangelical churches. That is to say, he argues for reading and interpreting the Bible with the understanding that it was written to an original audience and with equal understanding of the writing style and genre that each author employed.

The challenge of this book is not just a call to better hermeneutics, but a call for allowing the Bible to determine your conclusions through good hermeneutics and not through a predetermined grid of historical, systematic, or creedal theology. This book is written as a challenge to that way of thinking. It challenges the notion that we need something else to help us understand what the Bible says other than the Bible itself. Well, we have challenged that notion and we will continue to challenge it. We have come to a crossroads in history where people have lost faith in most institutions. They have lost faith in the church, the government, in education, and even in the family. People are looking for truth and the truth must be found in a source that is solid and reliable. Not something that man has written but something that has come from God. Scripture is the only source of truth, which is not the result of fallible man.

Therefore, we must be people of the truth even if that truth is not what you want to hear or believe. It is not the responsibility of Alan or anyone else except God to convince you if something is true or not. Yet you must believe it if it is true. Alan has presented to you in this book what he believes to be true, but you must do the work and search the Scriptures for yourself. I said these very words to a close friend of mine that does not hold the views expressed in this book. I told him that if it is true, then no matter how it disrupts his life, he must embrace it as true. We do not have the authority to determine what is true but we do have the responsibility of embracing truth.

I applaud you for reaching this point in the book and being willing to continue reading through some of the more difficult parts. If you have been intellectually honest while reading this book then your head has probably been spinning for a while and you are not sure which way is up theologically. That is okay. You are where I was when I was first confronted with these concepts, and sometimes it is still overwhelming as I learn more and more. Before you make your final decision on this book, I would like to suggest a few things:

1. Check your motives. Are you in search of truth or are you just out to prove Alan or full preterism wrong.
2. Re-read this book and take the time to search out the facts and be sure check the footnotes. You now know the major arguments and the gist of the conclusion, so take the time to do serious study before you decide to accept or reject the conclusions of this book.
3. Pray and ask God to make the truth plain to you and have the courage to embrace whatever the truth may be.

I would now like to address those that are reading this book for less than honest motives. There are a number of Federal Vision, New Perspectives on Paul, and preterists out there that debate and write so as to gain acceptance and to be given a seat at the orthodox table, so to speak. They know they will never be allowed to sit with the adults, so they are hoping for a seat at the kiddy table. Well, we are not interested in being *allowed* to sit at the kiddy table. We are going to sit at the picnic table and enjoy the freedom of the outdoors. All are welcome to join us.

Protestant Christianity does not have a Pope or any ruling body that determines orthodoxy. Christians are only required to believe what the Bible teaches, not what other Christians determine they can or cannot believe the Bible teaches. Now, some may say that this is proof that we are creating an entirely different Christianity, but we are not concerned with what they think we are doing. We are in search of truth, and that is all.

Finally, I would like to say that this book is just the first step. Jesus said, "If you abide in my word, you are truly my disciples, and you will know the truth, and the truth will set you free"…"So if the Son sets you free, you will be free indeed." I have never been as free as I am now. The truth that I am fully glorified, living in the completion of the New Covenant, has freed me beyond anything I thought possible. After I first learned the truth of full preterism, I struggled with the practicality of it, but I later realized that I was still looking for practicality in an Old Covenant framework. I will not lie: Initially, it was a tremendous challenge; but now it has become a great joy! Alan and I hope to share that process with you in our next book, *Living Our Lives With New Covenant Eyes.*

Until then, be of the Truth!

J. Jeremiah Thompson
Berkeley Springs, West Virginia
August, 2009

Appendix A:

DEMONSTRATING THE REQUIRED SENSIBILITY OF THE PRE-70 AD DATING OF THE SCRIPTURES

DIFFICULT TEXTS IN CONTEXT

Below are proposed interpretations of some passages that provide difficulty when the New Testament books are given a late date of composition. The intention here is to demonstrate that when the New Testament Scriptures are recognized as having an early date of composition, they make complete sense.

Hebrews 6

[4]For in the case of those who have once been enlightened and have tasted of the heavenly gift and have been made partakers of the Holy Spirit, [5]and have tasted the good word of God and the powers of the age to come, [6]and then *have fallen away, it is impossible to renew them again to repentance*, since they again crucify to themselves the Son of God and put Him to open shame.[142]

While teaching this text, many professors and pastors have given examples of people they know that have "fallen away." But when the question is posed to them, "Can that person you just described ever repent?", the answer is returned something like this: "Well, we can't know for sure, we have to leave that to God." But the problem is that this text tells us that these particular people cannot be renewed to repentance. So you cannot give examples of people like this followed with the words, "We have to leave that to God." If the example given fits the first part (i.e. have fallen away), then it has to fit the second part (i.e. impossible to renew them again to repentance).

This text, like other similar passages, has particular people within a particular setting in mind. There is a way to know who these people were. They can be defined very specifically without retreating to "leaving that to God." To put it simply, these were Jews who had the promise of the coming Messiah handed down to them from generation to generation, and had participated in God's dealings with Israel all of their lives. They were a special people to whom God chose to bestow His blessings. When the clear fulfillment of God's promise of the coming Messiah had arrived, dying and resurrecting, they rejected Christ and returned to the Old Covenant sacrificial system, thus "they again crucify to themselves the Son of God and put Him to open shame." Of course it was impossible to renew them again to repentance. They participated in all the baptisms of repentance, circumcision, Passover…and they still fell away. These are particular people in a particular time.

The following passages have the same type of explanation. They all become a lot easier to understand with a pre-70 AD dating. Consider the following:

2 Peter 2:1-9

¹But false prophets also arose among the people, just as there will also be false teachers among you, who will secretly introduce destructive heresies, even denying the Master who bought them, bringing swift destruction upon themselves. ²Many will follow their sensuality, and because of them the way of the truth will be maligned; ³and in their greed they will exploit you with false words; their judgment from long ago is not idle, and their destruction is not asleep. ⁴For if God did not spare angels when they sinned, but cast them into hell and committed them to pits of darkness, reserved

for judgment; [5]and did not spare the ancient world, but preserved Noah, a preacher of righteousness, with seven others, when He brought a flood upon the world of the ungodly; [6]and if He condemned the cities of Sodom and Gomorrah to destruction by reducing them to ashes, having made them an example to those who would live ungodly lives thereafter; [7]and if He rescued righteous Lot, oppressed by the sensual conduct of unprincipled men [8](for by what he saw and heard that righteous man, while living among them, felt his righteous soul tormented day after day by their lawless deeds), [9]then the Lord knows how to rescue the godly from temptation, and to keep the unrighteous under punishment for the day of judgment.

These false teachers are compared with the false prophets of Israel. The focus of what these false prophets and teachers did according to Peter was to *secretly* introduce destructive heresies (v. 1). First of all, in verse 3, Peter states, "By covetousness they will exploit you with *deceptive words*." Secondly, in verse 9 we see the sum of Peter's exhortation to the readers that the Lord does indeed know how to rescue the godly from trials. So, these false teachers, driven by their desire for power, sex, and money, said whatever was necessary to manipulate people into following them (cf. vv. 12-14). Thus, a sort of pseudo-comfort was presented to the people that it is better to deny Christ under persecution than to suffer.

These were men who *secretly* introduced these heresies. This, along with the *deceptive words* they used (v. 3), implies intentionality. They know that what they are teaching are heresies, but they teach them anyway. Thus, the reason these particular men are bringing swift destruction upon themselves has everything to do with the intentionality of introducing destructive heresies.

Of course, there is nothing said so far about these false teachers that some churches today do not see. So why does 2 Peter require a pre-70 AD dating? The key here is at the end of verse 1: "…bringing upon themselves swift destruction." This "swift destruction" should be compared to the destructions of the wicked in the three examples provided in verses 4-8: The angels were cast into hell, the ungodly in the ancient land during Noah's time were destroyed with a flood, and the ungodly in Sodom and Gomorrah were turned to ashes and condemned to extinction. These "swift destructions" were directly related to the particular trials that these ungodly people brought upon Noah and Lot.[143] And these swift destructions placed the ungodly under punishment until the Day of Judgment (v. 9).

The Day of Judgment coincides with the swift destruction of these false teachers because their swift destruction comes by means of that final judgment. But all of the examples given illustrate the same swift destruction. So the "swift destruction" and "the Day of Judgment" are not synonymous, it's just that the swift destruction that comes upon these false teachers is brought about by means of that Day of Judgment.

Verse 9 tells us that the Day of Judgment would come upon *all* those who were "held under punishment," which must include these false teachers. Those from the illustrations given were held under punishment in hell until the final judgment. What about the false teachers? Notice that each of these swift destructions were by no means small, or individualistic. They were huge destructions that affected large numbers of people and angels. It is not remotely like saying, "Pastor Bob and Pastor Dan and their families are false teachers that are bringing upon themselves swift destruction." The false teachers that Peter was talking about are connected to a larger sect of ungodly people than just a couple of teachers within a particular church.

Therefore, we should recognize the contextual argument of Peter and similarly understand that the swift destruction of these particular false teachers was directly related to the Judaizers (2 Pet. 2:14, "Accursed *children*", i.e. Old Covenant Jews) who were assisting in the persecution of Christianity under Nero by causing trouble amongst those who embraced the New Covenant. In essence, they were playing both sides of the fence: faithful to the Beast (Revelation 17; Israel is the woman riding the beast) and profiting from personal gain within the church. God made sure that they were kept from ever repenting, but continuing in their wickedness as punishment for indulging in the lust of defiling passion and despising authority (cf. Rom. 1). And sure enough, their swift destruction came with the Destruction of Jerusalem. Being Jews, they denied the Master who bought Israel by means of the remnant, and it was impossible to renew them again to repentance (cf. Heb. 6).[144]

1 John 5:16-17

[16]If anyone sees his brother committing a sin not leading to death, he shall ask and God will for him give life to those who commit sin not leading to death. There is a sin leading to death; I do not say that he should make request for this. [17]All unrighteousness is sin, and there is a sin not leading to death.

John tells us here that if anyone commits the sin leading to death, you should not pray for that. Of course, some argue that John is talking about biological death, and so you shouldn't pray for the biologically dead. While that is theologically correct, it is not what John is writing about.

John speaks two times very specifically about those who do not abide in Christ and love the brethren, but love the world instead: 2:18-23—They are antichrists who deny that Jesus is the Son of God; 4:1-6—They follow the spirit of the antichrist by denying that Jesus came in the flesh. In both of these places, John is talking about the heresy introduced by Cerinthus, namely, that "'the Christ' was thought to have come on Jesus at His baptism and to have departed at the cross."[145]

Because John writes in a literary style called "recapitulation"[146], our text (5:16-17) is about this same heresy. Following the spirit of the antichrist and denying that Jesus is the Son of God who came in the flesh is the sin that leads to death. John has already told his audience in 2:19, "They went out from us, but they were not really of us; for if they had been of us, they would have remained with us; but they went out, so that it would be shown that they all are not of us." The reason John says not to pray for the sin that leads to death is because these people were to suffer the same judgment as those of Hebrews 6 and 2 Peter 2. They rejected Christ to be the Son of God, following in the spirit of Cerinthus, the antichrist, which was "in the world already" verifying to them that it was "the last hour."

DATING OF REVELATION

The Book of Revelation also makes the most sense with a pre-70 AD date of composition. This next section is devoted to the dating of when Revelation was written. For a far more detailed analysis, read, *Before Jerusalem Fell: Dating the Book of Revelation,* by Kenneth Gentry. For those interested in further study of Revelation, consider reading the following books for a better understanding of the imagery within Revelation: *He Shall Have Dominion* by Kenneth Gentry; *He Shall Reign* by R. Dennis Campbell.[147]

The question about the date of the writing of Revelation has produced works defending both early (60's) and late (90's) dates. With great scholars on both sides of the issue, is it possible to determine when it was actually written? Kenneth Gentry has produced several extensive works regarding the dating of Revelation with no equal rival. The magnitude of reasons for an early date given by Gentry has even been the subject of an entire volume,[148] which no one has contended with the same degree of care and detail.[149] This is due to the fact that the arguments for a late date are few and weak at best. In fact, the majority of arguments that late-date advocates use to promote a late date are not actually strong arguments that verify a late date, but weak arguments against an early date. The bottom line is that a late date is maintained not because of the vast evidence in favor of it, but because if an early date for Revelation is correct, then Revelation stands to support preterism.

Some proponents of the late date bring into question the character of the preterists (both full and partial), arguing that we are working backwards from a predisposed eschatology, thus imposing upon Revelation an early date. For example, Robert Thomas states concerning Gentry, "*Predisposition* keeps him from seeing the book's theme verse as a reference to Christ's second coming" (italics mine).[150] However, due to the nature of the literary genre of Revelation, the preterist retains the burden of proof to find accurate evidence for its prophetic fulfillment in history. This is a far more difficult task than claiming that the literal events have not yet come to pass or claiming that these events are allegorically repeated events throughout history. There are no consequences facing the Premillennarian or the Amillennarian views that can be meted out until the proposed future Second Coming of Christ. On the other hand, the preterist must accurately portray a historical fulfillment for each and every event that he claims has been fulfilled in 70 AD. Thus, it is far more compelling to believe that preterism is a posteriori[151] to the dating of Revelation rather than a predisposition. So what must be said to convince the reader of an early date? Or better, what more could be said than has already been said by Gentry to convince the critics of an early date?

With the exceptional works produced by Gentry (and others), why add to an already conclusive set of works? For those who would most likely not read an entire volume consisting of the single subject matter of dating, this chapter will contain a brief synopsis of the arguments for an early date, perhaps some fresh arguments, and interaction with the critiques of the arguments.

An Agreeable Axiom

We begin with the following supposition: Proponents of a late date agree that an early date for Revelation is at least a possibility. George Eldon Ladd remarks, "There must be an element of truth in [the preterist] approach, for surely the Revelation was intended to speak to its own generation."[152] While Ladd critiques the preterist interpretation of Revelation, by concurring that it contains "an element of truth", he infers that Revelation was written before 70 AD, or at the very least, his statement infers that an early date is a possibility. Enough evidence has been brought to the table so as to eliminate the *impossibility* of an early date. No one could be foolish enough to deny this simple axiom. Because the interpretation of Revelation very much hinges on when it was written, it is important that the early date not only be shown to be possible, but also shown to be accurate. Then again, Mark Hitchcock believes the following:

The preterist dependence on the early date for Revelation is aptly stated by Winters. "When the interpretation depends upon the date, the interpretation can never be more certain than the date itself—if the date is wrong, then, of necessity the interpretation is wrong. The whole business of making the interpretation depend upon the date is therefore built upon a sandy foundation....But if the late date is correct, the whole approach that assigns Revelation as a prophecy fulfilled in the destruction of Jerusalem is false and must be totally rejected." The entire preterist system therefore rises or falls on the early date of Revelation.[153]

Obviously! This statement affirms nothing more than the fact that in order for prophecy to be prophecy, it has to be fulfilled after the date it was stated. We might as well say that building an interpretation from the prophecies in Isaiah cannot be based on the surety that Isaiah was written before the prophecies were fulfilled. Therefore, understanding Isaiah to be prophesying about Christ is building our interpretation upon a sandy foundation. This is among the most ridiculous forms of circular reasoning. Since an early date for Revelation is obviously required for preterism to stand, an early date will be demonstrated below.

Time References

Of particular importance for the dating of Revelation is the time references contained within the book itself. Consider the following examples: 1:1, "...the things that must *soon* take place"; 1:3, "...for the time is *near*"; 22:6, "...what must *soon* take place"; 22:7, "...I am coming *soon*", 22:10, "...for the time is *near*"; 22:12, "...I am coming *soon*"; 22:20, "Surely I am coming *soon*" (all italics mine). Jesus seems to be communicating an urgent message, repeating over and over, especially in the closing section of the book, that the fulfillment of the prophecies contained in Revelation were impending at the time of the writing. Much resistance is given to the preterist understanding of these time references. A glimpse of this resistance can be seen by Mark Hitchcock as he attempts to prove a futurist understanding of these time references. "The noun tachos and the adverb tachu occur eight times in the Apocalypse...Both refer to 'a very brief period of time, with focus on speed of an activity or event, speed, quickness, swiftness, haste.'" The point he goes on to make is that these words speak not of an impending nature, but of a speedy nature. So, according to Hitchcock, Jesus is very concerned to make sure that the readers of this letter are aware that when the prophecies of the book are fulfilled, they are going to be fulfilled very quickly. The nature of this argument is incorrect because the particular words that John uses are the only Greek words available to communicate the concept he wished to communicate. On the other hand, the Greek words that John used here actually communicate very clearly about impending fulfillment. Consider the remarks of noted Greek Scholar and church historian, Kurt Aland, regarding the word "tachu" (soon):

> In the original text, the Greek word used is tachu, and this does not mean "soon," in the sense of "sometime," but rather "now," "immediately." Therefore, we must understand Rev. 22:12 in this way: "I am coming now, bringing my recompense." The concluding word of Rev. 22:20 is: "He who testifies to these things says, 'surely I am coming soon.'" Here we again find the word tachu, so this means: I am coming quickly, immediately. This is followed by the prayer: "Amen. Come, Lord Jesus!" ... The Apocalypse expresses the fervent waiting for the end within the circles in which the writer lived – not an expectation that will happen at some unknown point X in time (just to repeat this), but one in the immediate present.[154]

Hitchcock summarizes Gentry's explanation that "the temporal expectation of the author seems to demand a preterist approach to Revelation."[155] He then critiques Gentry in the following way:

There are two problems with this understanding of tachos and engus in Revelation. First, these timing statements are strategically located to frame the entire content of Revelation. Both tachos and engus occur at the very beginning of Revelation and again at the very end, as seen in this table.[156]

Beginning of Revelation	End of Revelation
(The introduction, 1:1-8)	(The Conclusion, 22:6-21)
en tachei, 1:1	22:6 (en tachei), 22:7, 12, 20 (tachu)
engus, 1:3	engus, 22:10

Using this view of strategic framing, Hitchcock digs himself a hole. Follow carefully his next critique of Gentry:

> ...[Gentry] attempts to establish a soon beginning to the eschatological events in Revelation. But one cannot establish a beginning of all the events in Revelation within a few years of its writing. For instance in what sense did the final release of Satan (20:7-9) and the final judgment (vv. 11-15) begin soon after Revelation was composed? They did not. They are removed from A.D. 95 by almost two thousand years.[157]

By the same token, if these time references speak of a "speedy" fulfillment as opposed to an impending fulfillment, then in what sense does Hitchcock's rendering of the thousand-year reign happen speedily? It does not. So much for the framing theory. With or without the framing theory, in agreement with Hitchcock's rendering of the time references are William Mounce and George Eldon Ladd.

But when all is said and done, one key element keeps slipping through the cracks in this whole debate over the time references. That element happens to be the consideration of who the recipients of the letter were. Why would John write a letter to the churches about judgment and tribulation and the impending or speedy nature of those prophecies if the prophecies weren't intended for them directly? To this the Amillennarian answers that these time references do refer to the immediate recipients of the letter...as well as to every generation after.

In regards to the time references in Revelation, Simon Kistemaker, an Amillennarian, spends his time explaining the differences between the Greek words chronos and kairos. Both of these words are rendered "time" in English. Chronos refers to a duration of time: You are reading this book at this chronos. Kairos refers to an appointed time or season: Lord willing, tomorrow you will wake up at the kairos that you set your alarm clock.

Kistemaker believes that kairos, the word used in Revelation 1:3, should be understood to mean, "The time is near to make a decision." This is based on the understanding that the word kairos signifies an opportune time or a time of decision. But all of this becomes moot because the problem with this understanding of Revelation 1:3 is not with the word "time" but with the word "near." John is referring to the things of this prophecy that must "soon take place" (1:1). Supposing John meant, "The time is near to make a decision," the decision would still be in regards to the things that must soon take place. In addition, in 1:3, John includes the definite article with "time" so as to indicate a particular time, *the* time, not many times over and over again. *The* time for the prophecies in this book to be fulfilled "is near," and these things "must soon take place."

Arguing experientially, J Barton Payne "rejects the preterist limiting of 'the range of the book's applicability to the 1ˢᵗ Christian century.' He argues that 'this is a position, which, when held with consistency, denies all modern relevance to John's predictions.'"[158] What Payne and others who share his sentiment fail to realize is that any other position, when held with consistency, denies all contemporary relevance for the recipients of the letter.

Irenaeus

Irenaeus' (A.D. 130-202) renowned statement that has fueled this debate over the dating of Revelation is generally translated into English from the original Greek as follows:

> We will not, however, incur the risk of pronouncing positively as to the name of Antichrist; for if it were necessary that his name should be distinctly revealed in this present time, it would have been announced by him who beheld the apocalyptic vision. For that was seen no very long time since, but almost in our day, towards the end of Domitian's reign.[159]

The particular portion of interest from this statement revolves around the last sentence, "For that was seen..." Was Irenaeus referring to John or to the vision? While a strong case can be made for the referent being John,[160] the discrepancy in Irenaeus' statement makes this no place to build a fortress on one way or the other. While Gentry and many others show extremely valid and compelling reasons why this statement should be taken as referring to John and not the vision, who could possibly know exactly what Irenaeus meant? The late-date advocates not only attempt to make a case against an early date using this statement, but actually use it as one of their strongest arguments. What needs to be provided is better evidence than a statement that is not clear enough to determine what was originally meant. Way too much time and writing has been spent (from proponents of both positions) trying to prove what Irenaeus meant. Does the dating of Revelation really rest or fall on the words of a second century church father? If so, we're in a lot of trouble.

A Jewish Book

A stronger line of reasoning has to do with the elements consisting of the Temple in Revelation, the strong presence of Jewish Christianity, and the Hebrew flavor of the grammar. All three of these elements point to a Jewish focus. Corresponding to these, why is John measuring a Temple that is still standing if he wrote it after 70 AD? While many would argue that this is a future Temple, it seems that this would be a bit confusing without the mention of the fallen Temple, or the rebuilding of a new Temple first. Secondly, "The book of Revelation gives evidence that it was written during a time when there remained a strong Jewish, and even Judaizing, element in the church (2:9; 3:9; 7:4-8; 14:1; 21:12). The Jewish influence and threat dwindled rapidly after A.D. 70, and was hardly a factor in the late first century."[161] Thirdly, as Gentry has noted, "although John wrote in Greek, Revelation has long been recognized as one of the more 'Jewish' books of the New Testament."[162] Going on, Gentry quotes from a couple of notable sources:

> In Charles's introduction to Revelation, he included a major section entitled "A Short Grammar of the Apocalypse." Section 10 of this "Grammar" is entitled "The Hebraic Style of the Apocalypse." There Charles well notes that "*while [John] writes in Greek, he thinks in Hebrew.*" As Sweet puts it: "The probability is that the writer, thinking in Hebrew or Aramaic, consciously or unconsciously carried over semitic idioms into his Greek, and that his 'howlers' are deliberate attempts to reproduce the grammar of classical Hebrew at certain points."[163]

Why would Revelation contain such a strong Jewish focus if Jerusalem had already been destroyed?

The Beast of Revelation

Probably the greatest complaint against the preterist dating of Revelation revolves around the famous 666. Revelation 13:18 reads, "This calls for wisdom: let the one who has understanding calculate the number of the beast, for it is the number of a man, and his number is 666." The preterist claim is that the man, the beast, is Nero. The Hebrew rendering of Nero's name is Nrwn Qsr (pronounced Neron Kaiser). Each of the Hebrew letters contains a numeric value to them. Here are values for Nrwn Qsr: N = 50; r = 200; w = 6; n = 50; Q = 100; s = 60; r = 200; total = 666. One fascinating aspect of this cryptogram is that a textual variant in Rev. 13:18 reads 616 rather than 666.[164] Textual analysts ask if this variation was the result of a copyist's error or an intentional change to accommodate readers outside the scope of Revelation's initial Hebrew audience. The highly respected textual scholar Bruce M. Metzger says: "Perhaps the change was intentional, seeing that the Greek form Neron Caesar written in Hebrew characters (nrwn qsr) is equivalent to 666, whereas the Latin form Nero Caesar (nrw qsr) is equivalent to 616."[165]

One of the critiques to understanding 666 as the number of Nero is that it could also fit the names of other men throughout history. John Walvoord explains, "In attempting to solve the riddle of this verse, some have considered the phrase to represent Caesar, others Nero or Caligula."[166] Others believe that this will be the number of a man yet to come. The view held by Walvoord is that the number six in Scripture represents man qualitatively.[167] Still others, such as Simon Kistemaker, hold the view that the number six in Revelation represents falling short of perfection, whereby the beast, controlled by Satan, falls *really* short of perfection.[168]

The fact of the matter is that the number of the beast does not refer to Nero simply because he's the only possibility that fits that number. Nor does this provide any conclusive stronghold for the preterist position. Similar to other highly debated issues, this cannot be used as proof for the dating of Revelation one way or the other. However, the fact that Nero does indeed fit the number 666 supports an early date very nicely. And if Nero fits the bill, why continue to look for another fulfillment? But Kistemaker does not believe that Nero fits the bill. So let's examine his three critiques. He begins with the "problem" of the mortal blow:

> If we should understand the number 666 to refer cryptically to Nero, we have to ask why John writes openly

about the "seven hills" (17:9); Roman writers commonly used this expression to designate Rome. And if we say 666 equals Nero as the beast, then the context presents difficulties. First, one of the beast's heads had received a mortal blow administered by someone else (13:3), but Nero committed suicide, while the beast continues to live.[169]

First, if Roman writers commonly used the expression, "seven hills," to designate Rome, then why would one argue backwards and say, "John wouldn't refer to Nero cryptically because he doesn't refer to Rome cryptically?" It would make more sense to say that John is revealing something about who the beast is by giving a clear point of reference to Rome.

Second, if John were to speak the name of the beast without using symbolism, we would expect that he would also speak the name of Rome without using symbolism. But the fact of the matter is, he chooses to use the symbolism of Rome, and by that, produce for us a clear understanding of who the beast was by consistent symbolism.

Putting these two thoughts together, both the reference to Rome and the reference to Nero are symbolic. But one is cryptic, and one is not. The one that is not helps the readers to understand the one that is.

Kistemaker further argues that the Hebrew spelling, Neron, is unconvincing because it adds to the Greek spelling. But if John is warning Jews of impending judgment, would they not have spelled Nero's name with the Hebrew spelling?

Also, where does Revelation 13:3 indicate that the mortal blow was administered by someone else? What it actually says is that John saw one of the beast's heads *as if* it had been slain. The word hôs is the Greek word used here to tell us what this death appeared to look like. This word is used to produce a metaphor. It means "as or like." We see this same use of metaphors many times throughout the Scriptures. One such example is in Revelation 1:17: "When I saw Him, I fell at His feet as [hôs] a dead one." John was no more dead than was Nero slaughtered by someone else. John fell at the feet of Jesus like someone who is dead falls down. Nero was dead, but the wound that this brought to Rome looked like Rome was slaughtered. The emphasis isn't on who did the slaughtering, but rather on the fact that Rome looked completed defeated. Remove the head and the kingdom collapses.

So, John did not say that one of the beast's heads had received a mortal blow administered by someone else. He said that it was as if, or like, one of the heads had been slain. This fits best with the imagery of Revelation. The death of the beast's head was so devastating that it is described to appear like it had been "slaughtered to death" (lit.). Thus, it was amazing that the beast could come back from this devastation. Since the beast is Rome here, when Nero (who is also called the beast because Rome followed his dictatorship) suddenly died during the time that Vespatian, the next successor, was surrounding Jerusalem, it was indeed amazing that Rome was able to come back from this. John tells us that one of the beast's seven heads appeared to have been slain, but its (the beast's) mortal wound was healed. John did not say that the beast's head was healed, but that the beast itself was healed, "and the whole earth marveled as they followed the beast."

As Kistemaker goes into his second argument against Nero, he actually supports the interpretation above even though he attempts to give a different one. Consider how he moves from his first to his second argument:

> ...but Nero committed suicide, while the beast continues to live. Next, the fatal wound that had healed symbolizes a return to life. This clearly is Satan's parody of seeking to imitate Christ's resurrection.[170]

Kistemaker is saying the exact same thing that is argued above except he has a different conclusion. His statement concerning the beast continuing to live, symbolizing a return to life, stands to argue for the present author's conclusion. So this argument is moot.

Kistemaker's third argument accomplishes nothing for his position. In fact, he even argues well for the symbolic nature of the mark of the beast. Of course, due to his Amillennial theology, he makes the presupposition that the contrast is between Satan and Christ and leaves no room for the fact that "the dragon gave his power and his throne" to the beast (Rev. 13:2) which in turn causes the whole land to worship the dragon, "for he had given his authority to the beast" (v. 4). Would this not also constitute a contrast between Satan and Christ? As already stated, this third argument accomplishes nothing in support of a late date. Another moot point.

Thus far, the bill stands unscathed. So we'll move on to another approach that attempts to disprove the Neronic fulfillment.

The "Qualitative Man" View

Daniel Wallace argues in support of the "qualitative man" view. He states the following:

> If anthrôpou is generic, then the sense is, "It is [the] number of **humankind**." It is significant that this construction fits Apollonius' Canon (i.e., both the head noun and the genitive are anarthrous), suggesting that if one of these nouns is definite, then the other is, too. Grammatically, those who contend that the sense is "it is [the] number of a man" have the burden of proof on them (for they treat the head noun, arithmos, as definite and the genitive, anthrôpou, as indefinite – the rarest of all possibilities)…The implications of this grammatical possibility, exegetically speaking, are simply that the number "666" is the number that represents humankind.[171]

Now pay attention to his next statement: "Of course, an individual is in view, but his number may be the number representing all of humankind…" It seems as though Wallace wants it both ways. Perhaps a burden of proof is unnecessary if Apollonius' Canon is used to understand both the noun and the genitive to be definite. This clearly fits the grammar of the sentence and tells us that the number of *the* beast is the number of *the* man. This is not just any man. Nor is it mankind generically. It is the only man whom John has described as the beast. Adela Yarbro Collins writes: "First of all, the use of the word *psephizein* [*calculate*] is an indication that the number involves the process of gematria, i.e., adding the numerical value of the letters of a word. Secondly, the most natural way to understand *arithmos gar anthropou estin* [*for the number is that of a man*] (13:18) is that the number relates to the name of *some human individual*" (italics mine).[172]

This human individual is none other than the sixth king, "who now is" (Rev. 17:10) at the time of the writing of Revelation, namely, Nero. "By no calculation can the sixth king possibly refer to Emperor Domitian (81-96 AD),"[173] which is the time-frame usually given for the late date of Revelation. Here is the line of Roman emperors by a calculation that makes sense: 1. Julius Caesar (49-44 B.C.); 2. Augustus (27 B.C.-A.D. 14); 3. Tiberius (14-37); 4. Gaius (37-41); 5. Claudius (41-54); 6. Nero (54-68); 7. Galba (68-69); 8. Otho (69); 9. Vitellius (69); 10. Vespasian (69-79). Notice that Nero is the sixth king. And the seventh king "has not yet come; and when he comes, he must remain a *little* while" (italics mine). Galba's reign only lasted a year. Another coincidence? If so, we have a pile of coincidences that are getting very difficult to climb.

Patristic[174] Evidence

One of the other critiques of the Neronic theory is that, presumably, four German scholars proposed the name Nero Caesar as the man whose number is 666 for the first time in 1830.[175] Thus, if this critique was true, this theory is maintained without the support of any of the church fathers. Consider the following information from Francis X. Gumberlock's closing argument in his essay, *Nero Antichrist: Patristic Evidence for the Use of Nero's Naming in Calculating the Number of the Beast (Rev. 13:18)*:

> Present scholarship depicts the Nero theory of the number of the beast as having first arisen in Christian history among German scholars in the 1830's. The *Liber genealogus* [*or Book of Genealogy*, a fifth-century chronicle from North African

Christianity] attests that the name of Nero was being used by early Christians in their calculation of the number of the beast, which was 616 in their version of Rev. 13:18. This fifth-century African text, therefore, pushes back the date of the Nero identification some fourteen hundred years. Based on a statement in Irenaeus's *Against Heresies* about a "name…of him who is to come" that some Christians were using to arrive at the spurious number 616 instead of 666, it is very likely that Irenaeus in the second century knew of the Nero identification. This allusion in Irenaeus, along with the Nero theory contained in an unknown source from which the *Liber* quotes, may bring the date of this idea even closer to the time of the writing of the Book of Revelation. Therefore, against critics who regard the Nero identification as a novelty not to be found in the early church, the *Liber genealogus* shows that it did in fact exist in the earliest centuries of Christian history.[176]

Conclusion to the Dating of Revelation

The vast majority of evidence shows that Revelation was written before 70 AD, probably 65 or 66. Criticisms against the arguments for an early date fall short of amounting to anything of significance. These criticisms provide insufficient grounds for maintaining a late date because the late-date view of Revelation has no solid evidence in its favor. Because it is generally agreed upon that an early date is not impossible, whereas a late date is (if one is to remain honest and faithful to the meaning of words in the text), then the early date is the only valid starting point to build an interpretive foundation on. This is by no means a sandy foundation, but a foundation of solid rock evidence.

DATING OF OTHER BOOKS

John

The Gospel of John is frequently given a late date (i.e. sometime after 70 AD). Most every other book in the New Testament has significant support for an early date, even if scholars do not agree. We are not here looking for complete agreement, but rather, enough evidence to support that a pre-70 AD dating of all the books of the New Testament can be substantiated. Why this approach? Because as it is demonstrated in Part II of this book, the evidence of fulfillment of all of the prophecies in New Testament is found in the destruction of Jerusalem in 70 AD. In other words, the internal teaching of the New Testament Scriptures demands a fulfillment within one generation of their being written. No other event in history can fulfill these prophecies. Thus, the argument stands that if all of the New Testament books *can* have a pre-70 AD dating, then they *were* written before 70 AD. All that is required here is the possibility, for the possibility then demands certainty. Daniel Wallace, in his book, *Greek Grammar Beyond the Basics*, demonstrates that possibility, and therefore, certainty for us in the book of John using John 5:2:

> The text reads **estin** de en tois Ierosulumois ... kolumbethra ("Now there *is* in Jerusalem ... a pool"). Since eimi is nowhere else clearly used as a historical present, the present tense should be taken as indicating present time from the viewpoint of the speaker. The implication of this seems to be that this Gospel was written before the destruction of Jerusalem in 70 CE. Although many object to a pre-70 date for John's Gospel, they must, in support of their view, reckon with this text.

In a footnote, Wallace states the following:

> By arguing that estin is a stative present, we are admittedly going against the tide of NT scholarship. Generally, NT

scholars have attempted to circumvent the *prima facie* force of estin by adopting one of five approaches in this text: (1) estin is a historical present ...; (2) estin is an anomalous present ...; (3) the author erred, not knowing that the pool had been destroyed ...; (4) the pool of Bethesda must have survived the Jewish War ...; (5) the redactional view: John 5:2 belonged to an earlier stratum of the Gospel, only to go uncorrected in the final publication... Each of these views has severe problems. See Wallace, "John 5:2," 177-205.[178]

Charles Hill, Professor of New Testament at Reformed Theological Seminary, argues against Wallace as follows:

> ... I would take exception to the conclusion Wallace draws on 531 on the date of John's Gospel based on his use of estin in John 5:2, "Now there *is* in Jerusalem ... a pool". Wallace says, "Since the equative verb is nowhere else clearly used as a historical present, the present tense should be taken as indicating present time from the viewpoint of the speaker". Even if this is true, it may be no more than a phenomenological observation. Is there some reason why one could not or would not use an equative verb as a historical present? Eusebius, *HE* 2.23.18 relates that James' gravestone was still by the temple in Hegesippus' day, sometime in the second century. Thus, a) some things did survive the destruction in a.d. 70 and b) writers sometimes continue to speak of structures as if still there (here the temple) even long after they were destroyed.[179]

Hill's argument does nothing more than provide the possibility that Wallace is wrong, thereby implicitly admitting the possibility that Wallace is right. In the case with Scriptural dating, possibility produces certainty in favor of pre-70 AD dating. There is, however, further internal support to verify an early dating of John. Consider John 2:18-22. Jesus is discussing the destruction of His body as a sign to justify what

He had just done in the Temple. Jesus uses the language of the Temple as an analogy for His own body. The relationship between the death and resurrection of Christ and the Temple is too close to be missed. In fact, even the Jews that heard Him thought He was talking about the literal Temple. Whatever the case may be regarding their ignorance of Jesus' exact meaning, John decides to include an interlude about the resurrection of Christ here at the beginning of the Gospel to show that this prophecy had come true.

It is odd that nowhere in the Gospel of John does he record the destruction of the literal Temple as a fulfilled event, particularly since an allusion, such as the one found here in our text, would no doubt raise questions, if not produce a reminder of the fall of Jerusalem. This is especially true since this passage takes place in the Temple and since John, in a matter of fact way, with no commentary, states in the next verse, "Now when he was in Jerusalem at the Passover Feast…" It is quite odd that John would bring a statement about the fulfillment of the resurrection into the text here but not a statement about the fulfillment of the destruction of Jerusalem. Indeed, it would make more sense that the Gospel of John was written before 70 AD. The internal evidence of John in support of a pre-70 AD dating should be even more evident when we consider John 14-16, which is dealt with in sub-chapter 4A of this book.

1 John

It was noted earlier that 1 John 2:18 says, "Children, it is the last hour; and just as you heard that antichrist is coming, even now many antichrists have appeared; from this we know that it is the last hour." John states very plainly that it was the last hour and that many antichrists had appeared at the time of his writing. According to John, it was the last hour. Jesus said that antichrists would appear in the first century, prior to the destruction of Jerusalem (Luke 21:8, 20). At the time that John wrote 1 John, he states that the antichrists, which Christ prophesied would come before the destruction of Jerusalem, had appeared. In addition, according to John, it was the last hour. If 1 John was written after the destruction of Jerusalem, what event was about to occur after the "last hour" was complete? Jesus links antichrists with the destruction of Jerusalem and states that they would arrive on the scene *before* Jerusalem would be surrounded by armies.

The only way to substantiate a date for 1 John after 70 AD is if one can demonstrate that John is talking about different antichrists than Jesus was. And if that can be demonstrated, then one must further explain what "last hour" John was talking about. All things considered, what grounds would anyone have to state that John is not teaching about the same things Jesus was? If John is recording the fulfillment of Christ's prophecy, then the event that followed the "last hour" was the destruction of Jerusalem, for that is what Jesus prophesied would come following the appearing of the antichrists. First John not only has the possibility of a pre-70 AD dating from the internal evidence, but the probability, and therefore, the certainty. Finally, if 1 John was written after the Gospel of John, which is generally agreed upon, then this further solidifies that the Gospel of John was written before 70 AD.

SUMMARY

The fact that the New Testament Scriptures contain impending time texts requires a fulfillment of the prophecies attached to those time texts within one generation of their being written. The destruction of Jerusalem in 70 AD is the only event in history that could fulfill the prophecies of the New Testament. Therefore, if the books of the New Testament have the possibility of a pre-70 AD dating, then it produces certainty of that fact, for no other event after 70 AD could possibly have fulfilled the prophecies within the time frames given. The internal evidence of the highly debated books has been evaluated and produces this certainty. There is no reason to continue to cling to a post-70 AD dating for any of the books of the New Testament.

Appendix B:

INTELLECTUAL DISHONESTY

A final word must be said here regarding the intellectual dishonesty put forth in, *When Shall These Things Be? A Reformed Response to Hyper-Preterism.*[180] It is heartbreaking to see the level at which the futurists are willing to descend in order to protect the doctrine of the future (to us) second coming of Christ. For starters, the book uses the derogatory term of hyper-preterism when it does not apply. At least two of the contributors would call themselves partial-preterists in order to distinguish themselves from full preterists. But if they are partial preterists, then why must the full preterists be called hyper-preterists? If there are degrees of preterism, then certainly, there must be at least one degree between partial and hyper.

This is the same sort of thing that has occurred with Calvinism. Partial Calvinists, who hold to some of the five points of Calvinism, often refer to five-point Calvinists as hyper Calvinists. The degree between partial Calvinism and hyper Calvinism is skipped altogether. This is usually due to a misunderstanding of what five-point Calvinists believe. It is often thought that no five-point Calvinists believe that evangelism is necessary. Thus, they are called hyper Calvinists. Perhaps the term hyper Calvinist is necessary to distinguish between Calvinists who believe evangelism is necessary and Calvinists who don't. But just because a Calvinist holds to the five points of Calvinism does not make that person a hyper Calvinist. This is a term intentionally used to be derogatory towards Calvinism in order to make it appear extreme and outside the teaching of Scripture.

The same is being done with full preterism. Anyone that goes beyond partial preterism to full preterism is thought of to be a hyper-preterist. It isn't exactly clear what the motivation is behind this, but it could be a couple of things. The first possibility is that non full preterists do not actually understand what full preterists believe. This is clear form the series of "other questions" that Mathison asks in his book, *Postmillennialism: An Eschatology of Hope*. The large majority of his questions do not need answers because they aren't asking questions that are accurately directed at what full preterists actually believe. In fact, only one of his questions is worthy of an answer, and it is dealt with in chapter 5 of this book. However, lest full preterists be accused of simply dismissing his questions, let's take a look at the rest of them below.

> Did Christ "shed" his glorified human body and thus cease to be fully man? Or did his human nature cease to be a truly human nature by acquiring the divine attribute of omnipresence?[181]

In these two questions, Mathison requires full preterists to answer according to his required presuppositions. He plants the requirement that Christ had a *glorified* biological body at His ascension. Because Mathison does not seem very interested in actually hearing what full preterists are saying, he requires full preterists to answer his questions using his framework. So he leaves full preterists with only one option: Christ ceased to be fully man. No matter how these questions are answered, according to Mathison, the biological body is part of the nature of man and so he forces full preterists to answer his questions with his presupposition. These questions deserve no answers because full preterists don't begin with his presupposition. It is interesting, however, that Mathison poses a problem for the traditional view with these questions. Glorified or not, Mathison is stating that without the biological body, one ceases to be full man. So what of those who have died and gone to heaven? Are they sub-human, Zombies, aliens, what?

According to Mathison and the traditional view, they cannot logically still be human!

Below is series of questions from Mathison that can only be directed at full preterists who inconsistently believe that individuals today continue to be resurrected at the point of death:

> If Christians receive their resurrection bodies at the point of death, where do those resurrection bodies go? Do Christians go to be with Christ here on earth, or do they go to heaven? Do Christians wander around with Christ in their incorporeal resurrection bodies forever?[182]

Since Mathison remains stuck on his presupposition about biological bodies being resurrected, he causes his reading audience to think that full preterists can't answer these questions and therefore think that full preterism must be wrong. It is true that full preterists who hold to the resurrection view put forth in this book cannot answer the first question because we do not believe that Christians receive resurrection bodies at the point of death. Full preterists who hold to the resurrection view put forth in this book believe that we *are* resurrected bodies even before biological death.

The second question above illustrates this point again. Those who hold to the resurrection view put forth in this book believe that we are presently with Christ here on earth. When we die, we go to heaven. Full preterists explicitly teach that Christians go to heaven when they die.

Finally, Mathison's last question subtly dislodges his readers from the fact that even futurists believe that Christians who have died biologically do not presently have their biological bodies. Yet Mathison believes that they are with Christ. If Christians who have died biologically can "wander around with Christ" apart from their biological bodies for two thousand years and counting, then why can't they do so forever? Of course, it is doubtful that Mathison actually believes that Christians who have died biologically have been simply wandering around with Christ without their biological bodies. He very well knows that living with Christ in Heaven is far more than that. But even he cannot describe what life in Heaven is like because the Scriptures do not give us the details. So when Mathison figures it out, he can inform the rest of us so we can better answer his question.

Mathison then posits a series of questions regarding creedal authority:

> In light of the full-preterist rejection of creedal authority, we must ask whether the creeds contain errors about such doctrines as the trinity and the deity of Christ. If not, then are the creeds without error on these points? Is it not possible for a merely human document to be inerrant as a matter of fact without implying that its authors are incapable of error? Is there not a difference between claiming that someone "did not err" and claiming that he "cannot err"?[183]

Full preterists do not deny the creedal statements regarding the trinity and the deity of Christ. And the answer to all of his subsequent questions is obviously, "yes." Stating that a document has the possibility of being inerrant does not mean that it is. The set of questions here are driven to make his readers think that if one statement in the creeds is considered to be in error, then all of the creed must be thought to be in error. This is an illogical leap.

Following are the next series of questions that Mathison asks:

> If the "perfect" has come and we now see face-to-face rather than in a glass darkly (1 Cor. 13:10, 12), why do we have to grow in our understanding of doctrine? In the full-preterist system, it seems that the transitional period when Christ was away was more doctrinally stable than the present perfect age when Christ is here in fullness. Why did the coming of Christ in 70 lead to such a rapid doctrinal decay and confusion?[184]

Once again, full preterists have continually taught that the parousia of Christ had to do with our relationship with God, not with the expression of perfection on earth. These questions completely miss the teaching of full preterism.

Finally, Mathison asks his last series of questions:

> Pastorally, how does one tell the middle-aged mother of three whose body is riddled with cancer that in the present age there is no longer any death; that there is no longer any mourning, or crying, or pain; that all these things have passed away? How does one tell her little boy, who only wants his mother to come home, that there is no more pain, that God has wiped away every tear?[185]

Here again, full preterists have to answer Mathison's questions within his framework. Apparently, Mathison must believe that Revelation 21-22 has to be literal. But full preterists explain over and over again that the elimination of death, mourning, crying, and pain have nothing to do with our biological life on earth. These things cannot be any more literal of the New Heavens and New Earth than the description of the New Jerusalem coming down out of heaven adorned as a bride for her husband. Does Mathison really believe that there will be a literal bride's veil over the New Jerusalem? Does he believe that Jesus will actually marry a city? Surely, he does not. So why must the effects of what comes with the descent of the New Jerusalem be a literal expression on earth? It is because of his framework, which he attempts to force full preterists to submit to. In doing so, he plays on the emotions of his readers with these questions because they make full preterists look like mean bullies. Although we have answered Mathison, his questions make it apparent that he is not interested in honest debate and discussion.

Lastly, Gentry also critiques "hyper-preterism" in his book, *He Shall Have Dominion*. All of his critiques, which fill a total of six pages, have been dealt with extensively throughout this book, so there is no need to repeat the information in the form of responses here. There is one critique that he makes, however, that is very peculiar and self-defeating that needs to be brought to light. Gentry states the following:

"...hyper-preterism suffers from serious errors in its hermeneutical methodology. When a contextually defined passage applies to the A.D. 70 event, the hyper-preterist will take *all* passages with *similar* language and apply them to A.D. 70, as well. But similarity does not imply identity..."[186]

Now, pay very close attention to the example that Gentry gives to demonstrate his point: "...Christ cleansed the Temple twice and in virtually identical ways; but the two events are not the same."[187] Of course they aren't the same event, because there were two different times that Christ cleansed the Temple. But Gentry admits that both times that Christ cleansed the Temple were virtually identical. Why? Because they are both described using *similar* language. Therefore, Christ did not cleanse the Temple in two different ways, one spiritually, and one physically. Gentry inherently makes the obvious point that because *similar* language is used in both events that, therefore, both events occurred in the same manner.

The problem with Gentry's critique here is that He contradicts himself and concedes with the full preterist that similar language does indeed imply identity. The two events were "virtually identical" events because the similar language used to describe the two events demonstrates identity in the way both events occurred. Saying that two events are identical is not the same as saying that those two events are the same event. In addition, when *one* event is described in various passages using similar language, then the concept of identity can only be used in reference to the passages describing that one event, but not to the event itself, for more than one is necessary to speak of identity.

If Gentry wishes to follow his critique consistently in defense of a future (to us) parousia of Christ, he would have to argue that both comings of Christ (one in 70 AD and one at some time in the future) have to happen in virtually identical ways. Therefore, according to Gentry's reasoning, either both comings of Christ have to be invisible or both comings of Christ have to be visible. He can't have it both ways.

So who is the one actually suffering from serious errors in hermeneutical methodology? It certainly isn't the full preterist. When a contextually defined passage applies to the AD 70 event, full preterists will most definitely take *all* passages with *similar* language and apply them to AD 70 because Scripture only teaches one parousia of Christ.

So every one of Mathison's "other questions" have been dealt with, and Gentry helps demonstrate that full preterists actually have a consistent hermeneutical methodology. Perhaps now, as Mathison has already done in His recent book, *From Age to Age*, the term full preterism will be used instead of hyper-preterism, unless the form of preterism they are arguing against goes beyond the degree of full preterism.

The second possible motivation behind the derogatory term hyper-preterism is that those who use it know full well that this term would automatically turn people against full preterism before they understand what it is. This is far worse than misunderstanding or not listening. This is downright wrong. This sort of thing aims at gaining a sympathetic ear before it is earned.

This derogatory terminology, however, does not even come close to the other form of intellectual dishonesty put forth in *When Shall These Things Be?*[188] As has been already noted, at least two of the contributors are partial preterists. One of them is Keith Mathison and the other is Kenneth Gentry. Mathison is the editor of that volume. He enlists the authorship of ammillennialist, Simon Kistemaker, to make a case for a late date of Revelation and to provide an alternative interpretation of Revelation contrary to any degree of preterism, whether partial or full. Doesn't this seem a bit odd? If Kistemaker is right, and Revelation can be dated after 70 AD, then both Mathison's and Gentry's partial preterism falls along with full preterism. But both Mathison and Gentry believe that Revelation was definitely written before 70 AD. Gentry even wrote a book on the subject called, *Before Jerusalem Fell: Dating the Book of Revelation.* Yet, Mathison and Gentry are evidently content with Kistemaker's conclusion to his chapter:

> If it can be established that John wrote his book five years prior to that fateful date of A.D. 70, then the preterists

have some reason to be optimistic. But as long as the external evidence for a late date calls for serious consideration—for the witness of the early church fathers is strong—this optimism dissipates. And as long as careful exegesis of key passages in the Apocalypse demonstrates the validity of a date around 95—because compelling evidence is often found in the use of key words—the brightness of the preterist view dims. In short, this view needs incontrovertible evidence for an early date of Revelation in order to survive; without this evidence, it becomes tenuous.[189]

Yet, both Mathison and Gentry have contended that there is indeed incontrovertible evidence for an early date of Revelation. Again, this is the whole point of a 409-page work written by Gentry. So why include Kistemaker's chapter in a book against "hyper-preterism?" Could it be that Mathison and Gentry are so opposed to full preterism that they are even willing to sacrifice their own eschatological belief in order to destroy it? Then again, Mathison argues for a partial preterist understanding in his chapter of the same volume as Kistemaker. Could this simply be an oversight? It is highly unlikely, especially since Mathison was the editor. But even if that is the case, the chapters within the volume contradict themselves. On the other hand, if it isn't an oversight, then it is blatant intellectual dishonesty. Whatever the case may be, both Gentry and Mathison would take issue with Kistemaker's late date. And, as Kistemaker has pointed out, if the book was written before 70 AD, "then preterists have some reason to be optimistic."

Appendix C:

FULL PRETERISM IN A NUTSHELL

What is full preterism? This appendix will briefly summarize for the reader the doctrine of full preterism as it is argued for in this book. The way that full preterism will be summarized below is by way of contrast with the traditional view and will only touch on some of the broader points discussed in this book. The reason for this approach has to do with the fact that full preterism is rarely understood by those who oppose it.

Full preterism has a very different framework than the traditional view. The traditional framework has caused people to completely disregard full preterism simply because they can't understand how anybody could believe that Jesus visibly came out of the sky already and took away the world's biological pain, sorrow, and death. The reason this seems so ridiculous to people is because their framework demands a biological return of Jesus to eliminate tears, sorrow, and death from our biological bodies.

In essence, a lack of understanding of the full preterist framework has brought about a trend in thinking that full preterists have no hope. Yet both traditionalists and full preterists believe that there is life in heaven after biological death for all those in Christ. The difference is that traditionalists place their hope in the future biological parousia of Jesus to judge the living and the dead (plural) when the resurrection of their biological bodies (plural) is completed. Full preterists, on the other hand, believe that the hope of mankind was in the parousia of Christ to spiritually judge the living and the dead (plural) when the resurrection of the body (singular) was completed, which had to do with the restoration of our relationship with God that was lost in the Garden.

The whole hope of the traditionalist lies in what will happen with our biological bodies. Charles Hodge confirms this in his *Systematic Theology*: "The whole of daily life of the Christian is founded, [Paul] says, on the hope of the resurrection; not of the continued existence of the soul merely, but of the glorious existence of the whole man, soul and body, with Christ in heaven."[190]

Full preterists agree with Paul that the whole of daily life of the Christian was founded on the hope of the resurrection. But the resurrection was about passing from death (i.e. separation from God) to life (i.e. presence of God). So full preterists do not lack hope, they have a fulfilled hope that Jesus has guaranteed our entrance into heaven when we die biologically. The attack that full preterists have no hope comes from a belief in a false hope and a misunderstanding of what full preterism teaches. Therefore, it is important for those who hold to the traditional framework to actually understand what the full preterist framework teaches before they can claim that it has no hope or validity. Below are the contrasts between the traditional and the full preterist frameworks.

Traditional Framework	Full Preterist Framework
The parousia of Jesus is still future to us.	The parousia of Jesus occurred in 70 AD.
The parousia is defined as a *visible* 2nd coming of Jesus to earth.	The parousia is defined as the *invisible* arrival or presence of God among men.
Jesus has to come again to fix our biological bodies because sin directly brought about two deaths in the Garden: spiritual and biological. Jesus fixed spiritual death at His first coming, but He still has to fix biological death at His second coming.	There was only one death that came as a result of sin in the Garden: spiritual separation from God. Biological death is the natural order of God's creation and is nowhere taught in Scripture to result from sin. Biological death was always in the mind of God as the necessary means of taking people to heaven. Thus, the only fix that had to happen was the restoration of God's presence to His people through the elimination of The Sin and The Death of Adam, by which all mankind was condemned.
Man is defined as body *and* soul (and according to some theologians, body *and* soul *and* spirit). Therefore, the souls of men have to be reunited to their biological bodies (although the traditionalists have not demonstrated how people in heaven can be called "people" after biological death, and before we are restored to those biological bodies, if the biological body is part of the definition of what makes a person a person).	Man is defined as a body or a soul. These terms are used interchangeably in Scripture. The biological body is simply the instrument in which we live while on this earth. It does not define man. Therefore, after biological death, people live in heaven forever. Biological bodies are not needed in heaven.

The resurrection is defined as biological bodies coming out of their graves and being reunited to our souls. This, of course, must somehow include those who have been cremated. So the resurrection is not only about biological bodies coming out of the graves, but biological bodies being put back together after they have decayed into the ground. It is unclear as to whether the soul enters the body before it is resurrected or after it is resurrected because in order for there to be a body to enter into, it has to be put back together first. If this is the case, then the resurrection of biological bodies actually occurs apart from the soul.

Whatever the case may be, after our biological bodies are put back together, they are then changed to have different qualities, presumably according the pattern of the biological resurrection of Jesus, although this poses a problem for the change that will occur in the biological bodies of unbelievers.

This may seem to be a vague explanation of the traditional view, but it is truly presented with the same vagueness provided by the traditionalists themselves. Perhaps a couple of quotes might demonstrate this:

"At the last day... all the dead shall be raised up, with the self-same bodies, and none other (although with different qualities), which shall be united again to their souls for ever" (WCF, 32.2).

That is the extent of clarity the WCF provides on the matter.

"Scripture teaches us to look forward to a *bodily* resurrection, similar to the resurrection of Christ...It will include both the righteous and the wicked, but will be an act of deliverance and glorification only for the former. For the latter the re-union of body and soul will issue in the extreme penalty of eternal death" (Berkoff, *A Summary of Christian Doctrine*, 179).

The resurrection is defined as the simultaneous dying and rising of two modes of existence. The first mode of existence is separation from God (i.e. death). This mode of existence is the result of being in the body of Adam. The second mode of existence is being in the presence of God. This is the result of being in the body of Christ.

All were in Adam until the death and resurrection of Christ. After the resurrection of Christ, those who believed the Gospel were being raised out of death into life. The resurrection of all the dead was completed in 70 AD at the parousia of Christ. Those who were in Christ by faith entered into eternal life. Those who were still in Adam entered into eternal death.

This is also the extent of clarity on the matter provided by Berkoff in *A Summary of Christian Doctrine*. Apparently, both the righteous and the wicked are resurrected in their biological bodies, but the righteous will live forever in their bodies that have different qualities while the wicked will live forever, and die forever, in their bodies that have the same different qualities.

"...all unsaved people of all time will be raised ... to be judged and then cast into the lake of fire forever ... At their resurrection they will apparently be given some sort of bodies that will be able to live forever and feel the effects of the torments of the lake of fire" (Ryrie, *A Survey of Bible Doctrine*, 183).

To clarify, unsaved people are given some sort of bodies that are able to live forever and die forever at the same time.

This is the doctrine that traditionalists claim Paul teaches in 1 Corinthians 15. So Paul takes 58 verses to explain this doctrine and that's the best level of clarity that he was able to give.

Eternal death begins after unbelievers die biologically or when Christ returns, whereby they will have no more opportunity to believe and be raised out of spiritual death. Eternal life begins on earth for those who believe the Gospel because they have been raised out of spiritual death. The fact that people can still be raised out of spiritual death means that temporal death still exists. That temporal death will be thrown into the eternal death at the second coming of Jesus. Until then, people will be saved from spiritual death.	Since 70 AD, both eternal death and eternal life begin at biological birth for people respectively. At the parousia of Christ, the temporal death was thrown into the eternal death. Prior to the resurrection of Christ, everybody was in temporal death because temporal death was the universal status of every person. When the temporal death was destroyed in 70 AD, it was destroyed for everyone, both the believer and the unbeliever. Therefore, unbelievers were thrown into the same eternal death that the temporal death was thrown. The whole point of eternal death is that it is eternal and there is no resurrection out of it.
The judgment will be a *visible*, universal judgment for every person that has ever lived. Each person will stand before the judgment seat of Christ in their biological bodies, which will have different qualities that can live forever on earth or in Heaven (depending on the view that's held), or live forever while dying in hell.	The judgment was an *invisible*, universal judgment for all the nations in existence during the first century. At the parousia of Christ, all who had embraced the Gospel entered into eternal life, all who did not, entered into eternal death. Likewise, those who were in Hades were released and also entered into eternal life or eternal death.
At the future parousia of Jesus, all souls will be reunited to their biological bodies which will at that point be changed into immortal bodies. At that time, Jesus will visibly judge the living and the dead and will destroy all sin, sorrow, pain, and death in the biological body for those who are in Christ. This is the hope of every believer.	At the parousia of Jesus, the resurrection into the new mode of existence was completed, and the living and the dead were judged. Those in the body of Christ entered into eternal life; those remaining in the body of Adam entered into eternal death. Since the parousia of Christ, those who are in Christ no longer have sorrow, pain, or death in relation to God and our sins are no longer counted against us. The parousia of Jesus completed all that was necessary in order to give us entrance into heaven when we die biologically. There we will live forever and ever.

As you can see, the full preterist framework is considerably different than the traditional framework. Understanding what full preterists are actually teaching makes a huge difference in determining its validity. People fear what they don't know. There is no reason to fear full preterism because it is the only doctrine of eschatology that is consistent with the teaching of Scripture.

While it is sometimes claimed that the greatest weakness of full preterism is in its doctrine of the resurrection of the body, it is actually the traditional view that contains the weakness in its doctrine of the resurrection of the body. The reason the traditional view has so much vagueness in its doctrine of the resurrection of the biological body is because that is not what the Scriptures teach. Nowhere does Paul teach a doctrine of the resurrection of the biological body. Even after Paul spends fifty-eight verses in 1 Corinthians 15, ten verses in 2 Corinthians 5, and eight verses in Romans 6, traditionalists cannot clarify their doctrine of the resurrection of the biological body.

Full preterism, however, provides perfect clarity in line with Paul's teaching because Paul's doctrine of the resurrection of the body has nothing to do with biological bodies and everything to do with the resurrection of the body of Adam in Christ.

Bibliography

Aland, Kurt, and Barbara Aland. *The Text of the New Testament.* Translated by Erroll F. Rhodes. Grand Rapids: Eerdmans, 1987.

*Aland, Kurt, and Barbara Aland, *The Text of the New Testament, second ed.* Grand Rapids: Eerdmans, 1989 [1981 German original].

Adams, Jay E. *The Time is at Hand: Prophecy and the Book of Revelation.* Woodruff: Timeless Texts, 2000.

*Bauer, Walter, W. Arndt, F. W. Gingrich, F. Danker, *The Greek-English Lexicon of the New Testament and Other Early Christian Literature, second ed.* Chicago: University of Chicago, 1979.

Beale, Gregory K. "The Purpose of Symbolism in the Book of Revelation." Calvin Theological Journal 41 no 1 (April 2006) : 53-66.

*Berkhof, Louis. *A Summary of Christian Doctrine.* Edinburgh: The Banner of Truth Trust, 1938.

*Berkhof, Louis. *Systematic Theology: New Combined Edition.* Grand Rapids: Eerdmans, 1996.

Birks, Kelly Nelson. *The End of Sin: An Eschatological Odyssey into Teloarmatia.* Baltimore: Publish America, 2004.

*Birks, Kelly Nelson. "So Where's Your Proof?." Preterist Archive. http://www.preteristarchive.com/Hyper/ 2004_birks_mathison.html (accessed March 29, 2009).

Campbell, R. Dennis. *He Shall Reign.* Baltimore: Publish America, 2004.

*Currid, John D. *Genesis: Volume 1 Genesis 1:1-25:18.* Darlington: Evangelical Press, 2003.

*Curtis, David. "The Ascension and Promised Return." Berean Bible Church. http://www.bereanbiblechurch.org/transcripts/acts/1_9-11.htm (accessed March 19, 2009).

*Curtis, David. "The Feasts of the Lord." www.preterism.com. http://en.preterism.com/index.php?title=The_Feasts_of_the_Lord&printab (accessed March 24, 2009).

*Curtis, David. "The Resurrection from the Dead." Berean bible Church. http://bereanbiblechurch.org/transcripts/philippians/3_11.htm (accessed March 24, 2009).

*Dillard, Raymond B. and Tremper Longman III. *An Introduction to the Old Testament.* Grand Rapids: Zondervan, 2006.

*Frost, Samuel M. *Exegetical Essays on the Resurrection of the Dead: 2nd Revised Edition.* Xenia, Ohio: Truth Voice Publishing, 2004.

Frost, Samuel M. *Misplaced Hope: The Origins of First and Second Century Eschatology.* Colorado Springs: Bimillennial Press, 2006.

*Fruchtenbaum, Arnold G. "The Fall of Man." Ariel Ministries. http://ariel.org/dcs.htm (accessed March 28, 2009).

*Gentry, Kenneth L. Jr. *He Shall Have Dominion, Second Edition, Revised.* Tyler: Institute for Christian Economics, 1997.

*Gentry, Kenneth L., Jr. *The Beast of Revelation.* Powder Springs: American Vision, 2002.

*Gentry, Kenneth L. Jr. *Before Jerusalem Fell: Dating the Book of Revelation.* Powder Springs, American Vision, 1998.

*Green, David, ed., *House Divided: Bridging the Gap in Reformed Eschatology. A Preterist Response to When Shall These Things Be?* Ramona: Vision Publishing, 2009.

*Gumerlock, Francis X. "Nero Antichrist: Patristic Evidence for the Use of Nero's Naming in Calculating the Number of the Beast (Rev. 13:18)." Westminster Theological Journal 68 no 2 (Autumn 2006) : 347-60.

Harris, Gregory H. "Can Satan Raise the Dead? Toward a Biblical View of the Beast's Wound." Master's Seminary Journal 18 no 1 (Spring 2007) : 23-41.

*Harris, R. Laird, et al., eds. *Theological Wordbook of the Old Testament.* Chicago: Moody Publishers, 1999.

*Henry, Matthew. *Matthew Henry's Commentary on the Whole Bible.* Peabody: Hendrickson Publishers, 1991.

*Hill, Charles. "Notes on Wallace Readings." Paper distributed in his Greek exegesis course, Reformed Theological Seminary, Oviedo, Florida, 2008.

*Hitchcock, Mark L. "A Critique of the Preterist View of 'Soon' and 'Near' in Revelation." Bibliotheca Sacra 163 (October-December 2006) : 467-78.

*Hodge, Charles. *Systematic Theology: Vol. II.* Peabody: Hendrickson Publishers, 2001.

*Hodge, Charles. *Systematic Theology: Vol. III.* Peabody: Hendrickson Publishers, 2001.

*Horton, Michael. *A Better Way: Rediscovering the Drama of God-Centered Worship.* Baker Books, 2002.

Horton, Michael. *God of Promise: Introducing Covenant Theology.* Grand Rapids: Baker Books, 2006.

*Kelly, Douglas F. "Systematic Theology I: Scripture, Theology Proper and Anthropology." Notes given to students for the Systematic Theology I course at Reformed Theological Seminary Virtual Campus, received July 2, 2007, copyright 2003.

*King, Max. *The Cross and the Parousia: The Two Dimensions of One Age-Changing Eschaton.* Warren: Writing and Research Ministry sponsored by The Parkman Road Church of Christ, 1987.

*Kistemaker, Simon J. *New Testament Commentary: Revelation.* Grand Rapids: Baker Books, 2001.

*Noll, Mark A. *Turning Points.* Grand Rapids: Baker Books, 1997.

*Ladd, George Eldon. *A Theology of the New Testament, Revised Edition.* Grand Rapids: Eerdmans, 1993.

*Leithart, Peter. "Assurance, 1." De Regno Christi.

http://deregnochristi.org/2007/09/20/assurance-1/ (accessed March 27, 2009).

*Lewis, C. S. "The World's Last Night" (1960). In *The Essential C.S. Lewis*, ed. Lyle W. Dorsett. New York: Simon & Schuster Inc., 1996.

*Newberry, Thomas. *The Interlinear Literal Translation Of the Greek New testament*.

Logos Bible Software Edition: Libronix Digital Library System 1.1.1, 2008.

Mathison, Keith A. *From Age to Age: The Unfolding of Biblical Eschatology*. Philipsburg: P&R Publishing, 2009.

*Mathison, Keith A. *Postmillennialism: An Eschatology of Hope*. Phillipsburg: P&R Publishing, 1999.

*Mathison, Keith A. "The Shape Of Sola Scriptura." *Reformed Protestant* (2001).

*Mathison, Keith, ed. *When Shall These Things Be? A Reformed Response to Hyper-Preterism*. Phillipsburg: P&R Publishing, 2004.

*Metzger, Bruce. *A Textual Commentary on the Greek New Testament*, 2nd ed. Stuttgart: United Bible Societies, 1994.

Neall, Beatrice S. "Amillennialism Reconsidered." Andrews University Seminary Studies 43 no 1 (Spring 2005) : 185-210

*Noë, John. "An Exegetical Basis for a Preterist-Idealist Understanding of the Book of Revelation." Journal of the Evangelical Theological Society 49 no 4 (December 2006) : 767-96.

*Noë, John. *Dead in Their Tracks: Stopping the Liberal/Skeptic Attack on the Bible*.
Bradford: International Preterist Association, 2001.

Piper, John. *Desiring God*. Sisters: Multnomah Publishers, 2003.

Piper, John. *God is the Gospel*. Wheaton: Crossway Books, 2005.

*Piper, John. *The Pleasures of God: Meditations on God's Delight in Being God*. Sisters: Multnomah Publishers, 2000.

*Pratt, Jr., Richard L. "Hyper-Preterism and Unfolding Biblical Eschatology." *Reformed Perspectives Magazine*, Vol. 7, Num. 46 (Nov. 13-19, 2005): 1-30.

*Preston, Don. "Rethinking II Peter 3." www.eschatology.org.

http://www.donkpreston.org/index.php?option=com_content &view=article&id=345:rethinking-ii-peter-three&catid=34:new-heaven-and-earth&Itemid=61 (accessed March 22, 2009).

*Preston, Don. "The Second Coming: Why We Should Still Be Waiting."

www.eschatology.org. http://www.donkpreston.org/index. php?option=com_content&view=article&id=207:the-second-coming-why-we-should-still-be-waiting&catid=37:responding-to-the-critics&Itemid=61 (accessed March 23, 2009).

*Preston Don. "Questions on Romans 8 and the Redemption of the Body."

www.eschatology.org. http://www.donkpreston.org/index.php? option=com_content&view=article&id=574:question-on-romans-8-and-the-redemption-of-the-body&catid=66:your-questions&Itemid=180 (accessed April 9, 2009).

*Preston, Don. "What About the Creeds and Church History?" www.eschatology.org.

http://www.donkpreston.org/index.php?option=com_content &view=article&id=705:what-about-the-creeds-and-church-history&catid=116:topical-studies&Itemid=61 (accessed September 10, 2009).

*Preston, Don. "What is the Preterist View?" www.eschatology.org.

http://www.donkpreston.org/index.php?option=com_content &view=article&id=323:what-is-the-preterist-view&catid=110:preterist-introduction&Itemid=61 (accessed April 3, 2009).

*Preston, Don. "Your Questions Dec. 6, 2006." www.eschatology.org.

http://www.donkpreston.org/index.php?option=com_content &view=article&id=482:your-questions-dec-62006&catid=66:your-questions&Itemid=180 (accessed March 23, 2009).

*Pringle, William, trans. *Calvin's Commentaries: Vol. XVI: Commentary on a Harmony of the Evangelists, Matthew, Mark, and Luke.* Grand Rapids: Baker Books, 1999.

Riddlebarger, Kim. *A Case for Amillennialism.* Grand Rapids: Baker Books, 2003.

*Robertson, O. Palmer. *The Christ of the Covenants*. Phillipsburg: P&R Publishing, 1980.

*Russell, Bertrand. *Why I'm Not a Christian*. New York: Simon and Schuster, 1957.

*Ryrie, Charles Caldwell. *A Survey of Bible Doctrine*. Chicago: Moody Publishers, 1972.

*Sproul, RC. *Last Days According to Jesus*. Grand Rapids: Baker Books, 1998.

Stevens, Edward E. *Expectations Demand a First Century Rapture*. Bradford: International Preterist Association, 2003.

*Stevens, Edward E. *Questions About the Afterlife: Preterist Answers to Gary DeMar's Five Questions About the Afterlife*. Bradford: International Preterist Association, 1999.

*Sullivan, Michael J. "Kenneth Gentry's Prophetic Confusion & The Analogy Of Scripture." Tree of Life Ministries. http://treeoflifeministries.info/index.php?option=com_content&view=article&id=148:mike-sullivan&catid=35:preterist-eschatology-all-prophecy-fulfilled-by-ad-70&Itemid=77#_ftn25

*Thomas, Robert L. "Theonomy and the Dating of Revelation." Master's Seminary Journal 5 no 2 (Fall 1994) : 185-202.

*Toews, Brian G. and Todd J. Williams. *Knowing the Will of God: Mystery of Revelation*. Morrisville: Biblion Publishing, 1998.

*Wallace, Daniel B. *Greek Grammar Beyond the Basics*. Grand Rapids: Zondervan, 1996.

Walvoord, John F., and Roy B. Zuck. *Bible Knowledge Commentary*. Wheaton: Victor Books, 1985.

*Walvoord, John F. *The Revelation of Jesus Christ*. Chicago: Moody Publishers, 1966.

*Wilson, Douglas. "Final Assurance." Blog and Mablog. http://www.dougwils.com/index.asp?Action=Anchor&CategoryID=1&BlogID=4545 (accessed March 27, 2009).

*Wilson, Doug. "Gentiles Under the Law." Blog and Mablog. http://www.dougwils.com/index.asp?Action=Anchor&CategoryID=1&BlogID=4711 (accessed March 27, 2009).

Scripture Index

Exodus
2:24...44
6:8...44
16:10...316
19:9...316
20:11...120
23:25-26...120
34:5...316

Leviticus
12:6...34
16:2...316
26...171

Numbers
11:25...316
14:33-34...192

Deuteronomy
1:11...191
2:25...159
7:9...191
9:5...45
17:18...170
18:22...219-220
28...171
28:4, 5, 8...120
28:15-68...120
29:24...159
31:10-11...170
33:13...120

2 Samuel
5:4...192
22:10-12...86

1 Kings
11:42...192

2 Kings
12:1...192
13:23...45
22...170

1 Chronicles
14:17...159

Job
19:25-27...203

Psalms
18:9-12...86
36:35...315
37:4...62
50:10...191
78:69...182
84:10...191
90:40...191
104:3-4...86
110:1...88
148:1-6...182

Ecclesiastes
1:4...182

Isaiah
7:20...157
6:4...317
9:6...155
10:12...157
13...84
13:6...193
13:9-10...193-194
15-23...157
19:1...86
20:1-6...86
24:12...157
24:23...331
24-29...153, 157
25:8...158
26:16-18...187
26:19...158
27:13...153
28:15, 16, 18...158
34...165
34:4...331
43...184
51:5...193

Jeremiah
4:13...86
4:23...331
31:27-34...148
48:16...193

Ezekiel
7:7...193
30:3...86
30:18...86
32:7...331
37...125

Subject Index

Glossary

Amillennialism: The belief that Christ's reign during the millennium is spiritual in nature. At the end of the present age, Christ will return in final judgment and establish a permanent physical reign.

Apologist: One who offers an argument in defense of truth.

A posteriori: Relating to or denoting reasoning or knowledge that proceeds from observations or experiences to the deduction of probable causes. Simply put: Based on observation or experience.

Book of Life: The allegorical book in which God records the names and lives of the righteous.

Canon of Scripture: The complete set of sixty-six Biblical books inspired by God as the authoritative Word of God.

Church, The: The entire collective body of Christ of all ages.

Confession (of Faith): A detailed expression of stated beliefs.

Conjugation: The different forms of a verb as it varies according to voice, mood, tense, number, and person.

Covenant: A life and death bond sovereignly administered.

Covenantalism: The understanding that God deals with His people corporately and collectively through covenants.

Creed: A statement of beliefs.

Death: Separation from God, not to be confused with biological death.

Dichotomy: The belief that man is defined as biological body *and* soul.

Eisegesis: Introducing into a text one's own ideas.

Eschatology: The study of last things.

Exegesis/Exegetical: Interpreting directly from a text its actual meaning.

Federal Head: The representative of a group united under a federation or covenant.

Full Preterism: The belief that the coming of Christ following His ascension occurred in 70 AD, as did the resurrection and the judgment. These events were invisible to biological eyes for they were spiritual in nature. However, the destruction of Jerusalem was the visible event that verified the occurrence of the invisible events. The coming of Christ, the resurrection, and the judgment were the final resolution of separation from God and the restoration of mankind into the presence of God.

Futurist: One who believes in the future (to us) second coming of Christ, resurrection of the dead, and judgment of the living and the dead, but not necessarily in the resurrection of *biological bodies*.

Hades:The temporary location of the biologically dead prior to the resurrection. Hades was divided into two parts: Paradise and Hell or

Tartarus. Paradise was the part of Hades where the Old Covenant saints went after biological death. Hell was the part of Hades where the Old Covenant wicked went after biological death.

Heresy: A damnable belief contrary to orthodox religious doctrine, also known as the creeds. Once upon a time, however, heresy was not determined by the creeds, but by Scripture. That's actually how the creeds developed.

Hermeneutics: The art and science of studying the Bible.

Hyper-preterism: A derogatory term used against full preterists to claim that their brand of preterism is unbiblical because they don't agree with the creeds in the future second coming of Christ. Note that this term is used not because the view can actually be shown to be unbiblical, but simply because it goes against the creeds.

Judaizers: A sect of Jews who were zealous for the maintaining of the Old Covenant Law, and taught that it was necessary for Christians to obey that Law.

Legalism: An over-emphasis on law, but loosely defined as the adherence to additional laws not specified in the Bible.

Orthodox: Conforming to what is generally or traditionally accepted as right or true.

Overseer: One of the elders in the local church. An overseer functions as a guardian of doctrine.

Parousia: Coming, arrival, or presence. Usually translated into our English Bibles as "coming."

Partial Preterism: The belief that there was *an* invisible coming of Christ in 70 AD to destroy Jerusalem via Rome, but that there *will be* a visible, biological, second coming of Christ, along with a future resurrection and judgment.

Polity: A form of church government.

Postmillennialism: The belief that Jesus will return after the present thousand-year reign. Postmillennialists see the thousand years as a figurative term for a long period of time. During this thousand-year reign, the forces of Satan will gradually be defeated by the expansion of the Kingdom of God throughout history up until the second coming of Christ.

Premillennialism: The belief that Christ will return before His literal, physical, thousand-year reign on earth.

Preterism: See full preterism and partial preterism.

Recapitulation: A recycling of the same teaching, giving different information each time.

Soteriology: The study of salvation.

Systematic Theology:A discipline of Christian theology that attempts to formulate an orderly, rational, and coherent account of the Christian faith and beliefs.

Traditional View (the portion dealt with in this book): [Definition taken from the Westminster Confession of Faith, where all of the following is believed to take place in the future (to us) and "bodies" means, *biological bodies*.]

Chapter 32:
    I. The bodies of men, after death, return to dust, and see corruption: but their souls, which neither die nor sleep, having an immortal subsistence, immediately return to God who gave them: the souls of the

righteous, being then made perfect in holiness, are received into the highest heavens, where they behold the face of God, in light and glory, waiting for the full redemption of their bodies. And the souls of the wicked are cast into hell, where they remain in torments and utter darkness, reserved to the judgment of the great day. Beside these two places, for souls separated from their bodies, the Scripture acknowledges none.

II. At the last day, such as are found alive shall not die, but be changed: and all the dead shall be raised up, with the selfsame bodies, and none other (although with different qualities), which shall be united again to their souls forever.

III. The bodies of the unjust shall, by the power of Christ, be raised to dishonor: the bodies of the just, by His Spirit, unto honor; and be made conformable to His own glorious body.

Chapter 33:
I. God has appointed a day, wherein He will judge the world, in righteousness, by Jesus Christ, to whom all power and judgment is given of the Father. In which day, not only the apostate angels shall be judged, but likewise all persons that have lived upon earth shall appear before the tribunal of Christ, to give an account of their thoughts, words, and deeds; and to receive according to what they have done in the body, whether good or evil.

II. The end of God's appointing this day is for the manifestation of the glory of His mercy, in the eternal salvation of the elect; and of His justice, in the damnation of the reprobate, who are wicked and disobedient. For then shall the righteous go into everlasting life, and receive that fulness of joy and refreshing, which shall come from the presence of the Lord; but the wicked who know not God, and obey not the Gospel of Jesus Christ, shall be cast into eternal torments, and be punished with everlasting destruction from the presence of the Lord, and from the glory of His power.

Transfiguration:A complete change of form or appearance into a more beautiful or spiritual state.

Trichotomy: The belief that man is defined as body *and* soul *and* spirit.

True Israel:All of Abraham's descendants by faith whom Christ came to redeem, which includes both Jews and Gentiles.

Endnotes

Preface

[1] I attribute this analogy to my good friend and partner in ministry, Jeremiah Thompson.

[2] Keith A. Mathison, "The Shape Of Sola Scriptura," *Reformed Protestant* (2001): 147.

[3] Ibid, 280

[4] The view that Christ will return following the thousand-year reign of Christ, which we are in presently.

[5] Polity refers to a form of church government.

[6] Engle, Paul E., Steven B. Cowan. *Who Runs the Church? 4 Views on Church Government* (Grand Rapids: Zondervan, 2004), 26.

[7] Ibid, 44.

[8] Ibid, 60, italics mine. David Green clearly articulates Gentry's position here:

> We.... learn from Gentry that when Christians are confronted with preterism, it is "crucial" that they first go to the ecumenical creeds (orthodoxy) before they go to Scripture. And "only after" Christians decisively establish the fact (by means of the creeds/orthodoxy) that preterism is anti-biblical, may they then rightly go on to "consider" preterism exegetically and theologically in light of Scripture.

[David Green, ed., *House Divided: Bridging the Gap in Reformed Eschatology. A Preterist Response to When Shall These Things Be?* (Ramona: Vision Publishing, 2009), 4.]

[9] Kurt Aland and Barbara Aland, *The Text of the New Testament, second ed.* (Grand Rapids, 1989 [1981 German original]), 296.

[10] Keith Mathison, *Postmillennialism: An Eschatology of Hope* (Phillipsburg: P&R Publishing, 1999), 23.

[11] Ibid, 26.

Introduction

[12] http://www.personalpromisebible.com (accessed May 21, 2009).

[13] As you will see later in the book, this isn't to say that there is no personal relevance to individuals in the Bible. Individuals in Christ do benefit from what God has promised to His corporate people. But we must learn to recognize what each promise is teaching to the corporate people first before we attempt to apply those promises to ourselves. One of the most obvious dangers with putting our names in the text is that an unbeliever might get one of these Bibles with his or her name in the text and it may never be true for them if they never believe. Suddenly, unbelievers are gaining a false assurance of salvation. It's a good thing Personal Promise Bibles weren't around when Judas was alive. He would certainly have caught God in a contradiction.

Yet, the FAQ page of the Personal Promise Bible site states, "The Personal Promise Bible does not add to the scriptures but rather clarifies the meaning of the scriptures much the same way that the Amplified Bible clarifies the meaning of the text." If putting our names in the text clarifies the meaning of the text, then the required Biblical conclusion turns out to be universalism, especially since the Personal Promise Bible would have to subjectively put people's names in the verses so as not to contradict itself. Yet, as it stands, contradiction in the Personal Promise Bible becomes impossible to avoid. Consider the following example: In John 3:16, the Personal Promise Bible changes the word, "world," to a person's name, for example, Alan. But what would the Personal Promise Bible do with John 14:17, which reads, "...that is the Spirit of truth, whom the world cannot receive, because it does not see Him or know Him, but you know Him because He abides with you and will be in you."

As you can see, this verse poses a contradictory problem for the Personal Promise Bible . Would they change the word, "world," to Alan, or would they change the word, "you," to Alan? If they choose to translate the word, "world," as Alan, in order to remain consistent with John 3:16 (which they would have to, considering both verses are from the same book and same author), then Alan does not know Him because He does not abide with Alan. In addition, this would now contradict John 3:16 because in John 3:16, Jesus told Alan that God so loved Alan, that He gave His one and only Son, that Alan, believing in Him, should not perish, but have eternal life. John 14:17 changes all that when Jesus tells Alan that Alan *cannot* receive the Spirit of truth, because Alan does not see Him or know Him.

Unfortunately, this inconsistency and contradiction is not only done in the Personal Promise Bible . The majority of Christians actually read the Bible this way. The creators of the Personal Promise Bible just found a way to market what many people are already doing. One can see why understand how to read the Bible through New Covenant eyes is so important.

[14]http://www.thomasnelson.com/consumer/ product_detail.asp?sku= 071801975X (accessed May 21, 2009).

Chapter 1

[15]I say *"predominance* of having a personal relationship with Jesus" because a personal relationship with Jesus flows out of our corporate relationship with Jesus, not the other way around. The guarantee of our personal salvation and relationship with Jesus is grounded in the fact that we are connected to Christ by being connected to His corporate people. So the most important thing is not our personal relationship with Jesus. Our personal relationship with Jesus is a given if we are part of the corporate people that have a relationship with Jesus. The marriage of the Lamb to His bride, the Church, means that Jesus did not marry me as an individual, but His Church as a whole. The predominance of personal relationships has feminized Christianity. I am not married to Jesus. We, as a Church, are married to Jesus. This is why earthly marriages are such a great picture of Christ and the Church. But just because I, as an

individual, am married to my wife does not mean that I, as an individual, am married to Jesus.

[16] Taken from the JG Wentworth commercials.

[17] How does this make a difference? Understanding how God deals with man through covenants will help us to understand why the texts read like they do. What's with all the sacrificing in the Old Testament? What is the Old Covenant teaching? What does Abraham have to do with anything? When did the Old Covenant end and the New Covenant begin?

Of course, those questions only touch the surface. Some difficulties arise due to the far removal of our culture from ancient covenants as well as the failure of the church to pass on a knowledge of these covenants from generation to generation. Some recent studies have been done to try to revive an understanding of ancient covenants, but even with that, few of the recent studies agree. Yet, there are common elements that run through these studies that can help the reader grasp enough of what a covenant is in order to understand the Scriptures contextually.

A reading of some of these recent studies (such as Michael Horton, *God of Promise: Introducing Covenant Theology*) would prove very beneficial, providing a strong grasp on the essence of a covenant. A recommended starting point is, *The Christ of the Covenants* by O. Palmer Robertson. Robertson defines a covenant as "a bond-in-blood sovereignly administered" (4). Noting that there is disagreement among scholars, some think that a covenant is not (necessarily) sovereignly administered, but rather an agreement between two parties (equal or not). Some also disagree on the bond-in-"blood" part of the definition. Robertson, along with others, such as Richard Pratt from Third Millennium Ministries, see the covenants of Scripture rooted in the Suzerain Vassal treaties in play during Old Covenant times. The problem with this is that the Suzerain Vassal treaties were not established in the Garden of Eden when God established the first covenant with Adam. Presumably, these Suzerain Vassal treaties are based upon the concept of a covenant that is in the mind of God because that is where a covenant stems from. However, while this might be true, it is an unnecessary leap to assume that this is the case.

Here is a possible broad definition that seems basic enough to run through all the covenants of Scripture: A life and death bond sovereignly administered. Since the study of the exact nature of covenants is beyond the scope of this book, the reader is encouraged to spend some time studying what a covenant is and how God deals with His people though covenants.

[18] Brian G. Toews and Todd J. Williams, *Knowing the Will of God: Mystery of Revelation* (Morrisville: Biblion Publishing, 1998).

Chapter 2

[19] Raymond B. Dillard and Tremper Longman III, *An Introduction to the Old Testament* (Grand Rapids: Zondervan, 2006), 18.

[20] Requests for information should be addressed to:
Biblion Publishing, P.O. Box 1413, Morrisville, PA 19067, E-Mail: biblionpub@aol.com.

[21] Bertrand Russell, *Why I'm Not a Christian* (New York: Simon and Schuster, 1957), 16.

[22] Ibid.

[23] RC Sproul, *Last Days According to Jesus* (Grand Rapids: Baker Books, 1998), 13.

[24] RC Sproul further comments, "When [Russell] expressed his criticisms of the biblical text, he was speaking outside the field of his expertise. The problem, however, is that Russell's is not a lone voice in recent history. His criticisms are echoed by a multitude of highly learned specialists in the field of biblical studies" [ibid., 14].

[25] The art and science of Bible study (i.e. the approach one takes in Bible interpretation)

[26] A mystical interpretation of a word, passage, or text, especially scriptural exegesis that detects allusions to heaven or the afterlife.

[27] Doug Wilson, "Gentiles Under the Law," Blog and Mablog, http://www.dougwils.com/index.asp?Action=Anchor&CategoryID=1&BlogID=4711.

[28] Italics mine.

[29] Italics mine.

[30] Italics mine.

[31] Italics mine.

[32] Kenneth Gentry, *Before Jerusalem Fell: Dating the Book of Revelation* (Powder Springs: American Vision, 1998), 84.

[33] Peter Leithart, "Assurance, 1," De Regno Christi, http://deregnochristi.org/2007/09/20/assurance-1. Leithart includes the following comments that have been excluded from this quote:

We gain assurance by entering the "front door." What's that mean? The "front door" is the means of grace. God speaks to us in Word and Sacrament. He speaks graciously. He makes promises. He offers cleansing and fellowship, renewal and resurrection life. Gaining assurance by the front door means trusting that God is addressing me in Word and Sacrament, trusting that He is finishing His good work through those means, and believing that He is perfecting me in faith.

I have purposely excluded these comments because I take exception to the continuation of the sacraments after 70 AD. Yet, I agree with the rest of his conclusions.

Chapter 3

[34] This question does not produce a false dichotomy, though some believe it does. I believe that those who argue that this produces a false dichotomy are arguing from a desire to be worthy enough in and of ourselves to turn the pleasure of God towards us. But God's pleasure in His people, and the praises of His people, is grounded in His own pleasure in Himself. The reason why God enjoys the worship of His people is because our praises are applauding *Him*. John Piper is helpful here when he explains why God takes pleasure in obedience. If you substitute the words, *obedience* and *obey*, with the word, *worship*, in the following quote, you will see that the point remains the same:

God is happy with our obedience when our obedience is the overflow of our happiness with God. God is delighted with our obedience when it is the fruit of our delight in him. Our obedience is God's pleasure when it proves that God is our treasure. This is good news, because it means very simply that the command to obey is the command to be happy in God. [John Piper, *The Pleasures of God: Meditations on God's Delight in Being God* (Sisters: Multnomah Publishers, 2000), 250.]

God does not take delight in sinners in and of themselves. He takes delight in us only because He is the ground of that delight. In other words, He delights in us because of all that He has done and not because of all that we have done. So God enjoys the praises of His people, not because the praises themselves are wonderful, but because of the object of those praises, because our praises applaud *His* performance. As the heading of the paragraph from where the above quote was taken states: "WE ARE HIS PLEASURE WHEN HE IS OUR TREASURE."

[35] Michael Horton, *A Better Way: Rediscovering the Drama of God-Centered Worship* (Baker Books, 2002), p. 15.

[36] See John Piper, *God is the Gospel* (Wheaton: Crossway Books, 2005).

[37] See John Piper, *Desiring God* (Sisters: Multnomah Publishers, Inc., 2003).

Chapter 4

[38] Cited by Don Preston, "What About the Creeds and Church History?," www.eschatology.org, http://www.donkpreston.org/index.php?option=com_content&view=article&id=705:what-about-the-creeds-and-church-history&catid=116:topical-studies&Itemid=61

[39] Mark A. Noll, *Turning Points* (Grand Rapids: Baker Books, 1997), 155

[40] http://en.wikipedia.org/wiki/Galileo#Church_controversy (accessed August 6, 2009). Thanks to Jeremiah Thompson for condensing this important information about Galileo into a succinct paragraph.

[41] Whenever the term, preterist or preterism, stands alone, it is because the subject matter is agreed upon by both partial and full preterists. This will especially be the case in *The Dating of Revelation* section in appendix A.

Sub-Chapter 4A

[42] Calvin gives the following interpretation of this text:

These words cannot be understood in the sense which some have given to them as relating to the first mission, but embrace the whole course of their apostleship. But the difficulty lies in ascertaining what is meant by the *coming of the Son of man*...I look upon the consolation here

313

given as addressed peculiarly to the apostles. Christ is said *to come,* when matters are desperate, and he grants relief. The commission which they received was almost boundless: it was to spread the doctrine of the Gospel through the whole world. Christ promises that he will *come* before they have travelled [sic] through the whole of Judea: that is, by the power of his Spirit, he will shed around his reign such luster, that the apostles will be enabled to discern that glory and majesty which they had hitherto been unable to discover. [William Pringle, trans., *Calvin's Commentaries: Vol. XVI: Commentary on a Harmony of the Evangelists, Matthew, Mark, and Luke* (Grand Rapids: Baker Books, 1999), 457-58.]

Calvin, like everyone else with the futurist presupposition, not knowing how to explain this statement of Christ to his apostles, come up with interpretations that force the text into a particular mold instead of taking the straight-forward meaning of the text. Where does Jesus remotely imply, much less, state, that He would come over and over again when matters are desperate? How many comings of Jesus are there?

Further, if we take Calvin's correct understanding that the words of Jesus are "peculiarly to the apostles," then this supposed promise to come over and over again could only apply to them anyway. What is striking here is that the phrase, "coming of the Son of Man," as well as all other references to the coming of Christ in Scripture, is only interpreted in a similar way as Calvin by futurists in places that demand a first century coming of Christ. In all the other places where this exact phrase is used, futurist either interpret it to mean the Second coming of Christ (in our future) or the destruction of Jerusalem in 70 AD (i.e. partial preterists, who also hold to *another* second coming of Christ in our future). Interestingly, in texts that demand a first century coming of Christ, Jesus can come over and over again, but in texts that don't contain an immediate time statement, He can only come again once. Again, it is the futurist presupposition that forces this sort of double hermeneutic.

There is only one way to interpret this text honestly. The coming of the Son of Man occurred in 70 AD, before His apostles finished going through the cities of Israel. Calvin calls this interpretation "farfetched." But it's the futurist interpretation that's farfetched.

[43] Italics mine.

[44] What does "in just the same way" mean? First of all, the Greek word that is translated "lifted up" is "epairo." Epairo is a compound word from "epi" and "airo." In Acts 1:9, *epairo* is in the passive voice. This is important because this word appears to be consistently translated as "exalt oneself" or "be exalted" when used in either the middle or the passive voice respectively. That is, it is consistently translated that way except for in Acts 1:9. The *Theological Dictionary of the New Testament (TDNT)* states the following concerning this word: "2. In the figurative pass. sense of 'to raise up oneself' or 'to oppose'…, or 'to exalt oneself…"' (186). The TDNT gives a few biblical and extrabiblical references to support this definition: LXX 2 Esr. 4:19, which is in the middle voice; LXX Psalm 36:35, which is in the passive voice; 2 Cor. 10:5, which is in the passive voice; and 2 Cor. 11:20, which is in the middle voice. In addition to these, 1 Mac. 1:3 contains "epairo" in the passive voice and there it is combined with "hupsao", which also means exalted, and together form a parallelism, which is best translated, "he was exalted and his heart *was lifted up*." Was his heart literally lifted out of his chest? No, but it was exalted along with *him*. The LXX Hab. 3:11 contains the exact same form of the word as in Acts 1:9, and there, Brenton, in *The Septuagint with Apocrypha* translates it as "exalted": "The sun was exalted" (1108). As you can see, there are sufficient and probable grounds to translate *epairo* in Acts 1:9 as "was exalted."

Secondly, we see that "a cloud took him out of their sight." The Expositor's Greek Testament states the following regarding the cloud: "The cloud is here, as elsewhere, the symbol of the divine glory, and it was also as St. Chrysostom called it: "to ochema to basilikon … " (p. 57) which means, "royal chariot of the king." David Curtis, Pastor of Berean Bible Church in Chesapeake, Virginia, in "The Ascension and Promised Return," explains the "cloud" in Acts 1:9 in the following extended quote:

> The idea is not that Jesus disappeared in a white puffy cloud. When Luke writes, "A cloud received Him out of their sight," they would recognize in this that He had gone to God, Who, when He revealed Himself, regularly did so in a cloud:

And it came about as Aaron spoke to the whole congregation of the sons of Israel, that they looked toward the wilderness, and behold, the glory of the LORD appeared in the cloud. (Exodus 16:10 NASB)

The cloud indicated God's presence:

And the LORD said to Moses, "Behold, I shall come to you in a thick cloud, in order that the people may hear when I speak with you, and may also believe in you forever." Then Moses told the words of the people to the LORD. (Exodus 19:9 NASB)

And the LORD descended in the cloud and stood there with him as he called upon the name of the LORD. (Exodus 34:5 NASB)

And the LORD said to Moses, "Tell your brother Aaron that he shall not enter at any time into the holy place inside the veil, before the mercy seat which is on the ark, lest he die; for I will appear in the cloud over the mercy seat. (Leviticus 16:2 NASB)

Then the LORD came down in the cloud and spoke to him; and He took of the Spirit who was upon him and placed Him upon the seventy elders. And it came about that when the Spirit rested upon them, they prophesied. But they did not do it again. (Numbers 11:25 NASB)

So the idea of a cloud would speak to them of the presence of God. And they would further remember that when the Son of Man received His kingdom, He would do so in the clouds of heaven:

"I kept looking in the night visions, And behold, with the clouds of heaven One like a Son of Man was coming, And He came up to the Ancient of Days And was presented before Him. 14 "And to Him was given dominion, Glory and a kingdom, That all the peoples, nations, and men of every language Might serve Him. His dominion is an everlasting dominion Which will not pass away; And His kingdom is one Which will not be destroyed. (Daniel 7:13-

14 NASB)
Notice that the Son of Man "came UP to the Ancient of Days" and was "presented before Him." At that glorious event, Jesus receives His kingdom and sits at the right hand of God awaiting the conquest of His enemies.

The idea of Jesus going and coming "on the clouds," is familiar apocalyptic language of the prophets to identify Himself as God. Only God came on clouds, that was a claim to deity. Thus they may well have seen His entering the cloud as indicating His departing to His heavenly throne.

This was the Shekinah Cloud, which means that it was the cloud that hid the presence of God. It was the same cloud of smoke that Isaiah saw in Isaiah 6:4. It was the same cloud that led the Israelites through the wilderness. It indicated the presence of God:

And after He had said these things, He was lifted up while they were looking on, and a cloud received Him out of their sight. (Acts 1:9 NASB)

...Jesus is then said to have been "lifted up," which is the Greek word epairo, which, in its passive form, figuratively connotes the lifting up of someone in stature or dignity. The only other use of this word cited in BAGD, 1 Clem 45:8, does not denote a literal and physical elevation of the person, but instead describes the exaltation of someone.

W. Neil writes, "It would be a grave misunderstanding of Luke's mind and purpose to regard his account of the ascension of Christ as other than symbolic and poetic. He is not describing an act of levitation." [W. Neil, The Acts of the Apostles (London: Marshall, Morgan & Scott, 1973) 66.]

So a correct understanding of "He was lifted up while they were looking on, and a cloud received Him out of their sight," may not have anything to due [sic] with Jesus floating up in the air into a cloud, but may, in fact, speak of His exaltation into the presence of God. Either way, the main idea here is that Jesus is exalted to the right hand of God, a position of superiority over and above others.

Verse 10 is literally translated, "And while they were gazing into the heaven/sky of His going..." The text does not say that they were staring at Jesus going into heaven. It simply says that they were staring into the heaven of his going. It is very likely that what is meant here is that they watched the cloud depart into the sky (and possibly dissolve into the air). "In just the same way," then, means that Jesus would come again on the clouds of heaven with power and great glory (Matt. 24:30), that is, exalted to the glory of His Father. How did they see Him go into heaven? In a cloud. Jesus did not fly up, up, and away until He disappeared into the sky. There is no reason to understand the exaltation and the cloud to be consecutive events that followed each other, but rather, that the exaltation and the cloud were both simultaneous events where the cloud is the visible symbol that showed to the their biological eyes the invisible reality of His exaltation. In other words, the "and" connects the visible and the invisible into one event, producing a sign and a reality. In just the same way, at the parousia of Christ, the sign of the clouds would point to the reality of the Son of Man coming.

For a further analysis of the phrase, "in just the same way," see Don Preston, "What About in Like Manner?," www.eschatology.org,

http://www.donkpreston.org/index.php?option=com_content& view=article&id=701:what-about-acts-1-qhe-shall-come-in-like-mannerq&catid=91:study-by-passage&Itemid=61.

[45] Italics mine.

[46] Italics mine.

[47] C. S. Lewis, "The World's Last Night" (1960), in *The Essential C.S. Lewis*, ed. Lyle W. Dorsett (New York: Simon & Schuster Inc., 1996), 385.

[48] John Noë, *Dead in Their Tracks: Stopping the Liberal/Skeptic Attack on the Bible* (Braford: International Preterist Association, 2001), 44-45.

[49] This view is held by partial preterists.

[50] Mathison, *When Shall These Things Be?*, 183.

[51] It is further important to note that there is not a single text in the New Testament that teaches that the world would see Jesus again. There

are two texts that are often thought to imply this, but they do not, in fact, teach this:

1. Philippians 2:9-11: "⁹For this reason also, God highly exalted Him, and bestowed on Him the name which is above every name, ¹⁰so that at the name of Jesus EVERY KNEE WILL BOW, of those who are in heaven and on earth and under the earth, ¹¹and that every tongue will confess that Jesus Christ is Lord, to the glory of God the Father." There are two possibilities here. The first possibility is that we read this at face value, namely, that every knee will bow and every tongue confess. If this is referring contextually to those in the first century only (i.e. everyone alive at the judgment), then this would happen at the parousia of Christ in 70 AD. Further, there is nothing in the surrounding context that requires these verses to be fulfilled *only* at the parousia. Even futurists believe that every knee bows and every tongue confesses at the point of death, even before their doctrine of the future (to us) coming.

The second possibility is that we translate these verses in their subjunctive form as they are in the Greek. Young's literal translation has captured this subjunctive mood which reads as follows: "⁹wherefore, also, God did highly exalt him, and gave to him a name that [is] above every name, ¹⁰that in the name of Jesus every knee may bow—of heavenlies, and earthlies, and what are under the earth—¹¹and every tongue may confess that Jesus Christ [is] Lord, to the glory of God the Father." When translated this way, the tone of the text suggests that the bowing of the knee and the confessing of the tongue is not a forced action upon every knee and every tongue universally but rather, a willful bowing and confessing at the good news that Jesus is Lord. It is in this name of Jesus that knees gladly bow and tongues gladly confess. This interpretation seems to fit the general context best.

2. Revelation 1:7: "BEHOLD, HE IS COMING WITH THE CLOUDS, and every eye will see Him, even those who pierced Him; and all the tribes of the earth will mourn over Him. So it is to be. Amen." It has already been demonstrated, and will be demonstrated again, that "seeing" Jesus at His coming does not mean with physical, biological eyes. This would hold true even more so in the book of Revelation.

[52] Walter Bauer, W. Arndt, F. W. Gingrich, F. Danker, *The Greek-English Lexicon of the New Testament and Other Early Christian Literature 2nd ed.* (Chicago: University of Chicago, 2nd ed., 1979), 500-01.

[53] This question becomes even more important when we compare the verses discussing eschatology with a multitude of verses that contain the same grammatical structures and do translate mello as "about to." Why is that the verses that do not discuss eschatology seem to fit the most basic definition of mello, namely, "about to," but the verses that do discuss eschatology *never* do? This seems a bit convenient, does it not? Here is a thought to ponder: If translators today were living when these eschatological verses were first spoken by Jesus and the apostles, how would they translate mello? You see, without two thousand years to contend with, nobody would have considered the possibility that mello could mean anything else but "about to."

[54] Thomas Newberry, *The Interlinear Literal Translation Of the Greek New testament*, Logos Bible Software Edition (Libronix Digital Library System 1.1.1, 2008).

[55] Italics mine.

[56] Italics mine.

[57] As stated earlier, "about to" does not have to be the exact translation, but the translation should carry the meaning of "about to." In other words, mello should be translated in a way that carries the impending nature of the word. Another "meaning" of mello that is suggested in Greek Grammars is "wait" or "delay." This often leads people to believe that mello can mean that something definitely will happen, but that it can be delayed indefinitely. However, this is not what is meant by this suggested translation. The only verse in the Bible that could possibly have this meaning is Acts 22:16. The ESV uses "wait": "And now why do you wait? Rise and be baptized and wash away your sins, calling on his name." The NASB uses "delay": "Now why do you delay? Get up and be baptized, and wash away your sins, calling on His name." As you can see, even here, mello retains the idea of immediacy. Mello is never used in a context that proposes a waiting period.

[58] The translation in this verse containing "about to" is based on the textual variant that, based upon the consistency of Hebrews is, in all probability, correct.

Sub-Chapter 4B

[59] The following translations translate it this way: ESV, NIV, NLT, KJV, NKJV, Young's Literal Translation.

[60] See R. Dennis Campbell, *He Shall Reign* (Baltimore: Publish America, 2004); Kenneth L. Gentry Jr., *He Shall Have Dominion, Second Edition, Revised* (Tyler: Institute for Christian Economics, 1997); Keith A. Mathison, *Postmillennialism: An Eschatology of Hope* (Phillipsburg: P&R Publishing, 1999).

[61] Italics mine.

[62] Sproul, *Last Days*, 203.

[63] The obvious exception to this would be where Paul is referring to the body (singular) of one individual.

[64] Douglas F. Kelly, "Systematic Theology I: Scripture, Theology Proper and Anthropology" (notes given to students for the Systematic Theology I course at Reformed Theological Seminary Virtual Campus, July 2, 2007). Dr. Kelly puts forth the traditional view. It should be noted as we proceed, however, that both dichotomy and trichotomy are held by various theologians in the traditional camp. Dr. Kelly holds to dichotomy, but the opposing arguments that follow apply equally to trichotomy. These terms refer to the constitution of man, that is, they seek to answer the question, "What is man?" Dichotomy answers by saying that man is made up of body *and* soul; Trichotomy answers by saying that man is made up of body, soul, *and* spirit.

[65] This definition of man as a body *and* a soul is called dichotomy. Some hold that man is a body *and* a soul *and* a spirit, which is called trichotomy. While the arguments set forth in this book will primarily oppose dichotomy, the arguments apply to trichotomy as well.

[66] Louis Berkhof, *Systematic Theology: New Combined Edition* (Grand Rapids: Eerdmans, 1996), 216 (italics mine).

[67] (A) cannot equal (B) and equal (C) at the same time and in the same relationship if (B) and (C) are not equal to each other. According to Berkoff (and the traditional view), immortality (A) equals the non-possibility of death (B; 1 Cor. 15:50-57) *and* the possibility of death (C). It is the futurist presupposition that forces Scripture to define

immortality as both the non-possibility of death *and* the possibility of death. If immortality means both, then what does mortality mean then?

[68] Arnold G. Fruchtenbaum, "The Fall of Man," Ariel Ministries, http://ariel.org/dcs.htm.

[69] Charles Hodge, *Systematic Theology: Vol. II* (Peabody: Hendrickson Publishers, 2001), 118.

[70] Berkhof, 215.

[71] Even there, "The Second Death" of Revelation 20 is an extension of the first death, not a completely new death. The reason for "The Second Death" is because the first death was temporary and the second death brings about its permanence for the wicked.

[72] Samuel M. Frost, *Exegetical Essays on the Resurrection of the Dead: 2nd Revised Edition* (Xenia, Ohio: Truth Voice Publishing, 2004), 73. The original quote had the calculation mistake of 324,000,000. In a phone conversation with Sam Frost on May 17, 2009, he authorized the change to 324,000 in the quote in order that the reader's attention would not be drawn away from the main point of the content.

[73] Italics mine.

[74] Bold and italics mine.

[75] R. Laird Harris et al., eds, *Theological Wordbook of the Old Testament* (Chicago: Moody Publishers, 1999), 1.132.

[76] John D. Currid, *Genesis: Volume 1 Genesis 1:1-25:18* (Darlington: Evangelical Press, 2003). "The author employs an emphatic verbal construction [in Genesis 3:16]: It literally reads, 'Multiplying, I will multiply.' Many commentators understand this comment as merely referring to the pain associated with the labour involved in childbirth. However, it possibly refers to more than that short period. The Hebrew term for 'pain' can also have an emotional thrust, signifying 'grief' or 'vexation'. Thus it may represent the pain associate with the concept of a child born in rebellion against God, born in sin, and with the deterioration of the physical body" (132).

[77] Frost, *Essays*, 74.

[78] Presumably, the reason the traditional view requires that Adam had to pass a probationary period before he could have access to the Tree of Life is because if he ate of the Tree of Life, he could live forever. Thus,

since the traditional view imposes a probationary period into the text, then Adam couldn't eat of the Tree of Life until he passed the test because eating of the Tree of Life equals eternal life. Thus, Adam had to earn access to the Tree of Life (i.e. eternal life). But Genesis 2:16-17 does not allow for such a view: "The LORD God commanded the man, saying, 'From any tree of the garden you may eat freely; but from the tree of the knowledge of good and evil you shall not eat, for in the day that you eat from it you will surely die.'" Adam didn't have to earn eternal life. He was given it freely through the Tree of Life, the presence of God.
[79] In his *Systematic Theology*, Charles Hodge confirms this:

> The dead in the Old Testament are always spoken of as going to their fathers, as descending into "Sheol," *i. e.*, into the invisible state, which the Greeks called Hades. Sheol is represented as the general receptacle or abode of departed spirits, who were there in a state of consciousness; some in a state of misery, others in a state of happiness. In all these points the pagan idea of Hades corresponds to the Scriptural idea of Sheol. All souls went into Hades, some dwelling in Tartarus, others in Elysium. [Charles Hodge, *Systematic Theology: Vol. III* (Peabody: Hendrickson Publishers, 2001), 717.]

In Greek mythology, the home of the blessed after death was called "Elysium." "Paradise" is the equivalent term used in the New Testament. For example, Jesus told the thief on the cross, "Truly I say to you, today you will be with me in Paradise" (Luke 23:43). We know from Jesus' conversation with Mary Magdalene that He had not yet ascended to His Father in Heaven (John 20:17). Thus, the only other place that Jesus and the thief on the cross could have gone after they died biologically was Paradise in Hades. This lines up perfectly with the Hebrew idea of Sheol, where some were in a state of misery while others were in a state of happiness.

Tartarus is the Greek term employed by Peter in 2 Peter 2:4, which is often translated as "hell" in our English translations. The fact that Paradise and Tartarus/Hell defined two different states of being (and perhaps literally two parts of Hades divided by a gulf) is further seen from Jesus' teaching on the rich man and Lazarus in Hades in Luke 17:19-31.

[80] For the sake of clarity, it should be noted here that if man is defined as a body (within a body), it/he is indeed the seat of sin, and does become depraved.

[81] This answer was taken off of Gentry's facebook.com page, http://www.facebook.com/home.php#/photo.php?pid=52050&id=1668525845&ref=nf.

[82] Michael J. Sullivan, "Kenneth Gentry's Prophetic Confusion & The Analogy Of Scripture," Tree of Life Ministries, http://treeoflifeministries.info/index.php?option=com_content&view=article&id=148:mike-sullivan&catid=35:preterist-eschatology-all-prophecy-fulfilled-by-ad-70&Itemid=77#_ftn25.

[83] Robert Strimple, one of the authors of *When Shall These Things Be?*, recognizes this problem with the traditional view and proposes the following solution summarized by David Green: "Strimple teaches the non-humanity of the dead on page 337 (through a reference to Rudolf Bultmann and through a correction of Robert Gundry). According to Strimple, one of the reasons that Paul defended the resurrection of the body is because a departed believer is actually a *non-human* until he or she is physically resurrected" (Green, House Divide, 183).

[84] Quoted in David Curtis, "The Resurrection from the Dead," Berean Bible Church, http://bereanbiblechurch.org/transcripts/philippians/3_11.htm.

[85] Acts 2:31 provides further support that Jesus went to Hades at His biological death. See endnote 79 in this sub-chapter.

[86] Italics mine.

[87] David Curtis, "The Feasts of the Lord," www.preterism.com, http://en.preterism.com/index.php?title=The_Feasts_of_the_Lord&printab.

[88] Another passage regarding all rule and authority and power, is Colossians 2:13-15: "[13]When you were dead in your transgressions and the uncircumcision of your flesh, He made you alive together with Him, having forgiven us all our transgressions, [14]having canceled out the certificate of debt consisting of decrees against us, which was hostile to us; and He has taken it out of the way, having nailed it to the cross."

[15]When He had disarmed the rulers and authorities, He made a public display of them, having triumphed over them through Him." At the cross, Christ disarmed the rulers and authorities and triumphed over them. Surely, Paul does not mean that Christ literally disarmed the rulers and authorities in the earthly realm. He is speaking of the invisible realm. Thus it follows that in 1 Corinthians 15, Paul also means the final abolishment of all rule, authority, and power in the invisible realm.

[89] If the resurrection had to do with biological bodies this question wouldn't make any sense at this point. Paul had already established what the resurrected body of Christ was like in the first eleven verses. Plus, he discussed the Gospel with them in person. If his argument was that we are raised biologically after the pattern of Christ, then this question is not only redundant, but his answer doesn't fit the question.

[90] Verse 51 contains five textual variants that read as follows:
...we shall not all sleep, but we shall all be changed.
...we shall not all sleep, but we shall not all be changed.
...we shall all sleep, but we shall not all be changed.
...we shall all arise, but we shall not all be changed.
...we shall all sleep, but we shall all be changed.

The editorial committee of *The Greek New Testament* (UBS, 4th Revised Edition) gives an [A] rating to variant 1 above, which is the variant used in all standard translations of verse 51. An [A] rating means that they are sure that this was the original. Out of the four levels of certainty (A, B, C, or D), "the letter A indicates that the text is certain" (UBS, 3). If [A] is certain, than why so many variant readings? Ed Stevens helps us here by quoting and elaborating on Bruce Metzger's comments regarding this verse (in Edward E. Stevens, *Questions About the Afterlife: Preterist Answers to Gary DeMar's Five Questions About the Afterlife* (Bradford: International Preterist Association, 1999), 12-13):

> The reading which best explains the origin of the others is that preserved in (B, Dc, K, P, Psi, 81, 614, Byz Lect, syr-p,h, cop-sa,bo, toght, eth, and others). ***Because Paul and his correspondents had died, the statement "we shall not all sleep" seemed to call for correction.*** The simplest alteration was to transfer the negative to the

following clause (Sinaiticus, A*, C, 33, 1739, it-g, arm, eth, and others). *That this was an early modification is shown* by the artificial conflation of both readings in p46, Ac, and Origen; "oun" in G-gr may have arisen from a transcriptional blunder, "ou" [short diphthong] being read as "ou" [long diphthong]. The most radical alteration, preserved in several Western witnesses (D*, it-d,61, vg, Marcion, Tertullian, and others), replaces "sleep" with "arise", a reading which apparently arose to counteract (Gnostic?) denials of the general resurrection. [emphasis mine, ees]

From: *A textual Commentary On The Greek New Testament.* Companion vol. to the UBS Greek New Testament (3rd ed.) by Bruce M. Metzger. *United Bible Societies:* New York, 1971. Page 569.

There are two points in Metzger's statements needing emphasis:

1.The whole reason for the other variations (he says) was the historic reality that Paul and all of his contemporaries had died without seeing the general resurrection event occur (according to their concept of it). The late second century scribes and copyists evidently wanted to help Paul out of this jam. Paul had stated that not all the folks then alive in his day would die—some of them would live until the general resurrection. Since all of Paul's generation and everyone who had known them had died by the middle of the second century, the late second century scribes and copyists had a problem. They did not realize the general resurrection had occurred in connection with the destruction of Jerusalem in AD 70, so they believed Paul had made a mistake. Therefore, they felt the need to tamper with the text to disguise the supposed failure of the TIME implications.

2.Metzger shows at least one of these variants arose as early as the late second century, since it was included in the

Chester Beatty papyrus (p46) which could have copied an earlier one with the change in it. The change could have originally been made as early as mid-second century. This shows that the mid and late second century church leaders were already aware of and struggling with the non-fulfillment problem. It is not surprising that they chose to tamper with the TIME indicators rather than reinterpret their understanding of the NATURE of fulfillment. We still struggle with that faulty approach even today.

[91] Curtis, *Feasts*.

[92] "Hades" is the Greek rendering of the Hebrew, "Sheol."

[93] John 5, will be dealt with in more detail in chapter 5: Questions and Objections Answered.

Sub-Chapter 4C

[94] Italics and brackets mine.

[95] Italics and brackets mine

[96] Italics mine.

[97] Italics mine.

[98] Don Preston, "The Second Coming: Why We Should Still Be Waiting," www.eschatology.org, footnote 11, http://www.donkpreston.org/index.php?option=com_content&view=article&id=207:the-second-coming-why-we-should-still-be-waiting&catid=37:responding-to-the-critics&Itemid=61.

[99] Italics mine.

[100] Don Preston, "Rethinking II Peter 3," www.eschatology.org, http://www.donkpreston.org/index.php?option=com_content&view=article&id=345:rethinking-ii-peter-three&catid=34:new-heaven-and-earth&Itemid=61

[101] So Matthew 7:21-23.

[102] Don Preston, "Your Questions Dec. 6, 2006," www.eschatology.org, http://www.donkpreston.org/index.php?option=com_content&view=article&id=482:your-questions-dec-62006&catid=66:your-questions&Itemid=180.

[103] Who is the man of lawlessness? First, the man of lawlessness was alive in the first century. We know this because Paul tells us that he being restrained when Paul was writing (2 Thessalonians 2:6). So without question, the man of lawlessness was someone who was alive when Paul was alive. Second, Paul says that "the mystery of lawlessness is already at work" (v. 7). This is line with 1 John 4:3: "...every spirit that does not confess Jesus is not from God; *this is the spirit of the antichrist, of whom you have heard that he is coming, and now he is already in the world*" (italics mine). Paul and John are speaking of the same man, the antichrist. Both Paul and John say that he was alive in their time and that the spirit of the antichrist or the mystery of the man of lawlessness, was already at work before the antichrist had been revealed. In 1 John 2:18, John says, "Children, it is the last hour; and just as you heard that antichrist is coming, even now many antichrists have appeared; from this we know that it is the last hour." Since both Paul and John teach that the antichrist was coming, we know that Paul must be speaking of the same man that John is speaking of. We know that John is speaking of Cerinthus because Cerinthus was the agnostic leader that taught that the Christ came upon Jesus at His baptism and departed from Him at His crucifixion. And this is the heresy that John is dealing with in 1 John 5:5-10:

> [5]Who is the one who overcomes the world, but he who believes that Jesus is the Son of God? [6]This is the One who came by water and blood, Jesus Christ; not with the water only, but with the water and with the blood It is the Spirit who testifies, because the Spirit is the truth. [7]For there are three that testify: 8the Spirit and the water and the blood; and the three are in agreement. [9]If we receive the testimony of men, the testimony of God is greater; for the testimony of God is this, that He has testified concerning His Son. [10]The one who believes in the Son of God has the testimony in himself; the one who does not believe God has made Him a liar, because he has not believed in the testimony that God has given concerning His Son.

Third, Cerinthus claimed that an angel revealed to him that the Second Coming would usher in a literal reign of Christ in Jerusalem for a thousand years. Why would Cerinthus have to claim that an angel told him this is if this is what the apostles taught? One would think that he could just defer to the apostles to make his point. But the fact of the matter is, that Cerinthus used signs and wonders to get people to follow him, much like faith healers do today by playing on people's emotions. He used these signs and wonders to exalt himself to the status of being God. If the Christ left Jesus at His crucifixion, what reason would anyone who Cerinthus deceived have to believe that the Christ didn't descend upon him. And with Satan using Cerinthus (2 Thess. 2:9), he would have had the power to deceive people just like Satan, who was the prince of the power of the air (Eph. 2:2).

The phrase, "he takes his seat in the temple of God," is possibly figurative language used to denote the idea that Cerinthus would display himself as being God. The Temple only had one seat, the mercy seat, also known as the Ark of the Covenant. The Ark of the Covenant was were the presence of God resided. So Paul explains his figurative usage of the seat in the temple by telling us that it meant, "displaying himself as being God." Whether Cerinthus actually entered the most holy place is unknown, but it isn't beyond the realm of possibility since the veil was torn in two and entering the most holy place had no consequences after the death and resurrection of Christ (Heb. 10:19).

Conclusion of Chapter 4

[104] Of course, the predominate answer is "the Creeds." This answer has been adequately refuted already in various places throughout this book.

Chapter 5

[105] *A textual Commentary On The Greek New Testament.* Companion vol. to the UBS Greek New Testament (3rd ed.) by Bruce M. Metzger. *United Bible Societies:* New York, 1971. Page 569.

[106] Matthew Henry, *Matthew Henry's Commentary on the Whole Bible* (Peabody: Hendrickson Publishers, 1991), 636 (italics mine).

[107] Kelly Nelson Birks, "So Where's Your Proof?," Preterist Archive, http://www.preteristarchive.com/Hyper/2004_birks_mathison.html.

Concerning the Literal Rapture view within full preterism, Birks continues...

If historical/ physical corroboration is what some Christians want as to whether they are going to believe in Christ's teaching of the AD 70 parousia and a physical rapture is what is desired by some Preterists in order to try and deal with the "lack of documentation problem," (there was no one around to document the AD 70 parousia because they were all gone!) keep in mind that the literal rapture theory ALSO LACKS any outside documentation to substantiate it! So, if one is tempted to head in that direction because they cannot find historical documentation for an AD 70 parousia, keep in mind that the rapture proposition of AD 66-70 equally suffers from the exact same thing (the lack of historical corroboration)! So, it is no real option is it?

[108] Heb. 8:1-5; italics mine.

[109] Italics mine.

[110] Italics mine.

[111] Max King, *The Cross and the Parousia: The Two Dimensions of One Age-Changing Eschaton* (Warren: Writing and Research Ministry sponsored by The Parkman Road Church of Christ, 1987), 522.

[112] The same can be said regarding Paul's statement in verse 19: "For the anxious longing of the creation waits eagerly for the revealing of the sons of God." In what way does irrational creation anxiously long for, or wait eagerly for, anything?

[113] Don Preston, "Questions on Romans 8 and the Redemption of the Body," www.eschatology.org, http://www.donkpreston.org/index.php?option=com_content&view=article&id=574:question-on-romans-8-and-the-redemption-of-the-body&catid=66:your-questions&Itemid=180.

[114] Italics mine.

[115] It should also be noted that contrary to some translations, the New American Standard version accurately translates the word, "soma," in verse 23, as body in the singular rather than in the plural: "And not only this, but also we ourselves, having the first fruits of the Spirit, even we ourselves groan within ourselves, waiting eagerly for our adoption as

sons, the redemption of our *body*" (italics mine). In addition, verse 18 contains "mello" with the infinitive, which is not translated in our English translations: "For I consider that the sufferings of this present time are not worthy to be compared with the glory that is [about to] be revealed to us.

116 Mathison, *Postmillennialism*, 241.

117 Gentry, *He Shall Have Dominion*, 347.

118 See, for example, Homer Hailey, *Commentary on the Minor Prophets* (Grand Rapids: Baker Publishing, 1973); John F. Walvoord and Roy B. Zuck, *Bible Knowledge Commentary* (Wheaton: Victor Books, 1985).

119 Walvoord, *Bible Knowledge Commentary*, 1060.

120 Don Preston, "The Second Coming: Why We Should Still Be Waiting #1," www.eschatology.org, http://www.donkpreston.org/index.php?option=com_content&view=article&id=210:the-second-coming-why-we-should-still-be-waiting-1&catid=37:responding-to-the-critics&Itemid=61 (accessed March 31, 2009).

121See, for example, Isaiah 24:23; 34:4; Jeremiah 4:23; Ezekiel 32:7; Joel 2:11; 2:30-32.

122 Max King, *The Cross and the Parousia*, 575.

123 There is an interesting possibility that those who came out of their tombs after Christ's resurrection and went into Jerusalem (Matt. 27:52-53) were some of the Old Covenant Jews that had recently died and would have been known by those still living. The idea is that they appeared in Jerusalem to many as a sign of this very heavenly scene. They would have been witnesses to the fact that the Great High Priest was going to enter the most holy place "a second time" for the sins of the people and would therefore soon exit the most holy place for the last time (Heb. 9:23-28).

The fact that the curtain of the Temple was torn in two, from top to bottom, at His death (Matt 27:51), may have been a sign that the Shekina glory of God had exited the most holy place through the death of Christ in the flesh, thus symbolizing the exiting of the High Priest the first time. Christ was the Shekina glory of God in the flesh, and through His death in the flesh put an end to the sacredness of the most holy place in the Temple. "Therefore, brothers, since *we have confidence to enter the holy places* [in the earthly temple] by the blood of Jesus, by the new and living way that he opened for us *through the curtain, that is through his flesh*, and since we have a great priest over the house of God, let us draw near with a true heart in full assurance of faith, with our hearts sprinkled clean from an evil conscience and our bodies washed with pure water (cf. 1 Pet. 3:21-22). "Let us hold fast the confession of our hope without wavering, for he who promised is faithful" (Heb. 10:19-23; brackets and italics mine).

If this interpretation is correct, then since the veil was torn from top to bottom, this very likely demonstrates that God accepted the sacrifice of Christ, Himself being the final spotless Lamb that did not need His own sins forgiven and atoned for. Only the perfect High Priest could go in the first time on behalf of Himself and be accepted by God as the sacrifice that brings God and man together again. Thus, this tearing of the veil brought an end to the need for any more priests on earth. This High Priest could now enter the most holy place not made with hands on behalf of the people (Heb. 6:19-20) so that they could have eternal life in the presence of God restored and enter the most holy place in Heaven after biological death.

[124] Practically speaking, it is possible that these saints that went to Hades before going to heaven would continue to encourage the dead ones of the Old Covenant that their release was coming soon.

[125] "When we consider that 1 Corinthians was written a mere twenty-five years after the beginning of Christianity, and when we consider that the eschatological, first-fruits church was already partaking of the coming resurrection, and we consider the eager expectation in that era of the imminent fulfillment of the end of the Adamic ages and of the resurrection [of] the dead, we should expect that believers in that historical moment would refer to the vast multitudes that had lived and died before the advent of Christ as the '*dead* [ones].' This is not to say that the term 'the dead' in the New Testament was code for 'the dead of the Old Testament in contrast to dead Christians.' It is to say only that in that eschatological generation, if reference were made to the pre-Christian dead in contrast to the relatively few dead Christians (in about AD 55), the designation 'the dead' or 'dead ones' sufficed" [Green, House Divided, 195-96].

[126] Italics mine.

[127] Italics mine.

[128] See comments under the question, "Don't John 5:25-29 And Revelation 20:5 Teach Two Resurrections, One Spiritual And One Physical?"

[129] Don Preston, "What is the Preterist View?," www.eschatology.org, http://www.donkpreston.org/index.php?option=com_content& view=article&id=323:what-is-the-preterist-view&catid=110:preterist-introduction&Itemid=61.

[130] See the developed interpretation of 1 Corinthians 15:29 (sub-chapter 4B of this book) for a similar and fuller explanation of covenantal incorporation.

[131] Young's Literal Translation.

[132] Richard L. Pratt, Jr., "Hyper-Preterism and Unfolding Biblical Eschatology," *Reformed Perspectives Magazine, Vol. 7, Num. 46* (Nov. 13-19, 2005): 1.

[133] Ibid, 2.

[134] Ibid.

[135] Mathison, *When Shall These Things be?*, 122-123.

[136] Ibid., 131.

[137] Ibid., 132.

[138] Ibid., 136.

[139] Ibid., 151.

Chapter 6

[140] Again, this is no different than the traditional view of election. The slight variance between the two views is that the traditional view teaches that the elect inherit eternal life when they believe and the full preterist view teaches that the elect already have eternal life before they believe. Either way you look at it, only the elect have eternal life anyway.

[141] For an argument concerning the issue of the elimination of sin on earth, see Kelly Nelson Birks, *The End of Sin: An Eschatological Odyssey into Teloarmatia* (Baltimore: Publish America, 2004).

Appendix A

[142]Italics mine.

[143] The particular recipients of the angels' persecution are uncertain. But based on the context, it is implied that during such a time, "...the Lord knows how to rescue the godly from trials (v. 9)..." It is possible that the recipients of their persecution were the godly Angels.

[144] See the developed interpretation of 1 Corinthians 15:29 (sub-chapter 4B of this book) for a similar and fuller explanation of covenantal incorporation.

[145] Douglas Wilson, "Final Assurance," Blog and Mablog, http://www.dougwils.com/index.asp?Action=Anchor&CategoryID=1&BlogID=4545.

[146] Recapitulation: A recycling of the same teaching, giving different information each time.

[147] While neither of these works put forth the full preterist understanding of Revelation, they do provide a terrific perspective on the imagery in Revelation.

[148] Kenneth L. Gentry, Jr., *Before Jerusalem Fell: Dating the Book of Revelation*, 3rd ed. (Powder Springs: American Vision, 1998).

[149] Robert Thomas has written a very brief rebuttal in *Theonomy and the Dating of Revelation*. Master's Seminary Journal, 5 no 2 (Fall 1994) : 185-202. He deals with but a select few of Gentry's arguments, mostly attempting to refute Gentry's theonomic view in order to discredit the early date.

[150] Ibid, 1.

[151] Relating to or denoting reasoning or knowledge that proceeds from observations or experiences to the deduction of probable causes.

[152] George Eldon Ladd, *A Theology of the New Testament, rev. ed.* (Grand Rapids: Eerdmans, 1993), 672.

[153]Mark L. Hitchcock, *A Critique of the Preterist View of "Soon" and "Near" in Revelation*, Bibliotheca sacra 163 (October-December 2006) : 469.

[154] Kurt Aland, *A History of Christianity*, vol. 1: *From the Beginnings to the Threshold of the Reformation*, trans. James L. Schaaf (Philadelphia: Fortress, 1985), 88. Quoted in Gentry, 139.

[155] Hitchcock, 471.

[156] Ibid.

[157] Ibid.

[158] J. Barton Payne, *Encyclopedia of Biblical Prophecy* (Grand Rapids: Baker, 1973) 593. Quoted in John Noë, *An Exegetical Basis for a Preterist-Idealist Understanding of the Book of Revelation*, Journal of the Evangelical Theological Society 49 no 4 (December 2006) : 767.

[159] *ANF* 1:559-560. Quoted in Gentry, 47.

[160] See Gentry, *Before Jerusalem Fell*, 45-67.

[161] Keith Mathison, *Postmillennialism: An Eschatology of Hope* (Phillipsburg: P&R Publishing, 1999), 145.

[162] Gentry, 209.

[163] Ibid., 209-10

[164] Mathison, 261. Also, Gentry, 198-203. Also, Kenneth Gentry, Jr., *He Shall Have Dominion* (Tyler: Institute for Christian Economics, 1997), 422. Also, Kenneth L. Gentry, Jr., *The Beast of Revelation* (Powder Springs: American Vision, 2002), 42-43.

[165] Bruce Metzger, *A Textual Commentary on the Greek New Testament*, 2nd ed. (Stuttgart: United Bible Societies, 1994), 676.

[166] John Walvoord, *The Revelation of Jesus Christ*, (Chicago: Moody Publishers, 1989), 209.

[167] Ibid.

[168] Simon J. Kistemaker, *New Testament Commentary: Revelation* (Grand Rapids: Baker Books, 2001), 31.

[169] Ibid.

[170] Ibid.

[171] Daniel B. Wallace, *Greek Grammar Beyond the Basics* (Grand Rapids: Zondervan, 1996), 254 (Only brackets containing transliterations mine).

[172] Adela Yarbro Collins, *The Combat Myth in the Book of Revelation* (HDR 9; Missoula, Mont.: Scholars Press, 1976, 175. Quoted in Francis X. Gumerlock, *Nero Antichrist: Patristic Evidence for the Use of Nero's Naming in Calculating the Number of the Beast (Rev. 13:18)*, Westminster Theological Journal 68 no 2 (Autumn 2006) : 347.

[173] Mathison, 145.

[174] Meaning early Christian theologian (i.e. Church fathers).

[175] Kistemaker, 31.

[176] Francis X. Gumerlock, *Nero Antichrist: Patristic Evidence for the Use of Nero's Naming in Calculating the Number of the Beast (Rev. 13:18)*, Westminster Theological Journal 68 no 2 (Autumn 2006) : 360.

[177] Daniel Wallace, Greek Grammar Beyond the Basics, P. 531.

[178] Ibid.

[179] Charles Hill, "Notes on Wallace Readings" (paper distributed in his Greek exegesis course, Reformed Theological Seminary, Oviedo, Florida, 2008).

Appendix B

[180] For a detailed and devastating response to *When Shall These Things Be?*, read David Green, ed., *House Divided: Bridging the Gap in Reformed Eschatology. A Preterist Response to When Shall These Things Be?* (Ramona: Vision Publishing, 2009), where the authors demonstrate the overwhelming contradictions throughout *When Shall These Things Be?*

[181] Mathison, *Postmillennialism*, 243.

[182] Ibid.

[183] Ibid.

[184] Ibid.

[185] Ibid.

[186] Kenneth L. Gentry, Jr., *He Shall Have Dominion: Second Edition*, (Tyler: Institute of Christian Economics, 1997), 557.

[187] Ibid.

[188] For detailed and vivid demonstration of the intellectual dishonesty put forth in *When Shall These Things Be?*, read David Green, ed., *House Divided: Bridging the Gap in Reformed Eschatology. A Preterist Response to When Shall These Things Be?* (Ramona: Vision Publishing, 2009).

[189] Mathison, When Shall These Things Be?, 254.

Appendix C

[190] Charles Hodge, *Systematic Theology: Vol. III* (Peabody: Hendrickson Publishers, 2001), 773.